EUROPEAN POLITICS
Political Economy and Policy Making in Western Democracies

D1279625

EUROPEAN POLITICS
Political Economy and Policy Making in Western Democracies

Robert A. Isaak

School of Advanced International Studies
The Johns Hopkins University
Bologna Center

ST. MARTIN'S PRESS • New York

Tried. 9.95/19.90 (2 copies) 9/16/85

*To Karl and Erika
and their children
Gudrun, Uli, and Birgit*

Preface

Although Western European societies are among the most advanced in the industrial world, in the late twentieth century their adaptive capacities have been overwhelmed by an unprecedented rate and intensity of change. Following a period of prosperity and abundance, which promised to provide the basis for citizens in the West to transcend basic economic and security needs, Westerners found themselves faced with political and economic insecurity caused by recession, unemployment, government and energy crises, and terrorism. The promise of upward mobility was replaced for many by the perception of diminishing life chances and the prospect of lower standards of living. Much of the generous social welfare legislation—unemployment and medical insurance and state pensions—seemed thrown suddenly into jeopardy with declines of productivity, birthrates, and economic growth. Politics became a question of merely attempting to cope with institutional change, rather than trying to steer it. Democratic majorities shifted their focus from ideals to costs.

Politics has become inseparable from economics. As the interdependence of political and economic relationships became obvious on the global level during the oil and economic crises, the interaction between the political and economic spheres became more clear domestically as well. Investment incentives, tax cuts, social costs of nuclear energy, oil prices, pay-offs for working and not working in specific ways—all of these issues are both political and economic. To talk about politics without dealing with political economy is no longer to speak about the real world.

My aim in this book has been to redefine politics in terms of political economy, looking at the age-old phenomenon of power through a new pair of glasses hopefully better focused to clear the blur of our times. I believe the book will meet a need that exists in the area of comparative government for a text that treats the political economies of the major countries in the common market comparatively. I have kept the quantitative aspect of the book as limited as possible, since numbers often deter people from becoming involved in the all-too-human problems of political economy. Students who have never taken a formal course in politics, economics, or mathematics should be able to understand almost anything that is said, although levels of understanding differ depending on one's background and interest. In short, if the book gets beyond the grasp of the general reader, I have failed.

Those looking for the basic elements of politics and comparative government seen through the shades of political economy will find them here. Those at a more advanced level will also find the fundamentals of policy making in the largest European political systems— West Germany, France, Great Britain, Italy, and the Common Market itself. Each of these systems is approached from a different hypothesis of how political economic change is managed (or mismanaged). And those most interested in theory can begin with the speculative concluding chapter on comparative political economy.

In the years during which this book was written, my view of comparative policy making and political economy was enriched at four institutional settings: The Institute on Western Europe and The Research Institute on International Change, both at Columbia University, The Pace University Graduate School of Business, and The Johns Hopkins University School of Advanced International Studies, where I currently teach Comparative European Political Economic Systems and West European Integration at the Center in Bologna, Italy. Although my debts to students and colleagues are too numerous to mention, Don Puchala, Mark Kesselman, Lewis Edinger, James Livingston, Seweryn Bialer, Wilfred Kohl, Norman Graham, Ralph Hummel were particularly important in helping me complete this long project. Some may recognize portions of lectures given at Columbia University, Tufts University, Lafayette College, Pace University, SUNY at Oswego, and Johns Hopkins University SAIS in Washington and Bologna, where student and faculty reactions helped to refine my arguments. Carol Anne Ryan, Deanna Horton, and Alan Asay provided invaluable research assistance. Bert Lummus of St. Martin's Press and my wife, Gudrun, helped to make this a better book. Whatever faults it has are my own unique contribution.

R.A.I.
Bologna

Contents

Chapter 1
Comparative Politics and Policy Making

"A slow sort of country!" said the Queen. "Now, here, you see, it takes all the running you can do, to keep in the same place. If you want to get somewhere else, you must run at least twice as fast as that!"
—Lewis Carroll, *Alice's Adventures in Wonderland*

In the late twentieth century institutions are deceptive masks, disguising the relativity and uncertainty that result from the rate and diversity of socioeconomic change. "Power" and "legitimacy" are not fixed concepts but relative ones, created and destroyed by politicians who are adept at working through the cracks of obsolete bureaucracies. They often cover their real intentions with colorful spectacle. But such illusions do not last long, and the political structures are eventually revealed to be superficial. When the magic is gone, so often is respect for the entire political system. In all this confusion the only thing everyone is willing to recognize, regardless of differing points of view, is the inability of individuals and institutions to cope with rapid, widespread change.

Many observers of the political process find themselves in a situation resembling Kierkegaard's chess game, feeling like the piece that is not allowed to move, yet knowing that their health, if not their survival, may depend on breaking the rules of the game, moving somewhere, somehow. In Paris union-organized steelworkers demonstrate against job cuts planned jointly by the government and the steel industry. But the demonstration is exploited by other disenchanted individuals, the "trashers" or *autonomes*—the new-style artists of French political violence who harass the police with slingshots, wear Arab scarves to ward off tear gas, smash store windows, and steal whatever they can. The authority of the social order, symbolized by government and industry, is challenged by the counterorder of the working class, represented by the unions; this, in turn, is undermined by anarchic individuals out for immediate gain and a sense of significance.

1

This breakdown or decay of the differing status order systems of postindustrial societies is not just political; it is economic. Particularly in Western Europe, it is no longer possible on many issues to separate the government from industry, industry from the unions, the unions from anarchists, and the whole political economy from the individual demands and interest groups of which it is composed.

In some European nations, left-wing movements gather strength in reaction to outmoded institutions that frustrate the social needs and opportunities of the masses. Elsewhere, conservative trends appear in reaction to expansive welfare systems that hamper productivity, stimulate inflation, and strangle individual freedom with bureaucratic red tape. The inevitable contradictions of postindustrial societies make citizens ask whether Western democracies are decaying or whether they are painfully evolving new solutions to cope with social, economic, and cultural change.

Governments, multinational corporations, and other organizations are not omniscient structures but symbols of past and present relationships among human beings. It is true that they help fix the rules of the game, and they appear to be unavoidable entities. But half of the reality of political economy is what goes on behind the official rules of the game in the black market behind the black-and-white one. When free people in the West see that the rules of the game no longer make sense in terms of their own life chances, they begin to dodge the rules, make up their own rules, or leave the country. Under increasing economic pressures human beings adapt, and thus society's long-term costs are increased by individuals' short-term efforts to maximize personal benefit. Political thinking is inevitably opportunistic in this sense, which is why politicians make the most of all opportunities, both legal and borderline. They know, after all, that the official rules are actually the compromises of other politicians. They know that those with the most bargaining power in the existing system have the best chance of getting their own way.

THE BASIC ARGUMENT

Even granting that leaders and citizens who act to further their life chances regardless of the rules are acting out of free will, structural obstacles remain. The residues of old institutions and habits frustrate the needs of some and protect the interests of others. Three levels of structure are considered in this analysis of European policy making and political economy: the *substructure* of psychocultural modes, values, and ideology; the *infrastructure* of socioeconomic productivity, transportation, labor relations, and technology; and the *superstructure* of visible social and governmental interaction, voting behavior, party coalitions, government policy making, and economic bargaining. These structural levels proceed from that which is least conscious of values to the most visible level of government pomp and circumstance.

The basic hypothesis relating these structural levels to the changes occurring in European politics today is that *the greater the perceived or anticipated social change, the more the conservative impulse to preserve the status quo pushes policy options up to the superstructural level and the more difficult collective learning or adaptation becomes.* In *Loss and Change* sociologist Peter Marris demonstrates that when people undergo severe loss or extreme change in their lives they respond to a conservative psychological impulse by attempting to recover stability through old values and patterns. But what may be a necessary strategy for an individual in a disintegrating situation may make collective coping with change almost impossible—each person clings to his or her own interests and habits instead of helping the society move toward needed adjustment. Effective learning or adaptation, in short, involves change at the substructural and infrastructural levels, where it is least likely to occur if the threat of short-run loss is perceived as greater than the promise of long-term benefit for the whole community. If the Greek philosopher Heraclitus lived today, threatened by a thousand new rivers that could wash away whatever was familiar, he would probably hang on to what he's got.*

But the human capacity to adapt to change is as paradoxical as Heraclitus's observation that you cannot step into the same river twice. While some people resist change when there is too much of it to cope with, using old patterns as shields, others look to those who are adapting the fastest as models. Still others try to bypass all rules and achieve their ends immediately through violence or extortion. Progress poses a relative question: Is the winner the person who loses least of the old or the one who gains most of the new? For example, is it better to resist the sacrifice of national identity for the sake of European integration or to lead the European-integration movement in order to better exploit it to meet future national needs? What is needed is an expansion of the

---

*Marris writes of "the conservative impulse": "We accept resistance to change as a fact of life. We expect civil servants to be defensive when challenged by innovators, or peasant farmers to react with suspicion to new techniques. . . . When we argue about the need for social change, we tend to explain conservatism away as ignorance, a failure of nerve, the obstinate protection of untenable privileges—as if the resistance could be broken by exposing its irrationality. But when we turn from general questions of policy to the experience of people in society as they struggle to maintain their hold on life, the conservative impulse . . . is as necessary for survival as adaptability: and indeed adaptability itself depends upon it. For the ability to learn from experience relies on the stability of the interpretations by which we predict the pattern of events. We assimilate new experiences by placing them in the context of a familiar, reliable construction of reality." P. Marris, *Loss and Change* (New York: Pantheon, 1974), pp. 5–6.

basic hypothesis that relates structures to change, an expansion that enables us to examine the politics of costly national choices and highlights the payoffs for both resisting and adapting to change.

A *hypothesis* is a testable proposition derived from a theory. To explain and predict human behavior, theories must be selective and focused, aiming at the historical conditions of their time. The understanding we want is an understanding of an insistent present. The use of the past is to equip us for the future. We have little time for dry abstraction unless someone shows us that it can provide recipes for action to help solve our problems here and now. Otherwise, we are left feeling that we are eating the menu instead of the meal.

A *theory*, then, is a useful reduction of the complexities of reality designed to explain certain things and to be used for specific purposes. The set of problems that are most immediate and demanding for most nations appear to be economic in nature: In a world of scarce resources, who has most of his or her needs satisfied and who does not? We want to know how specific systems of human-need satisfaction and payoffs—that is, *political economies*—work and who benefits most.

The nuclear family often fails to cope with social changes, a failure that is symbolized by high divorce rates, low birthrates, and desertion of older family members. Larger social organizations—nation–states— have even more difficulty coping effectively with change. Even the wealthiest and most powerful nations find their efforts to achieve political and economic independence frustrated by interdependence, as the current resource and energy shortages make clear. Nor has the formation of larger regional organizations such as the European Community* solved these national difficulties in advanced industrial states. Old values and habits, substructural ruts, prevent the national "family" from learning from its past collective mistakes to cope more effectively with present problems, let alone future dilemmas. Outmoded transportation and communication systems and outdated ways of organizing work—that is, obsolete infrastructural technologies— physically block whatever aspects of the political economy have not already been blocked by self-defeating psychological attitudes, like a car that doesn't have the capacity to shift gears even if the driver wants to do so. And the superstructures of governmental, industrial, and labor bureaucracy are often occupied with nothing but unsolved problems carried up from these lower substructural and infrastructural levels. The overuse of bureaucracy as a panacea for social problems reminds one of the psychologist Abraham Maslow's observation:

*The European Community was founded in 1958 by the Treaty of Rome for economic and political cooperation and is made up of nine member nations: France, West Germany, Italy, Belgium, the Netherlands, Luxemburg, the United Kingdom, Ireland, and Denmark. Three more nations will join soon: Greece, Spain, and Portugal.

"I suppose it is tempting, if the only tool you have is a hammer, to treat everything as if it were a nail."

In an era of limited national capacity to cope with rapid social change, it may be most fruitful to compare the politics of various countries using a learning theory that focuses on the different payoffs of their political economies. In this view *comparative politics* can be defined as the analysis of alternative systems of learning by paying, that is, different systems of trade-offs. In any society, the citizen who wants to satisfy basic needs is confronted with limited information, time, and resources and is therefore dependent on the options presented by the economic and political market. The citizen is qualified for certain jobs and not others. Some educational and social opportunities are open to each person; others are not. Individual life chances can be viewed at any particular moment as a structured set of options that the political economy of a society presents to each individual, a sort of custom-designed menu for each class of people. Sociologists call this socioeconomic hierarchy of options stratification. And, as we will see later, much of political and economic life depends on whether people think they are going up or down the stratification ladder.

From the individual point of view, then, political economy is the politics of costly choices. Each person becomes politically conscious when he or she feels and articulates the tension between needs and values on the one hand and existing conditions, or social facts, on the other. Choices in such situations always involve costs in time, energy, or money. I may choose to become a life insurance salesman for the money at the cost of free time and what I consider a creative occupation. Another person may decide to become a teacher or an artist who values free time at the cost of a lower salary and less material comfort. Some societies may make the costs of becoming an artist so high that few people take this option, most preferring blue-collar work or white-collar bureaucracy. Life chances, in short, are presented to us by society as trade-offs between different kinds of benefits and costs.

From the perspective of political economy political systems can be seen as distributions of individual life chances structured by payoffs for certain kinds of choices or behavior. Each political economy is a learning system: people adapt to the opportunities presented to them by society or pay the price. If enough people refuse to accept the given options, demonstrations, strikes, or revolutions may result. For example, in 1968, when a sufficient number of students and workers decided that French society was restricting their opportunities and making the costs too high, they held a series of demonstrations and strikes that led to President de Gaulle's resignation.

At certain historical moments an individual's opportunities may open up or the person may decide not to accept the payoff system that society presents. But certain kinds of behavior—social, economic, and political behavior—almost always pay off more than others. The individual has little, if anything, to do with this system of rewards and punishments. Each person is born into the system. But to succeed in a national society, to satisfy personal needs and objectives, each person must cope with the existing rules of the game. The three basic strategies are (1) to use the system as it exists, (2) to organize others to achieve reforms aimed at sweetening the life chances of one's own class or group, or (3) to seek to destroy or leave the system for the sake of radical values. Novelist Aleksandr Solzhenitsyn, for example, was frustrated by the rules of the game of his native nation–state, Russia, and found out about other nations with different rules, with payoff structures more consistent with his own beliefs and objectives. Solzhenitsyn now writes and publishes novels in Vermont. For him, the trade-offs for freedom were too costly in the USSR; he preferred to gain more liberty in the United States even though this meant paying certain social costs in terms of the way of life he was used to.

SUBSIDIARY HYPOTHESES

To the basic hypothesis linking social structures to change (i.e., the greater the change, the greater the overload on the superstructure and the lower the degree of collective learning or adaptability), a subsidiary set of hypotheses can now be added. As overload and breakdown in the political economy system become more widely perceived by the mass public, people will tend to (1) hang on to what they have to protect their life chances against further change or (2) press for more radical short-term change to benefit their individual or group life chances immediately or (3) switch back and forth between (1) and (2), depending on whether their personal interests are affected by a specific issue or change and whether there is sufficient uncertainty as to the outcome of the social conflict to make it worth taking some risks.

In sum, times of uncertainty and rapid change inspire both "conservative" and "radical" impulses, which are paradoxically mixed to yield an ambiguous centrist voting pattern in postindustrial societies. This pattern, in turn, stimulates further uncertainty. As change undermines the legitimacy of the existing system of stratification in a society, individuals turn increasingly to realistic bargaining behavior, looking for their individual payoffs for resisting or adapting to change on a case-by-case basis. People increasingly vote their interest both on the market and in the voting booth rather than merely taking a certain party, ideology, or set of conventional rules of behavior for granted.

To view a political economy as a learning system is to focus on the objective gathering of information regardless of the analyst's particular ideological bent. Ideology is a relatively frozen set of beliefs that is used as a basis of political action to promote certain class interests. As a deliberate distortion of social perception, ideology obstructs the learning process by confusing what one wants with one's chances of getting it. Utilities or values are mixed up with probabilities or likelihoods in a particular historical situation. Although ideology is undoubtedly necessary for coherent political action, the analysis phase must be separated from this action phase if such biased action is to be most effective in the real world. Human beings can never be "value free," nor should they be. But social scientists must learn the arbitrary discipline of analyzing the historical situation to sort out the determined from the indeterminate, to accurately assess the probabilities of success for freedom of action in certain circumstances for the sake of certain values.

In this sober analytical sense, the interpretation of a political economy as a learning system stresses certain questions: What is to be learned? According to which criteria? What is the cost–benefit balance between different kinds of human behavior and policy decisions? Who benefits most and pays least for a pro-productivity policy? for a pro-redistribution policy? What information is crucial to permit a government to learn fastest from its mistakes? How can the life chances of the majority of the people in a particular cultural framework be maximized, given historical traditions, social conditions, popular values, and working styles? How can domestic political economies best be reorganized to adjust to changes in the international economic environment? How can political economies be aimed toward changing this environment for the sake of the national interest?

These questions can help indicate the optimum political economy for a particular society under certain conditions. Once posed, they can be answered by hypothetical solutions designed to be tested in the actual political economies being investigated, that is, by empirical hypotheses. From concepts to questions to falsifiable hypotheses, the scientific method becomes the ultimate learning tool for human beings to check their theories of reality against how it actually works.

The scientific method is useful in that it forces us to learn more efficiently from our mistakes than we normally would—a critical advantage in an era when we are bombarded with more information and social change than our minds can cope with. Let us say, for example, that I decide to sell my car. My initial instinct might be to go to my local used-car dealer and ask what he will give me for it and to sell it to him, figuring that I could not get much more elsewhere, since he looked up its value in the Blue Book, and being too lazy to take the trouble to shop around. Everyday thinking means taking things for granted, accepting habitual routines without question, without testing the assumptions on which behavior is based.

Using the scientific method, on the other hand, forces the decision maker not to take things for granted and to test assumptions against facts in a systematic way. The first step of the scientific method is to state the problem as clearly as possible: When and where should I sell my car in order to make the most money? The next step is to frame tentative answers (or hypotheses) to each part of the question in a form that can be tested in the real world: If I wait two years after buying a new car, then I will make the most money when I resell it. This *if–then* statement is a useful format in that it points toward causes: 100 percent of the time that I do X, Y follows. However, since few cases are strictly causal—that is, true or certain 100 percent of the time—it is often better to put hypotheses in probabilistic or correlational terms, such as "the more . . . , the more . . ." or "the more . . . , the less . . .": The more I paid for my new car in the first place, the more money I will get back (proportionately) if I wait longer than two years to sell it.

Both of these hypotheses can be "tested" in the next step of the scientific method by calling up as many used-car dealers as possible to find out how much they pay for a certain make and year of automobile when it is two years old and when it is more than two years old. This data-collecting phase permits me to prove or disprove my hypothesis in the particular case of my car: a learning-by-paying experience in that the more I learn, the less I will have to pay (or the greater the benefit or payoff to me). In large part the scientific method consists merely of getting into the habit of putting everyday assumptions into "the more I do X, the more Y will happen" kind of statements and then checking the facts in the particular case to see whether such working hypotheses hold water.

In everyday life the costs of not using the scientific method to learn from experience as fast as possible seem great enough. But in national political economies the costs are multiplied many times and often affect the lives of millions of people. In socialist countries, for example, it is usually assumed that the equal distribution of goods through centralized planning is just as important as the greater production of goods (if not more so). The ideological stress is on just division of the existing pie. But for the benefit of equality of distribution people often pay costs in terms of individual freedom and collective productivity. In capitalist nations, on the other hand, it is usually assumed that greater productivity and efficiency, achieved through the competitiveness of capital markets, are more important than equal distribution of the goods produced. The ideological focus is not on the division of the existing pie but on the creation of more pie. However, for the benefits of greater production and more individual freedom people pay costs in terms of inequality and social injustice.

The scientific method is useful for pinpointing costs and benefits over time in specific societies, capitalist or socialist. It can be used, for example, to ask, What are the individual costs and benefits of living in Italy today? for whom (the rich, the middle class, or the poor)? in Germany? France? England? How does the Common Market affect the learning-by-paying structures of each of these countries? Is a new form of political economy emerging that avoids the negative costs of capitalism and socialism in these nations? Or is the political and social turmoil there merely a battle among old forms, with predictable swings of the pendulum from left to right and back again?

KEY CONCEPTS OF COMPARATIVE POLITICS

A theory is always based on certain key concepts, which in turn are used in different combinations to form testable hypotheses. The great eighteenth-century philosopher Immanuel Kant, for example, created his theory of reality out of three key concepts: time, space, and cause. Without assuming the existence of these concepts, he argued that human beings cannot operate meaningfully in the empirical world.* Similarly, at least five key concepts appear to be indispensable in order to compare different nation–states: psychocultural modes (or *motivations*), political and social institutions (or *structures*), political-economic codes (or *bargaining behavior*), domestic and foreign policies (or *collective decision making*), and regional and global constraints (or *systemic parameters*). These five elements are necessary, if not sufficient, to predict the bargaining power of nations in the world economy.

As figure 1-1 indicates, past experience colors the substructure of each national society, which is dominated by the psychocultural modes (values, ideology, etc.) of the political culture. The substructure, in turn, provides the driving force of collective motivation for the creation and operation of the infrastructure, which is made up of "hidden" political and social structures and political-economic bargaining patterns (work traditions, transportation, communication and plant technologies, educational and class structures, etc.). The infrastructure provides the basis and impetus for the superstructure of official political and social institutions and political-economic bargaining and establishments (government, corporations, unions, etc.), which, in turn, transform the "inputs" from the lower levels into "outputs" of domestic and foreign policies deriving from official political-economic decision making. Such policy outcomes work their way through both regional and global levels of opportunity and constraint as each European na-

---

*In his classic work, *The Critique of Pure Reason* (1781), Kant argued that concepts without empirical content are meaningless whereas empirical reality without concepts to interpret it is unintelligible.

Figure 1-1 Sources of the National Political Economy

The Future

Global Constraints and Opportunities

Regional Constraints and Opportunities

Present Foreign Policy Outcomes

Present Domestic Policy Outcomes

Present Domestic Policy Outcomes

Super-structure

Infrastructure

Substructure

The Past

⟶ Input–Output
⟵‖‖‖ Feedback

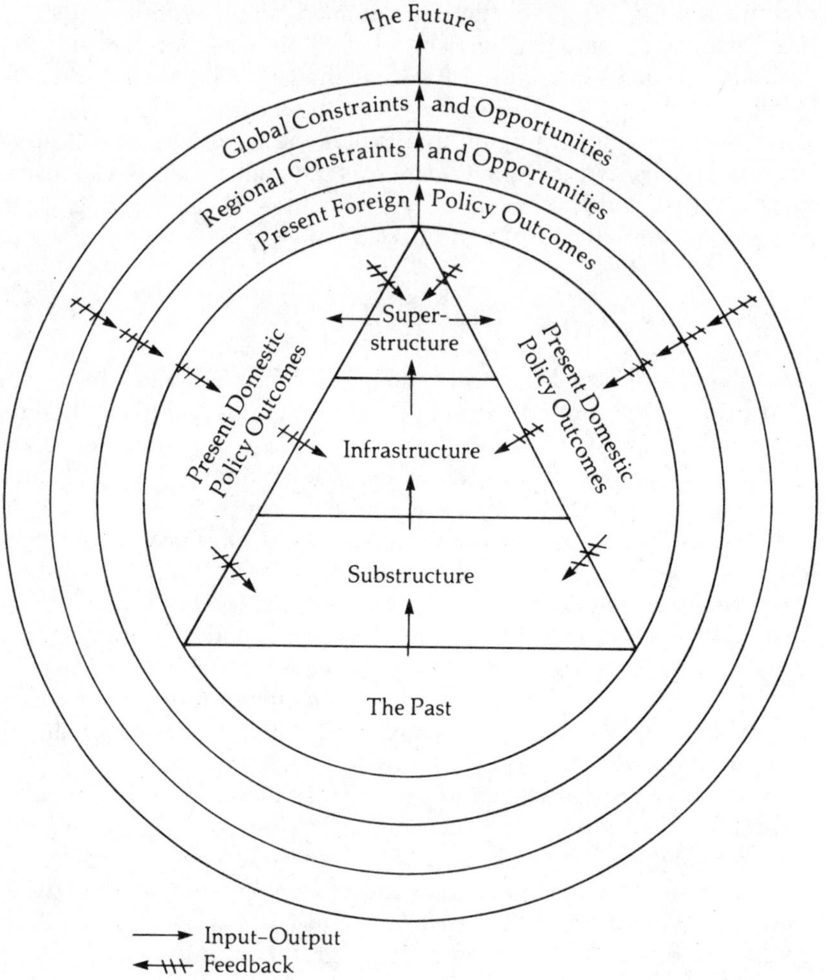

tion devises strategies for coping with and using the European Community "club," on the one hand, and the economic and political conditions of the global political economy, on the other. The overall result is a national impact on the history of interaction and interdependence among nation–states; in short, on "the future."

At each of these different national, regional, and international levels there are *feedbacks* to the national political economy, that is, reactions from the environment and other nations in it to the policies and actions of the nation in question. Collective national learning occurs to the extent that the national political economy has the capacity and will to process this feedback information effectively, transforming its domestic structures, processes, and policies in order to adapt to constant changes in the regional and global environment. The costs of not adapting to such changes in the long run, as well as the short-term benefits for certain national groups in resisting such adaptation, constitute the focus of this study.

Power is a social relationship in which some people can have more of their needs satisfied than other people. The conversion of the potential power of a nation into the actual power to use its resources and capabilities to promote the national interest in a specific situation depends on effective learning or adaptation in terms of feedback and change. To learn fast from experience is to become better able to satisfy one's needs. Economists call this collective national ability adjustment.

The epitome of a powerful nation would be one with a dynamic, achievement-oriented political culture; stable social and political institutions; an effective entrepreneurial bargaining style; a collaboration of domestic and foreign policies that permits steady domestic growth and social improvement along with aggressive export trade; and a strategic position in regional and world affairs due to the possession of enough economic or military potential to permit some degree of self-sufficiency. No Western European nation possesses all of these attributes by itself; West Germany comes closest. Even if all the Common Market nations could be coordinated in crucial policy areas, they would not constitute a superpower. In fact, even if the dream of a united Europe is fulfilled, the region will remain a halfway house of diffuse potentialities and vulnerabilities, not a full-fledged bargaining bloc on an equal par with the United States or the Soviet Union.

Political Culture: Psychocultural Modes or Motivations

The primary element in the bargaining power and political economy of a nation is *political culture*—the cluster of values, norms, and traditions that slants human behavior one way rather than another. The nature of political culture is revealed in Benjamin Cohen's tongue-in-cheek description of the perfect European: "He or she has the humility of a Frenchman, the punctuality of an Italian, the sense of humor of a German, the gastronomic good taste of an Englishman, the temperance of an Irishman, the generosity of a Dutchman, the good grooming of a Belgian and the world outlook of a Luxemburger."

Politics is social action that seeks to solve the tension between human needs and social facts in a particular cultural world.[1] Social facts, or existing social conditions, are marked by scarcity and deprivation, motivating human beings to ease their dissatisfaction by organizing politically. Human needs, according to Abraham Maslow, include bodily needs, security, love or belonging, self-esteem, and self-actualization—

in order of priority.[2] If I am not starving, I can worry about the bullets flying over my head; when the bullets stop, I can make love; when my basic physical security and belongingness needs are met, I have time to cultivate my self-worth or, if I am lucky enough to match my talents with the right opportunity, to self-actualize. And of course it is possible to have all of these needs, or a mix of them, simultaneously. However, the modes of expression of human motivation resulting from these needs vary from one culture to another because of differences in tradition and collective experience. Political culture thus slants and colors our needs, causing us to act one way rather than another.

In *Civilization and Its Discontents* (1930) Sigmund Freud defined culture as the product of the tension between the needs or drives of the individual as consciously directed by the ego and the existing norms or laws of a particular society, that is, the superego. An upwardly mobile middle-class person tries to make his way without breaking the laws of his society or violating its informal taboos; in the same society an artist may perceive her actualization to lie in continual rebellion against those very norms and taboos. Moreover, as anthropologists have shown, "No culture in its totality is a commodity or export. This is why any people who, by any method, whether by conquest or persuasion, assume that they can cause another group to change its entire way of life, are building policy on a psychological unreality. . . . Culture is not a straitjacket."[3] So much for the exportation of American capitalism, Chinese socialism, and the German economic miracle.

Human *needs* are universally recognized physical and psychological prerequisites for healthy human existence, and can be satisfied. *Values*, on the other hand, refer to what human beings want, regardless of what they actually need, and cannot be satisfied because people tend to want more than they need. The distinction between needs and values is critical in analyzing human motivations and political culture, since human needs, by their very nature, are universal, whereas values tend to be culturally specific and are not universal in the way they cluster in people's priority scales. Theoretically, it is possible for social scientists to identify a universal human-need scale, including both individual and social needs, with verifiable limits, and this holds the promise of some cross-cultural basis for public policy making.

Individual motivation derives from a mix of needs and values aimed at maximizing both the individual's life chances and those of the group to which he or she belongs. This applies to members of both majority and deviant groups. Take, for example, General Charles de Gaulle of France, who identified his own need for security and self-esteem with French cultural supremacy and attempted to maximize the life chances of both himself and his people in bargaining with other nations.[4] Similarly, terrorists in Western Europe have formed international groups such as "Terror International" to satisfy their mutual needs regardless of their national backgrounds or specific objectives.

Just as language is the skin of a political culture, each individual is a crucible of his or her psychocultural milieu. *Personality* refers to how an individual integrates his or her needs and values to form an identity. Such integration is based on a person's biological, psychological, and sociological circumstances.[5] From a Freudian point of view, although people's biological and psychological makeup determines their drives (i.e., how they mobilize their energies), the facts of the social and cultural world reinforce certain of these drives and tensions and reduce others. Such a political-culture explanation may lie behind the apparent contrast between the frequency of bizarre individual acts of violence in the United States (e.g., haphazard shootings or murders of young women) compared to collectivist acts of group violence in Western Europe (e.g., kidnapings). Deviants work out the frustration of their life chances in the existing social system by selecting modes of rebellion or violence that their own culture has more or less preselected for them. Americans tend toward individualist modes, Europeans toward collectivist modes.

The experiential aspect of knowing another culture is usually underestimated in comparing political systems. Political philosopher Eric Voegelin wrote: "Human society is not merely a fact, or an event, in the external world to be studied by an observer like a natural phenomenon. . . . It is a whole little world . . . illuminated with meaning from within by the human beings who continuously create and bear it as the mode and condition of their self-realization."[6] To view individuals from different cultures as "little worlds illuminated with meaning" is to recognize their social existence and values as well as their physical existence and movements.[7] This subjective aspect is what distinguishes social science from natural science. For example, sociologist Max Weber defined a social event, in contrast to a natural event, as an existential or physical occurrence *and the significance with which it is imbued,* that is, facts *plus values.* He went on to say that "there is no absolutely 'objective' scientific analysis of culture . . . [or] of 'social phenomena' independent of special and 'one-sided' viewpoints according to which— expressly or tacitly, consciously or unconsciously—they are selected, analyzed and organized for expository purposes."[8]

Take the example of a tree that falls over in the middle of a desert isolated from all human observation: this is a natural or physical event. But if the tree should fall on a telephone line the occurrence is immediately imbued with social significance (assuming that someone is cut off or notices that the line is down); the natural event is transformed into a social event as individual human beings ascribe meaning to it. By making the psychocultural modes of motivation explicit in various cultures it becomes possible to compare the similarities and differences in the ways individuals from different places ascribe meaning to events, and to distinguish universal needs and behavior from culturally specific values and customs. To understand the role of individual and group behavior in comparing political systems, we must take literally the saying "When in Rome, do as the Romans do."

Social and Political Institutions: Structures

When human beings organize to satisfy their needs and solve their problems, they create social relationships. After some time these social relationships become routines or taken-for-granted social facts: they become institutions. *Political institutions* are patterns of problem solving used over and over again that are relevant to people's political problems (or what they perceive as problems). Parliaments, constitutions, legal systems, armies, and welfare administrations are political institutions. Patterns in the social environment that constrict or reinforce what individuals can do to satisfy their needs, on the other hand, are *social institutions*. Although personal values may highlight an individual's ideal life chances, social institutions shape his or her real life chances. Typical social institutions include social class and status. *Social class* is how much one has of what there is to get—an individual's location in a social hierarchy as compared with others who also want what he or she wants. *Social status,* on the other hand, is where others *think* an individual is in the social hierarchy: how much they think a person has of what there is to have. Whereas class measures *objectively* how much money people have, how they earn it, what they spend it on, and their family and educational background, status is a *subjective* measure of the deference accorded to a person by others. For example, an aristocrat who has lost his or her money may still be accorded status. Social institutions such as class and status are the basis of potential political power for both individuals and groups.

Of course, other social facts exist that frustrate the needs of the individual citizen in addition to political and social institutions: existing values, personalities, and rules of the game. The social values of others often limit and reinforce the individual's behavior, depending on peer group pressures and what behavior is considered socially acceptable where the individual lives and works. Moreover, individuals often find themselves caught in value changes taking place in the society so that they do not know where to turn. Recent comparative studies indicate a shift in values among young people in Western industrial democracies away from materialistic, work-oriented, public-spirited values and toward private satisfaction, leisure, meeting the need for belonging, and for intellectual and aesthetic self-fulfillment.[9]

Similarly, changes in the rules of the game can be disorienting. The rules of the game are the taken-for-granted problem-solving procedures of any political world. In Western capitalist democracies, for example, the rules of the political economy provide that individuals may initiate economic or business activity up to the limits of state laws and informal norms of "proper" behavior. In socialist societies, on the other hand, the economic initiatives do not lie with the individual as much as with the state itself. In the United States anything is allowed unless it has been restricted by the state, whereas in the Soviet Union nothing is permitted unless it has been initiated by the state. Not to understand such differences in the rules of the game can lead to clear-cut economic losses. Thus, Raymond Vernon points out that if American policy makers use Western concepts like tariff protection, antidumping laws, most-favored-nation treatment, currency convertibility, and patent licensing, originally adapted for the American rules, in bargaining with the Soviet Union, they may find themselves further upsetting America's trade and monetary position as well as undermining agreements with its European allies. Bargaining strategies are different among entrepreneurs than among *apparatchiks* (socialist bureaucrats).[10]

How these different types of social facts—social institutions, political institutions, existing values, rules of the game, and personalities—cluster in a particular situation determines the potential bargaining power of an individual in his or her nation, and of the nation in negotiating with other nations. A nation like West Germany, for example, has a great deal of potential bargaining power, given its upper-class socioeconomic status in Europe; its stable political institutions; its work–save–invest social values; its ability to shape the Common Market's economic rules of the game in such a way as to preserve its export market; and its recent dynamic leaders, Chancellors Willy Brandt and Helmut Schmidt, who have often proven surprisingly successful in transforming West Germany's potential power into actual power. Existing social facts structure the social world in a way that gives certain individuals and groups greater potential power to satisfy their needs and maximize their values than others. Your real life chances depend on where you are standing in the hierarchy of social facts.

Given existing structures of social facts, there are two basic ideologies suggesting how they should be interpreted: those that ultimately seek to conserve existing social and political structures for the sake of stability, and those that ultimately seek to adapt existing structures to rapidly changing social and environmental conditions for the sake of maximizing the life chances of a greater number of human beings. Perhaps the best example of the conservative view of comparative analysis is the "overloaded" systems model popularized by Michel

Crozier, Samuel Huntington, and Joji Watanuki in their report to the Trilateral Commission on the governability of democracies.

In this report, published as *The Crisis of Democracy*, the authors paint a gloomy picture of once-stable democratic systems in Western Europe, the United States, and Japan headed for breakdown or decline because their governmental capacity to cope has become stagnant while the social demands on their democratic structures have increased in both quantity and intensity. Their argument is that the conjunction of contextual (environmental) or social trends and challenges intrinsic to democracy itself have overwhelmed democratic governmental systems with demands and pressures that are beyond their capacities. Contextual threats include factors like diplomatic defeat, worldwide inflation or recession, increasing dependence on resources from abroad—any changes in the distribution of economic, military, and political power in the world that affect the interests of a democratic state. Demands resulting from social structure and social trends include factors such as the increasing concentration of wealth in the hands of a few individuals; polarization between ethnic or regional groups; intellectuals attacking the corruption, materialism, and inefficiency of democracy; and changes in cultural values away from a work orientation and public spiritedness toward private satisfactions and leisure. By intrinsic challenges to democracy the authors of the Trilateral Commission report mean that "democratic government does not necessarily function in a self-sustaining or self-correcting equilibrium fashion. It may instead function so as to give rise to forces and tendencies which, if unchecked by some outside agency, will eventually lead to the undermining of democracy."[11]

The Trilateral Commission report's pessimistic view of democracy as tending to do itself in, as needing to be checked "by some outside agency," has the ominous ring of an authoritarian managerial elite that finds it difficult to tolerate the ambiguous inefficiencies and loud demands of democracy and longs for order and structural stability above all else—including individual freedom. Indeed, it can be argued that Western industrial democracies have fallen on hard times and lost legitimacy and stability not because of too much democracy but because of too little: corrupt, unresponsive, and unrepresentative elites have often led their peoples down technocratic garden paths that undermined the possibility of democratic participation and morale-building consensus without solving pressing problems. An example is the apparent popular rejection of more nuclear power plants in France, Italy, Austria, and West Germany after years of administrative indifference to protests by anti-nuclear groups. Rather than viewing democracy as an inherently unstable structure, it may be best to restore its original meaning: government by and for the people.[12]

Political-Economic Codes: Bargaining Behavior

A comparative analysis focusing on existing structures and over-loaded systems is not wrong so much as aimed the wrong way: to describe existing structures and the limited capacities of political systems is critical, but to overstress these elements is to focus on reactions to social change (i.e., in terms of the past) rather than on adaptations to anticipated social change (i.e., in terms of the future). To be responsible for the future of its people, a government must think and plan in terms of the problems they are likely to face and adapt existing structures in advance in ways that will improve the life chances of as many citizens as possible. The "poverty of historicism," as Karl Popper would put it, can have serious ethical consequences.[13]

The question is how to learn from the past without being trapped by it. Popper's point is that history is a bad guide for predicting the future, since we cannot know what people in the future will know and, therefore, what alternatives they are likely to choose. On the other hand, there is a tenacity about past traditions and existing institutions that often makes technological innovation seem superficial, like new gimmicks on an old façade. What counts most in policy analysis is to identify how past cultural forces and present institutions are apt to be mixed by decision makers in planning strategies for the future. Strategy is the futurity of present decisions—a cost–benefit calculation that aims at the long term. In this sense no strategy is a tacit strategy, just as non-decision-making is decision making: history will go on behind one's back and dole out costs and benefits regardless of any individual's intentions. But the critical focus is on the limited freedom people have to influence events in their behalf, to bargain for their future. Political economy provides a useful way of studying such collective bargaining behavior and the national strategies involved in costly choices.

In terms of Sigmund Freud's theory of civilization, political economy can be viewed as the superego incarnate: Political economy sets the rules for the transformation of potential into actual bargaining power and for payoffs or punishments. Thus, the focus is not on *any* human behavior but on that which is paid off or punished. In postindustrial Western societies like the United States and the European Community countries, this means focusing on bargaining behavior in which the material hedonism (the psychocultural motivation to seek pleasure and avoid pain) of Westerners comes together with the institutional structures of capitalistic liberalism and social democracy, resulting in concrete acts to be compared and evaluated in terms of the payoffs to the individual on the one hand and to the community, region, and world on the other. Such individual action and the reward structure behind it is, indeed, the *real* focus of most living politics: the collective decision making that results in specific domestic and foreign policies.

The concrete result of past bargaining or collective decision making in the public sphere is the budget. Over half a century ago economist Rudolf Goldscheid wrote that "the budget is the skeleton of the state stripped of all misleading ideologies." The present budget of a government, together with tax and other fiscal laws, represents the present public distribution of goods and services throughout the society. From this there emerge two basic conflicting ideologies of political-economic bargaining that are characteristic of all industrial societies—one that focuses on the redistribution of present benefits and one that seeks to maximize the production of future benefits.

The Politics of Equality vs. the Politics of Productivity

The political-economic doctrine of the Left is the politics of equality, focusing on a more equal distribution of goods, services, and opportunities in the present. In terms of motivation, the egalitarian ideology argues that *because of* past inequalities political action should emphasize the redistribution of life chances in the present for the sake of social justice.

The political-economic doctrine of the Right is the politics of productivity, stressing the maximization of economic growth and industrial and technological development in the future. Individual freedom to .stimulate productive work through the incentives of a relatively free market is seen to be more important than social justice. The productivity ideology has a future-oriented motivation: in order to create more wealth and productivity in the future, political action should organize society in the way that is most likely to increase production and industrial and technological growth.[14] If this means the continuance of an unequal hierarchy of life chances in society, with the rich and competent receiving the greatest benefits, so be it. The capitalist argument is that everyone, rich and poor, will be better off with greater productivity.

Modern capitalist societies appear to go through various stages of development with regard to these conflicting views of time, motivation, and value priorities. Early industrialization seems to have a consumption orientation; it is concerned with the present. Late industrialization stresses investment, with an accent on the future.[15] Postindustrial societies come finally to a stalemate between these two perspectives as some people become so well off or hedonistic that they want to live and consume in the present rather than sacrificing and saving for the future while others, out of habit, responsibility, or belief, have a greater propensity toward savings and are more concerned with investing for the future than with living in the present. As Professor

James Kurth has noted, capitalist societies today are characterized by awkward governing coalitions of groups oriented toward the past (e.g., small farmers) and the future (e.g., forward-looking industrialists), who are united in their opposition to groups oriented toward the present (those who want a fairer redistribution of goods for consumption now).[16] The inequalities resulting from these governing coalitions provoke predictable reactions from the groups that are out of power, as can be seen in Italy and France today. Political economy, then, is the existing payoff structure resulting from the constant bargaining between the Left and the Right.

Domestic and Foreign Policies: Outcomes of Collective Decision Making

Industrial political economies are perhaps best understood as mixtures of the politics of productivity and the politics of equality. They mix stimulants for the industrial sector with payoffs for the social sector. The industrial sector is dominated by exchange economics made up of two-way transfers of goods, services, or values—as in business deals. The social sector, in contrast, thrives on grants economics, which consists of one-way transfer payments such as taxes, welfare, and foundation grants. The domestic and foreign policies resulting from such political-economic mixtures are interrelated. Some policies, for example, stress payoffs to domestic demand, whereas others give higher payoffs to export trade. And the relative value and stability of a nation's currency has much to do with unemployment and economic stability at home as well as with the price of exports abroad.

Two policy areas symbolize the political-economic drama of our times: *social policy*, representing the politics of equality, versus *industrial policy*, representing the politics of productivity. Social policy includes such issues as health, education, welfare, transportation, and subsidies for the arts. Economist Kenneth Boulding has shown that social grants are motivated by both love and fear. Gifts are grants given out of love of one's fellow human beings and the desire to integrate the human family. Tributes are grants paid out of fear of blackmail or violence by the repressed and dispossessed if they are not "paid off" to keep them quiet. Since about one-third of many industrial economies consists of grants or one-way transfers, and since this percentage of the total is rising, no theory of comparative politics is complete if it leaves out matters of social policy.[17]

Industrial policy, on the other hand, includes such issues as economic-growth policy, inflation controls, management–labor relations, and legislation affecting the size, power, freedom, and tax base of corporations. It is traditionally concerned with two-way exchange economics and, in the West, with the "free-enterprise system." Whereas, as mentioned earlier, social policy (and the politics of equality) focuses on redistribution of the existing economic pie, industrial policy (and the politics of productivity) stresses the production of more pie. Politics is the collective decision-making process that seeks to solve the tensions between social and industrial needs on the one hand and the finite limits of social facts and resources on the other. The extent to which a certain structure of inequality is necessary for efficient production and management in advanced industrial societies, whether capitalist or socialist, is perhaps the central political-economic question of the late twentieth century.

Foreign Policy as an Extension of Domestic Policy

In our era of interdependence the traditional distinction between domestic and foreign policy has collapsed. The breakdown of the Bretton Woods international economic system, the rise of commodity cartels, the spread of recession and inflation throughout the world, the global grain and energy shortages, the proliferation of nuclear weapons—all of these problems have melted the boundaries between domestic and foreign policy making. Yet as Professor Peter Katzenstein of Cornell has noted, many political analysts have failed to take this development into account:

> It has struck me as odd that the recent shift from military to economic issues in international politics was not accompanied by a corresponding shift from foreign to domestic political analysis. Plausibility speaks for adopting a type of analysis which differs depending upon whether it deals with the sandbox of the strategist or the pocketbook of the entrepreneur. Since the primary constraints on government policy have shifted away from the international and toward the domestic level, foreign and domestic affairs have become closely intertwined. Analysis of contemporary foreign economic politics is inadequate as long as it focuses only on the "internalization" of international relations: the "externalization" of domestic structures is also of great importance.[18]

Viewed as an "externalization of domestic structures" or policies, foreign policies become comprehensible as attempts by national elites to maximize the life chances of people in their own nation. The love-or-threat motivations for social policy at home become the incentives for aid to developing countries and allies abroad, whereas the economic-growth objectives of domestic industrial policy become efforts to increase exports by seeking government contracts, devaluing currencies, or other means. France is a classic case of a national government that sets foreign policy as much as possible on the basis of domestic needs and interests, to such an extent that the French President even travels throughout the world scaring up business contracts for French industry. The fact that global economic, security, and political conditions sometimes frustrate these efforts does not stop the efforts or change the domestic source of foreign-policy motivation: social facts at the regional and global level are seen merely as obstacles to or instruments in the effort to achieve domestic objectives.

Regional and Global Constraints or Systemic Parameters

The extent to which domestic-policy objectives are constrained by regional or global conditions depends on how benign such conditions are or how much they can be used to promote a state's interests. After World War II, for example, in a regional and global situation that seemed extremely unfavorable to France, General de Gaulle managed to manipulate France back into the circle of big powers and, later, to use the regional framework of the Common Market to set up rules of the game that would benefit French agriculture. At the time people from other countries thought of de Gaulle as some kind of nationalistic megalomaniac. But from a detached, retrospective viewpoint his policies worked to maximize French interests. Similarly, the Germans used the Common Market framework to incorporate their own economic and political power and make their export-oriented foreign economic policy more palatable to nations that were still smarting from the memory of aggressive German nationalism.

Of course, the unstable global economic system of the past decade cannot be considered "benign," and many nations find the constraints on their foreign-policy options unbearably real. In the mid-1970s, for example, the British watched in horror as the value of the pound sterling fell rapidly ("beginning its descent into hell," as one Englishman put it). Although much of the pound's weakness at that time could be attributed to ineffective domestic social and industrial policies, the immediate cause of its precipitous fall appeared to be withdrawal of investments by Arab oil producers seeking to cash in on some old-rich turf only to discover that it was more old than rich.[19] But the control of so many petrodollars on the global market certainly gives Arab oil producers a greater national bargaining position in the world political economy and has been used to create surprising constraints on otherwise powerful nations such as the United States and major Western European nations.

On the other hand, in what appeared to be a disastrous economic situation from a regional and global perspective, Italians initially refused to change their behavior patterns even in the face of government austerity policies: "What austerity?" said Dario Armelini, the owner of a store near the Pantheon in downtown Rome. "No one is paying attention. Just look at all the cars going by. Italians continue to spend, to eat imported steaks, just like before. They refuse to feel the sting."[20] Indeed, perhaps the most effective part of Italian domestic–foreign policy in the world economic crisis of the 1970s was Italy's strategy of using its weakness to great advantage. Fearing that Italy might go totally communist and break away from the NATO bloc, West Germany, the United States, and others continued to bail it out with loans. Global academic theorists might learn a thing or two from experienced Old World players: people usually behave in terms of what pays off in the short run regardless of possible long-term consequences. If decadent consumption and celebration of the present seems to work, why not live it up?

Another example of the effectiveness of ignoring global and regional realities as long as they stay benign is the security dilemma in Western Europe. The Western conventional forces are greatly outnumbered by Eastern bloc troops, yet this does not cause either the Western Europeans or the Americans to respond with an adequate increase of Western conventional forces. Depending on theater nuclear weapons, which neither answer the challenge to conventional threats nor are likely to be used for fear of nuclear war, the Western Europeans continue to concentrate on their economic and social problems and take their security for granted. And to the armchair academic theorists who lose sleep at night worrying about the global balance of power, a typical Old World European might turn and say, "Really, you must try some St. Nicolas-de-Bourgueil. 1976 was an excellent vintage year for Val de Loire reds, you know. . . . "

But despite the short-term national interests responsible for much of European day-to-day policy making, the leaders of Western European nations are profoundly aware of the long-term importance of regional cooperation if Western Europe is to function as an effective bargaining bloc in world politics. The European Economic Community (EEC), or Common Market, has already established an effective club of privileged members that can increase their individual economic power by taking common stands on issues both inside and outside the community. For example, in the Lomé Convention of 1975 the nine Common Market countries agreed to give forty-five African countries privileged access to the market of the EEC for all of their products. Such exclusive agreements between particular regional blocs can have significant long-term effects on the economic and political map of the world and help transform Western Europe's economic power into real political influence.

Another positive indicator of the Common Market's economic power was the 1978 agreement between West Germany and France to establish a common EEC currency stabilization system based on a community unit of account (the European Community unit, or ECU). This agreement was made possible by a common international "threat" (the instability of the dollar and the world monetary system and U.S.–European frictions) and by similarities in the domestic political-economic policies of West Germany and France (an effective consensus between Chancellor Helmut Schmidt and President Giscard d'Estaing after the Left's loss in the spring 1978 French elections). Whether or not this European monetary system, which began officially in 1979 with eight EEC countries, will eventually lead to the long-awaited European monetary union may be less important than the effects of the existing pragmatic consensus on the world's monetary system.

The European Parliament for all Common Market countries elected in June 1979 may further the cause of unity in the Western European bloc by building transnational popular support for Europeanism. On the other hand, it may also have the effect of diluting the elitist management of European power with democratization and interest group squabbles, which would make the European Community more egalitarian while complicating its attempts to achieve unified foreign-policy positions. The egalitarianism-versus-effectiveness trade-off is becoming increasingly critical in foreign policy as well as in domestic political-economic decision making, for the domestic and foreign arenas have become inseparable.

The thrust of the argument here is that old categories—domestic versus foreign policy, comparative versus international politics, capitalist versus socialist political economies—have become so intermingled in the advanced industrial societies of Europe as to lose their utility. It may be more fruitful to compare national political-economic strategies in coping with change in a world as interdependent as ours has become. By focusing on the bargaining power of particular nations at specific historical moments, we may be able to come closer to predicting which of these strategies will be most successful in the long run— and at what cost in either productivity or redistribution, wealth or social justice.

In these terms, national indifference to selective regional and international realities often constitutes a deliberate strategy for managing change. In the late twentieth century the nation–state is so permeated by social and technological change and so dependent on so many factors that are beyond its control that national decision makers would face a hopeless task if they tried to take everything into account at once and to act on all fronts simultaneously. Indeed, the great advantage of a learning-by-paying or political-economic model of the management of change is that it gives policy makers in "overloaded democracies" criteria for coping with a storm of alternatives and pressures.

The learning-by-paying model, viewed conservatively, is one of anticipated loss: how can national policy makers lose least by adopting certain policies rather than others? What costs can be anticipated, and how accurately can their range be measured? What kinds of costs must be prepared for that are beyond the possibility of recognition at this time? Which costs must be paid for now—in either the public or the private sector—that are likely to become unbearably expensive later, when inflation drives their prices up? Which short-term costs can be safely ignored or postponed until the situation becomes more clear?

Viewed liberally, the learning-by-paying model is one of possible gains—or lost opportunities: how can national policy makers best use their present limited resources to invest for long-term gains that will match or do better than inflation? Which short-term investments now will bring the greatest long-term payoff for the nation? Which changes are on the horizon that can be adapted to immediately by national leaders and elites on the superstructural level and, in turn, can have a symbolic effect on the possibility of future change at the infrastructural and substructural levels? Which infrastructural changes must be attempted immediately to head off hopeless dependency on others in the future? Which dependencies must be assumed to be inevitable in order to free resources in these areas for investment in projects with great long-term potential for national need satisfaction?

In eras of rapid social change and perceived loss and status deprivation, most people revert to a conservative impulse that induces them to keep up old relationships and continuities in order to maintain psychological, if not social, equilibrium.[21] The primary task of a learning approach to political economy is to determine which of these conservative psychocultural impulses should be supported by the government for the sake of stability, order, and legitimacy and which should be opposed or redirected by political leadership to prepare people for inevitable changes that must be made for the sake of the nation's survival as an effective bargaining unit. The democratic representatives of a well-managed nation should aim for a dynamic equilibrium between productivity and redistribution, between entrepreneurial economic planning for the future and a juster distribution of opportunities and benefits in the present. The cases of West Germany, France, Britain, Italy, and the European Community provide useful illustrations of good and bad policy strategies under different conditions in the continual human struggle to create a state of both prosperity and social justice.

NOTES

1. The theory behind this definition of politics is spelled out in R. P. Hummel and R. A. Isaak, *Politics for Human Beings*, 2nd ed. (North Scituate, Mass.: Duxbury Press, Wadsworth Publishing Co., 1980).

2. Beginning with the most basic needs, Abraham Maslow's empirically grounded need hierarchy is defined as follows: (1) physiological needs: food, water, rest; (2) security needs: physical and psychic security; (3) love needs: warmth, affection, inclusion; (4) self-esteem needs: positive evaluation of the self by the self and others; (5) self-actualization needs: fulfilling one's highest potential, superior perception of reality, increased spontaneity and creativity, increased identification with the human species. See Abraham Maslow, *Motivation and Personality* (New York: Harper & Row, 1954). For cross-cultural empirical support of the universality of Maslow's need hierarchy, see Joel Aronoff, *Psychological Needs and Cultural Systems* (Princeton, N.J.: Van Nostrand, 1967), and Jeanne N. Knutson, *The Human Basis of the Polity* (Chicago: Aldine-Atherton, 1972).

3. Melville J. Herskovits, *Cultural Relativism* (New York: Random House, Vintage Books, 1973), p. 71.

4. For the analysis of de Gaulle and other world leaders as psychocultural leaders who seek to satisfy their own needs and values by satisfying those of their peoples, see R. Isaak, *Individuals and World Politics*, 2nd ed. (North Scituate, Mass.: Duxbury Press, Wadsworth Publishing Co., 1980).

5. See Robert W. White, *Lives in Progress* (New York: Holt, Rinehart and Winston, 1966), pp. 1–26.

6. Eric Voegelin, *The New Science of Politics* (Chicago: University of Chicago Press, 1952), p. 27. See also Charles W. Anderson, "System and Strategy in Comparative Policy Analysis: A Plea for Contextual and Experiential Knowledge," in William B. Gwyn and George C. Edwards, III, eds., *Perspectives in Public Policy-Making* (New Orleans: Department of Political Science, Tulane University, 1975).

7. See R. Isaak, "The Individual in International Politics: Solving the Level-of-Analysis Problem," *Polity*, 7, no. 2 (1974).

8. Max Weber, *The Methodology of the Social Sciences*, ed. Edward A. Shils and Henry A. Finch (New York: Free Press, 1949), p. 81.

9. See Ronald Inglehart, "The Silent Revolution in Europe: Intergenerational Change in Postindustrial Societies," *American Political Science Review*, 65 (December 1971), 991ff.

10. Raymond Vernon, "Apparatchiks and Entrepreneurs: U.S.–Soviet Economic Relations," *Foreign Affairs*, 52, no. 2 (January 1974), 249–262.

11. Michel Crozier, Samuel Huntington, and Joji Watanuki, *The Crisis of Democracy: Report on the Governability of Democracies to the Trilateral Commission* (New York: New York University Press, 1975), p. 8.

12. See R. Isaak, *American Democracy and World Power* (New York: St. Martin's, 1977).

13. See Karl Popper, *The Poverty of Historicism* (Boston: Beacon, 1957).

14. This differentiation of political-economic motivations is based on sociologist Alfred Schutz's distinction between "because-motive" *(Weil-Motiv)* and

"in-order-to-motive" *(Um-zu-Motiv)*. Schutz defined the "in-order-to-motive" as considering the whole action (characterized by the complete purpose envisioned) apart from any given phase. The "because-motive," on the other hand, refers to an event lying in one's past that led him to project a particular act. See Alfred Schutz, *Collected Papers*, vol. I, *The Problem of Social Reality*, "Common-Sense and Scientific Interpretation of Human Action" (The Hague: Martinus Nijhoff, 1973), esp. pp. 19–22.

15. See Charles Maier, "The Politics of Productivity: Domestic Sources of American International Economic Policy After World War II," paper presented at the Conference on Foreign Economic Policy of Advanced Industrial States, Cambridge, Mass., October 28–30, 1976. Reprinted in Peter Katzenstein, ed., *Between Power and Plenty* (Madison: University of Wisconsin Press, 1978).

16. Professor James Kurth of Princeton's Center for Advanced Studies made this observation at the conference cited in note 15.

17. See Kenneth Boulding, *The Economy of Love and Fear* (Belmont, Calif.: Wadsworth, 1973).

18. Peter J. Katzenstein, "International Relations and Domestic Structures: Foreign Economic Policies of Advanced Industrial States," *International Organization*, 30, no. 1 (Winter 1976), 2.

19. See "Gloom Is Spreading as Problems Grow in World Economy," *New York Times*, November 1, 1976, pp. 65, 67.

20. Alvin Shuster, "For the Italians, Many Appeals, Few Sacrifices," *New York Times*, October 31, 1976.

21. Peter Marris, *Loss and Change* (New York: Pantheon Books, 1974).

Chapter 2
West Germany:
A Social-market Economy

The West Germans are becoming more conservative—that is the way they are voting—and less eager for change in their lives than they were, say, 10 years ago. Wealth and the traditional virtue of hard work seem to go together still, even for the richest among them.
—Craig R. Whitney, *The New York Times*, November 13, 1976

In southern Europe, around the Mediterranean, there has been a movement toward the political left with the goal of changing intransigent economies that frustrate the life chances of the masses. In northern Europe, a shift to the right has taken place, stimulated by the discovery of the hidden economic costs of fulfilling the social needs of so many people in the form of welfare, unemployment benefits, and other transfer payments. West Germany* is probably the most important of the northern European countries that have moved in a conservative direction, since it is seen as the economic model of success by people in other European countries who envy its ability to keep inflation and unemployment relatively low while maintaining a high standard of living and a steady rate of economic growth. West Germans, in short, are seen as the rich of Western Europe.

Why did the Germans become so rich so fast after suffering a disastrous defeat in World War II? Various theses have been suggested to explain "the German economic miracle," each accenting a different aspect of the total picture. Some say that this fast rise in economic and political power was due to psychocultural factors—attitudes toward work, saving, investment, and order. Others stress political and social institutions, suggesting that a residue of fascist institutions was restructured and that an aggressive free-market economy was then erected on this foundation. Another explanation focuses on political-economic strategies and bargaining power. According to this view, the Germans astutely sought to tie up the industrial market in Western Europe

*See appendix, p. 210, for political-economic events of West Germany.

through the Common Market while throwing most of their national energies into the world export markets and new industrial technology. Still others highlight particular domestic and foreign policies, such as using the United States and the Common Market as security and political umbrellas, thereby freeing energy for domestic recovery and hiding the nation's growing strength. Finally, some look to outside regional and global conditions, arguing that the German miracle was a real miracle, more a question of chance and good luck than a matter of policy: the division of Germany forced the West Germans to push their exports in order to make up for their lost domestic market, and American capital helped finance this concentrated entrepreneurship.

Although all of these factors played a role, people throughout the world would like to know exactly how they came together to produce the consolidation of wealth and power that makes West Germany the model of a postindustrial capitalist democracy balancing social-need satisfaction with industrial growth. Is the German "miracle" a pattern that others should follow, or is it a one-time occurrence whose relevance is passing? Everyone wants a miracle, but to what extent is it wise for other countries to use this one as a basis for national planning?

The West German case raises many other intriguing questions as well. Who benefits most within German society today? Who benefits least? What are the implications of this political-economic system for other European countries? for the world? A brief examination of contemporary West Germany and its origins may shed some light on such questions.

WEST GERMAN POLITICAL CULTURE: MOTIVATIONS

The German philosopher Friedrich Nietzsche said that there is something peculiar about the Germans insofar as no matter what one says about them one is bound to be partially right. But beyond this diversity and complexity, a certain picture emerges from the history of German development, a picture that reveals a tradition of conservatism that does not deny liberalism so much as it overwhelms it. For German conservatism is not merely a momentary "world view" but a deep-rooted philosophical *Weltanschauung*—an almost untranslatable German term for a world view with "overtones of ideology, of a tendency towards, but not necessarily a fulfillment of, a systematic, comprehensive view of the world."[1] A *Weltanschauung* is a comprehensive and carefully articulated world view that has the potential to become a philosophy of life or an ideology for action.[2]

The roots of contemporary German ideology go back to the days of the Roman empire, which did not include the German tribes, which means that the German culture was never Latinized. Tacitus distinguished among Nordic Teutonic and Roman character types. Unlike the British and French, but like the Italians, the Germans unified as a nation–state quite late. At the beginning of the nineteenth century, Germany was still made up of more than 300 separate principalities. In *Lineages of the Absolutist State,* the historian Perry Anderson suggests that the passage of European nation–states from feudalism to absolutism to modern industrial societies did not eliminate feudalism so much as it extended feudal traditions in other forms, preserving the nobility in one form or another. This was particularly true in Prussia, the largest and strongest of the German states. The nationalistic literature of Johann Gottlieb Fichte, Josef Görres, and Ernst Moritz Arndt prepared the German political conscience for the unification movement. Metternich's balance-of-power strategies cast a conservative shade over Europe, nurturing German conservatism. The liberal exceptions to this trend, such as the revolution of 1848 and the founding of the Weimar Republic in 1919, are notable for their failure.

The historical tradition of philosophical idealism, exemplified by Immanuel Kant, was no match for Chancellor Otto von Bismarck's military and diplomatic strategies for uniting Germany under the domination of the conservative Prussian state, a goal that he accomplished in 1870. Bismarck announced to advocates of parliamentary democracy that "it is not speeches and majority resolutions but iron and blood" that are critical to the survival of a nation. By defeating Austria in 1866 and France in 1870, Bismarck eliminated the major opponents to German unification under Prussian hegemony. Since Prussia made up two-thirds of the territory of the new nation–state, Bismarck resolved the potential conflict between the federal and Prussian administrative authorities by making the Prussian bureaucracy the core of the state's administrative system. He then used this system to introduce social policies such as compulsory health and accident insurance for workers and disability and old-age pensions, making Germany the first European nation to take such steps. These popular social payoffs consolidated the legitimacy of the feudal–military elites of the new Germany. Bismarck's Prussian-dominated absolutism established a political culture of conservative order and civil-service control that helps explain West Germany's stability, order, and efficiency even today.

The Weimar Republic, established after World War I with one of the most democratic constitutions that has ever been written, attempted to resurrect Germany's liberal philosophical and political heritage. But social and economic instability, particularly lack of leadership and the incredible inflation of 1922, undermined the German liberals, preparing the way for the rise of Hitler and national socialism. Shocked that they had lost the war and resentful of the Versailles Treaty, which unjustly held them solely responsible for the war and demanded reparations that they could hardly begin to pay, the German people were overwhelmed by social change and uncertainty. Inflation soared, and political factionalism made social life unpredictable. The conservative impulse of the lower middle classes to recover their sinking status, combined with their fear of the power of big business and big unions, became the basis for the populist fascist movement.[3] Hitler promised revenge for the Treaty of Versailles and a black-and-white ideology of anticommunism and German nationalism in brilliantly orchestrated propaganda campaigns mixed with threats of violence and terror. And he exploited the weaknesses of the Weimar Republic to the hilt.

Hitler's ideological vision was conservative, racist, and militaristic, drawing on the conservative basis prepared by Bismarck and the Prussian Junker nobility and promising salvation from the present chaos. Referring to the First German Reich of the Holy Roman Empire and the Second German Reich of the Hohenzollern Empire of Bismarck, Hitler promised a Third German Reich that would last 1000 years. His charismatic appeal was based on state worship, race worship, and hero worship, culminating in the *Führer*—a majestic leadership role designed for a dictator like himself. By 1932 Hitler's National Socialist Party (the Nazis) drew one-third of the vote. When no constitutional majority could be found to rule Germany through the parliament as the Weimar Constitution anticipated, President von Hindenberg ruled through an emergency clause in the Constitution (Article 48), according to which he could issue decrees that had the force of law without parliamentary approval.

In 1933 von Hindenberg asked Hitler as the leader of the largest German party to form a coalition government. Once he had been made chancellor, Hitler proceeded to destroy the republican and parliamentary structure of the political system by pushing von Hindenberg to expand his emergency powers under Article 48. But by March of 1933 Hitler was able to rally only about 44 percent of the vote, despite his use of storm troopers to harass and terrorize the opposition. For more legitimate power under the Weimar Constitution, Hitler needed the passage of an Enabling Act, which required a two-thirds vote in parliament. To achieve this he arrested about 100 opposition members of parliament, and when von Hindenberg died he declared himself *Führer* by merging the offices of Chancellor and President. All parties but the Nazi party were declared illegal. Dissidents and minorities such as the Jews were systematically eliminated from Nazi society. Hitler constructed a dynamic economy based on heavy industry and armaments, eliminated unemployment, and built superhighways for tanks and trucks. He took over Austria and Czechoslovakia through intimidation and then attacked Poland, beginning World War II in 1939.

After the war, Western liberal capitalism was superimposed on the remains of the old conservative order without really severing the traditional connections among social, economic, and political institutions, despite "de-Nazification" efforts by the victorious Allies. This heritage helps explain the present political importance of German banks (particularly the central bank or *Bundesbank)* and the government's ownership of large shares of some major corporations. Despite Allied efforts to decentralize German political and social institutions in the coal, steel, chemical, and banking industries, strong incentives for concentration remained. The fifty largest firms increased their share of total industrial turnover from 25 percent in 1954 to 42 percent in 1967. The conservative framework inherited from the past provided a domestic consensus and a basis for national economic policy that allowed the Germans to throw their full energies into the export market. They were, after all, precluded by the Allied occupation from undertaking strong political or military development. Meanwhile, many of West Germany's competitors were still desperately groping for some kind of domestic political and economic consensus.

But if the West Germans were so conservative, what explains the often risky entrepreneurial drive that clearly had much to do with Germany's miraculous economic recovery? This too can be explained in part by the perception of status deprivation by a proud people with a long tradition of superiority. Indeed, Peter Marris has demonstrated that acute senses of loss, change, and status deprivation provide the impulse for innovative entrepreneurship, which he identifies as a *conservative* impulse:

> Entrepreneurship seems to depend on a delicate balance of handicap and potential advantage. . . . The innovator is driven by a self-protective impulse: he changes the world, so as not to have to change himself. He seeks out the situations which will confirm his self-image. . . . Even at the point in history where people attempt something new, their underlying motive is still, in a sense, conservative. They displace into original enterprises the purposes they have learned from the society in which they grew up, but cannot satisfy within its orthodox framework. The rewards they hope to win may in themselves be highly conventional—the successful entrepreneur courts acceptance by established good society, acquiring its manners and the trappings of its status.[4]

After World War II the Germans displaced their political and military power drives into entrepreneurial, export-oriented economic drives, just as they transferred their "illegitimate" German nationalism into the "Europeanism" of Common Market ideology. The traumatic experiences of loss, humiliation, and disorder were turned with concerted, conservative energy into economic gains, material status, and industrial order and efficiency of the first magnitude. Conservatives are conditioned to anticipate loss, and its experience drives them to try even harder to find security through incremental gains and innovative undertakings. The center may not hold, but it will always be sought: victory *will* be grasped from the jaws of defeat, even if it is an economic symbol of power, order, and superiority rather than a military one. For example, the perception of insecurity provided by the Soviet threat combined with this "need" for entrepreneurship motivated West German industrialists to invest heavily in South America in the 1950s. Today any claims that such investments represented company foresight in the economic sense should be salted with the security motivations of that period, which led anxious human beings to seek out a safe zone to hedge against an uncertain future.

The economic success of West Germany is, in part, embodied in a psychocultural mode of the ideal typical *modern:* an aggressive manager with a social conscience and a cool head who knows how to use charm to help balance the budget and how to exercise decisive will where charm fails. It has been noted that Marlene Dietrich's movies "remain alive largely because we value coolness more than unrestrained passion."[5] The same German cultural conditioning may explain the international respect accorded to the cool style of some West German political and economic managers, such as Chancellor Helmut Schmidt, who have made liberal social policies go down more easily by cloaking them in fiscal conservatism, the aura of technocratic expertise, and the traditional valuation of the whole community over the interests of any particular member or group.* Even the flat, bureaucratic language of official West German political dialog seems well suited to take the politics out of politics, to damp controversial issues to the point at which they become so boring that they are accepted out of indifference.

The postindustrial style expressed through the West German psychocultural mode may be a universal way of managing modern political economies that have had their traditional norms undermined by "legal–rational" forms of industrialization and bureaucratic organization. Such postindustrial economies have developed to a technological phase in which the legal–rational forms are, in turn, undermined by the establishment of a *technological* society based on an apolitical ideology—the belief that cool-headed technocratic elites must solve prob-

---

*Other German leaders, such as Herbert Wehner, Walter Scheel, Helmut Kohl, and Franz Joseph Strauss, do not have a "cool style." But neither do they have the degree of respect accorded to Schmidt by the managers of other postindustrial political economies.

lems that have grown too complex to be resolved by the common sense of the citizenry.[6] Thus, the German subsystems of "purposive–rational action" and scientific technique may best be understood as a more universal phase of Western modernization, which usually develops beyond the capacity of democratic politics to control the technocracy.[7] West Germany's unique development of political conservatism (mirrored in East Germany by a conservative Stalinist socialism) is but a particular national culture's way of reflecting a more universal psychological conservatism, what Marris calls "the tendency of adaptive beings to assimilate reality to their existing structure, and so to avoid or reorganize parts of the environment which cannot be assimilated."[8] This "conservative impulse" of postindustrial development is what holds together the seemingly contradictory elements of "conservative" free-market entrepreneurial capitalism and "liberal" social democracy and community transfer payments that make up the successful social-market economy of West Germany.

But if postindustrial economic success depends on a flexible, conservative set of social beliefs and motivations, West Germany's unusually conservative *Weltanschauung* may give it a particular edge in world economic competition, just as Japan's conservative world view helps explain its economic success. The comfortable efficiency of the German social order stimulates economic growth and productivity in peacetime, much as it has darker implications in times of war, when respect for German coordination and comradeship becomes fear of the German army and the potential for authoritarianism. Among the many studies of the German psychocultural milieu since the war, one of the most fascinating, if not controversial, is a comparison of American and German values based on the attitudes of schoolboys toward achievement and obligation. In this study David McClelland reduced the findings to different value formulas summing up the psychocultural values of Americans in contrast to Germans.

McClelland's American value formula—or what a typical individual American might say to sum up the norms according to which he or she is supposed to fulfill his or her obligations to self and society—goes like this: "I want to freely choose to do well what others expect me to do." The critical elements here are four: (1) free choice rather than institutional control, (2) action over thought or belief, (3) achievement to do something *well* once an activity is chosen, and (4) other-directedness or conformity—freely choosing to do what *the others* do or want you to do. In contrast, the value formula explaining the individual and social code of proper behavior of an ideal–typical German, says McClelland, would be: "I must be able to believe and do what I should for the good of the whole." Rather than beginning with the "I want" of individual desire or ego typical of Americans, the German begins with "I must,"

Table 2-1 Strengths and Weaknesses of American and German Value Codes

	Normative Ideal	Virtues	Sources of Strain	Excesses
United States				
Obligation to self	Achievement, self-actual-ization	Full use of individual capacities	Blockage of individual desire by group needs	License
Obligation to society	Other-directedness	Humanitar-ianism	Inability to get consensus, changing norms	Over-conformity, lack of original-ity, identity diffusion
Germany				
Obligation to self	Individual self-direc-tion (will power)	Self-disci-pline, work over pleasure, sacrifice of personal impulses	*Überforderung,* demanding too much of the indivi-dual	Arrogance, pride
Obligation to society	Loyalty to an idealistic code of decency	Order, organ-ization	Necessity for rationaliza-tions to get compliance, determining source of authority	Totalitar-ianism, "An order is an order," loss of individu-ality

SOURCE: David C. McClelland, "The United States and Germany: A Comparative Study of National Character," excerpted from D. McClelland, J. F. Stuff, R. H. Knapp, and H. W. Wendt, "Obligations to Self and Society in the United States and Germany," *Journal of Abnormal and Social Psychology,* 56 (1958), 245–255; reprinted in D. McClelland, *The Roots of Consciousness* (New York: D. Van Nostrand, 1964), pp. 62–92. Copyright 1958 by the American Psychological Association. Reprinted by permission.

implying a primary commitment to abstract social standards or obligations outside of himself or herself. In this light individual wanting alone is seen as selfish and the focus becomes *will power,* or "being able" to do what you should, and on *community obligation or duty*—what you should do is good for the whole community, not just yourself. McClelland sums up the strengths and weaknesses of the American and German value codes in table 2-1.

Of course, important changes in West German and American value priorities undoubtedly have taken place since McClelland published his study (in 1958), and such a study can be criticized for running the risk of giving scientific validation to national stereotypes. Despite these drawbacks, social scientists have confirmed some of McClelland's findings. The sociologist Daniel Bell, for example, has argued that the license of countercultural values and life styles (like beatnikism and the hippie movement) has resulted from the successes of American capitalism and may actually undermine the capitalist political economy in the future: capitalism may succeed so well that it does itself in as increased leisure allows more and more people to give up the work ethic for the sake of momentary pleasure and hedonism.[9]

Clearly, Bell's analysis applies in some ways to contemporary West German culture as well, especially given the great impact American cultural and life style patterns have had on young Germans since the war. But in West Germany this "diffusion phenomenon" has been countered by a reaffirmation of traditional values and conservative beliefs.[10] Cultural, sociological, and literary studies demonstrate an increasing West German national consciousness.[11] And interviews reveal that the rich in West Germany have acquired and preserved their wealth through a combination of the traditional value of hard work and a conservative approach to business and politics—with a bit of luck thrown in. Some observers believe that the West Germans are becoming more conservative and less eager for change than they were a decade ago, as indicated by voting trends in the late 1970s in general and the designation of Franz Joseph Strauss as the 1980 Christian Democratic candidate for chancellor in particular.[12]

But on what basis can McClelland's German "value formula" and its more recent variations be called conservative? Or, more broadly, what assumptions allow one to move from specific psychocultural values to a general *ideology*, a frozen set of collective beliefs used as the basis for political action in a particular society? "Left" and "right" or "liberal" and "conservative" must be defined in a way that is universal enough to allow for changes in cultural values and yet remain meaningful. In this larger, historical sense ideology is perhaps best viewed as a love affair between people and a set of ideas that they believe to represent the solution to their problems. Such a view underscores the emotional and experiential aspects of ideology as well as its cognitive and intellectual elements. The psychologist Silvan Tomkins has gathered interdisciplinary evidence demonstrating that to be "to the left" is to be in love with humanity as an end in itself, whereas to be "to the right" is to be enthralled with a standard beyond humanity (a creed, norm, or vision) for which people must discipline themselves. Tomkins spells out this universal ideological polarity:

Man is an end in himself versus man is not an end in himself: the valuable exists independent of man. . . . On the left he conceives himself to be an end in himself, to be of ultimate value; he wishes to be himself and to realize the potentialities which are inherent in him. On the right man is at best neutral, without value, independent of him, and he may become valuable by participation in, conformity to, or achievement of this norm.[13]

Glancing again at table 2-1 you will observe that typical German values are profoundly conservative, or "to the right": self-discipline and sacrifice for the sake of duty to an idealistic order or abstract code of decency; compliance for the sake of the whole community. The whole is assumed to be greater in significance than the sum of its individual parts, in contrast to the more leftward-leaning, "liberal" American values, which locate the meaning of action in individual choices that then add up to make the whole community.

This interpretation of the German political culture explains both right-wing and left-wing extremes, since they both qualify as "conservative" in Tomkins's system-first sense: both East and West Germany set the social order before the individual, one on a Marxist basis and the other from a similar Bismarckian–fascist heritage together with a conservative capitalism. At the least, the implicit conservatism of both East and West Germany in relation to their exceptional postwar economic achievements suggests that political culture cannot be excluded from a sufficient explanation of what makes a national political economy work the way it does.

WEST GERMAN SOCIAL AND POLITICAL INSTITUTIONS: STRUCTURES

Social and economic *structures* are old social relations (or *processes*) that have become institutionalized into routines, norms, laws, and bureaucracies. But since structures still, in part, constitute the active process of people reverting to "conservative impulses" in order somehow to cope with rapid change, they cannot be understood merely in outward physical terms: their outward appearance is merely the concrete symbolization of deeper psychological, anthropological, and mythological meanings of "structures" to a particular people at a certain historical moment. In this sense the psychocultural mode of German conservatism can be viewed as a *substructure,* a motivational *milieu* of collective cultural experience to which individual Germans often return. On this "invisible" heritage has been built the *infrastructure* of West Germany's contemporary social-market economy, the social, industrial, transportation, and resource framework that makes economic productivity and exporting possible. The final, most visible layer is the *superstructure* of governmental, industrial, and labor institutions and processes that attempt to manage the German political economy as a collective unit on a day-to-day basis. These three structural layers are dynamically interrelated, often to the point of being inseparable. West Germany's social economy can be explained only by tracing their roots in both the German past and the Western tradition of political economy.

Few would dispute that the contemporary German situation has to some extent been shaped by Bismarck's successful consolidation of an industrial and imperial state in the nineteenth century. The present German civil service and social-security system can be directly traced to that period. But more important, this critical phase of industrial consolidation, which would make possible a successful capitalistic, democratic political economy in West Germany, was also typical of the modernization of other Western industrial democracies: England, France, Italy, and the United States, among others. Liberal capitalistic democracy is based on an imposed social order or equilibrium (a set of sub-, infra-, and superstructures). This is anything but "democratic" in the pure majority-rule sense of that term.[14] Nor do the similarities end there. In an examination of the relationship between big business firms and Western democratic governments in the 1970s, Raymond Vernon concludes that

> the national policies of the leading European countries toward their large enterprises have taken on greater similarities than they had a decade or two earlier. Moreover, the similarities have included not only those of substance but also those of process and style. In brief, there has been a growing tendency to use large national enterprises in an effort to solve specific problems, as if they were agencies of the state. And there has been a related tendency to develop methods of governance that have reduced the role of the parliamentary process and elevated the role of specialized groups such as large enterprises and large unions.[15]

Parliamentary democracy appears to be *structurally* dominated by corporate, union, and technocratic management. "Managers and experts replace politicians, functionaries replace citizens, administration replaces politics, psychological power replaces ideological power, corporations, public or private, replace, or become superior to nations or the state."[16] *Apolitics* replaces politics in advanced stages of Western modernization: the ideology of managerial expertise replaces the democratic ethos of mass participation by everyday citizens in the solution of public problems.[17]

Yet if the most meaningful structures in Western European industrial governments today are managerial and administrative rather than political or democratic—if these are the startling similarities among Western governments—what are the differences that explain West Germany's distinct economic success and stability relative to other European nations? How do the West Germans do it?

The answer has already been implied: In an era when rational efficiency, effective economic management, and apolitical domestic stability have become the bases for national economic and political power, West Germany's psychocultural tradition, socioeconomic structure, social-market economy, export-oriented foreign policy, and Europeanist ideology put this nation in an ideal position. In a time of incredible social change, a system with the capacity to impose a pattern on reality is naturally apt to do better politically and economically than one that is divided within itself. While chaos often provides opportunities for dictatorships, rapid social change provides opportunities for well-organized bureaucracies and technocratic elites. West Germany's communal "conservative impulse" following the dislocations of World War II has been effectively incorporated into a social order and a political structure to make the German "economic miracle" possible.

Unlike other Western industrial economies, German industrialization in the nineteenth century was largely due to state economic institutions; Germany was not presented with a full-fledged capitalist economic system until after World War II. So just as the Germans had a long heritage of paternal authority in family relations, Germany had a tradition of state authority in political-economic relations. In addition to this underlying background of state-controlled stability, the basis for the dramatic postwar economic recovery depended on West German willingness to accept the historical concentration of wealth and property in West German society as well. As the economist Georg Küster has noted,

> The recovery of the economy was greatly helped by two factors: by substantial initial state aids for private industry; and by the fact that the old prewar structure of capital and wealth in Germany was almost wholly retained. In 1948, the Federal Republic began with a private economy "whose structure was the same as, and whose degree of concentration was only minimally lower than, that under the rule of National Socialism; and this private economy was left to the 'free play of forces.' " The experiment of the social market economy, therefore, involved an element of reversion and restoration: "When the Germans began to reconstruct their economy, they built upon the familiar structural foundation and plan, much of it invisible to the naked eye, as if guided by an archeologist who could pick his way blindfold about some favourite ruin."[18]

In short, after World War II the Western allies imposed a democratic government and a capitalist economy *on top of* a relatively undisturbed substructure of sociocultural attitudes toward state authority and existing economic interests. The apolitical acceptance of the postwar socioeconomic structure by the West German people assured the domestic stability that allowed the erection of an effective free-market economy and an aggressive export trade policy, which, combined with more socially conscious and progressive economic policies, resulted in the "economic miracle."

THE GOVERNMENT FRAMEWORK AND PARTY SYSTEM

Traditionally, the West German government is described in terms of institutional structure rather than political-economic bargaining power. In 1949 the Federal Republic of Germany, or West Germany, was created out of the American, British, and French zones of occupation, while the Soviet zone became the German Democratic Republic, or East Germany. Berlin, of course, was split between East and West, and West Berlin is still formally under the jurisdiction of the Americans, British, and French. The institutional structure of the Federal Republic was founded with the Basic Law of 1949, supposedly a temporary set of organizational rules to remain in effect until Germany could be reunited; it was not a formal "constitution." But institutional frameworks take on a reality of their own over time, a reality that is not always intended by their creators.

The purpose of the Basic Law was to set up rules of the political game that would avoid the weaknesses of factionalism that had undermined the Weimar Republic after World War I and would prevent the reestablishment of dictatorship through too much centralized power. For the sake of stability a representative rather than a direct democracy was set up. This made the average citizen's participation indirect and granted significant powers to the executive branch. For the sake of freedom, however, this executive power was offset by a federal system of national, regional, and local governments that shared power, and by a quasi-American system of checks and balances among the executive, legislative, and judicial branches of government. The same moderate balance between freedom and stability is found in the Basic Law's guarantee of majority rule, on the one hand, and on the other, protection of minority rights from government representatives who might try to infringe upon them for the "state's interest" or the "people's will." The Basic Law can be amended with a two-thirds majority vote of both houses of the legislature, and this has often been done in order to make relatively minor changes.

Unlike all the other major states in Europe, the Federal Republic has a federal structure rather than a centralized one. The *Bund*, or federation of the national branches of government, is jurisdictionally separated from the *Länder*, the ten constituent regional states, each of which has its own constitution, parliament, and government. To these ten states is added the city of West Berlin, which has a special status. Although the regional states are subject to national regulations, in this decentralized, federal structure the *Länder* governments are responsible for their own police and educational systems. Much radio and television also falls under the *Länder* jurisdiction, as do all residual powers not explicitly delegated to the federal government. While federal law is preeminent over state law, this is balanced by the required assignment of elected *Länder* representatives to key positions in the federal system, for example, in the selection of the federal president and justices and in the policy making of the *Bundesrat*, or federal council.

At the federal or national level, the Federal Republic has a bicameral (two-house) legislature: the upper house, or *Bundesrat*, with 45 members appointed by the *Länder* and West Berlin governments, and the lower house, or *Bundestag*, the nation's main legislative body, with 518 deputies elected for four-year terms through a mixed system of direct voting and proportional representation. The upper house cannot be dissolved the way the lower house can, and its constitutional powers are greater than those of the French Senate or the British House of Lords. All drafts of legislative bills from the federal government must be submitted to the upper house before they go to the lower house, and most bills passed by the lower house need the consent of the upper house to become law. Even federal executive ordinances and emergency executive government must be approved by the federal council.

The lower house, or federal diet, is formally the more important of the two federal legislative bodies. It is the prime lawmaking chamber and the main instrument for popular control of the federal government. Comparatively, the powers of the *Bundestag* appear to be greater than those of the French National Assembly, but not as great as the authority of the British House of Commons. The powers of the diet are checked by judicial review and by the right of the executive branch to use the veto when the chamber goes beyond its budgetary proposals, as well as by the federal structure of the Basic Law.

The executive branch, known as the *Bundesregierung* or federal government, is led by the *Bundeskanzler* or chancellor, who is elected by an absolute majority of the *Bundestag*. The chancellor has more power than any other individual in the West German system. He or she appoints the other ministers and cannot be impeached or forced to resign unless an absolute majority of the diet agrees in advance on a replacement in a "positive vote of no confidence." The chancellor is less dependent on the legislative majority than in a simple parliamentary system but more so than in the American presidential system. This exclusive chief of the federal government has primary responsibility for governmental policies and activities, but cannot appoint or remove ministers and advisors at will, without information requested by the legislature. The chancellor may, however, veto bills that go over his or her budgetary limits.

The *Bundespräsident*, or federal president, in contrast, is a symbolic figurehead who acts on the chancellor's advice and is elected constitutional head of state by the *Bundestag* together with elected members of the *Land* parliaments. Selected for a five-year term, the federal president has no significant policy-making responsibilities and is prohibited from engaging in "partisan" activities. Furthermore, he or she can be impeached by the Federal Constitutional Court if such proceedings are initiated by a two-thirds majority of either house.

The Federal Constitutional Court, the supreme court of the Federal Republic, deals exclusively with constitutional conflicts. Its sixteen justices take up complaints by individuals and organizations and are bound only by the Basic Law. The lower level of the regular court system is headed by the Federal Court of Justice, an appellate court. Unlike the American system, the West German judicial system does not often use trial by jury, and most of its proceedings are generally kept anonymous.

On the superstructural level institutional descriptions like these may seem dry. But the reason for this blandness is that the real drama is often hidden from view: the interlocking social and economic institutions from the Nazi past were basically accepted in the present without notice, making possible the incredible rise of West Germany's economic and political power. Naturally, American textbooks have not emphasized this fact too much, since it might point toward the failure of the American effort to "democratize" the West German people politically and to "liberalize" their economic system during the occupation period. Even more disconcerting was the possibility that effective democratic capitalisms could be established on stable fascist socioeconomic bases (Japan? Spain?)—a conclusion that would not exactly square with official American liberal ideology.

All at once the pieces begin to fall in place. The inherited and reinforced stability of the German socioeconomic system is a critical (if not the key) factor in explaining postwar West German phenomena such as the consensus and similarity of the major political parties; the passivity of labor unions; and the state's ability to control inflation, dampen unemployment, and stimulate an export-oriented economy. The socioeconomic consensus around a conservative *Weltanschauung*, in short, has paid off handsomely.

Take the parties, for example. Since World War II West German politics has been dominated by three parties: the Christian Democratic Union (the CDU and the affiliated Bavarian CSU—Christian Social Union), the Social Democratic Party (SPD), and the Free Democratic

Party (FDP). Parties that do not receive at least 5 percent of the vote are not allowed in Parliament. The CDU/CSU draws its support from the upper and upper-middle classes; from church believers, especially Catholics; from the business community; and from the elderly. From 1949 until 1969 this party's appeal to the affluent, the traditional, and the right of center allowed it to lead the West German political system. The Christian Democrats accomplished this by maintaining a coalition with the small Free Democratic Party, which is supported by middle-class and independent voters. Konrad Adenauer, Ludwig Erhard, and Kurt Georg Kiesinger were the three Christian Democratic chancellors during this period.

In 1972 the Social Democrats were able to replace the Christian Democrats, turning to the Free Democrats for a coalition after a short "grand coalition" with the Christian Democrats. The SPD draws strength basically from blue-collar workers, trade union supporters, government employees, young people, and nonreligious groups. In the 1970s the SPD provided West Germany with two chancellors—Willy Brandt and Helmut Schmidt—but the party's Marxist heritage slipped increasingly into the background. Management and productivity edged out redistribution and social justice, particularly under Schmidt. The SPD leaders knew that they could replace the dominant Christian Democratic Union in the government only if they projected a conservative image that did not threaten a highly successful status quo.

This acceptance of tradition also explains why the transition from a CDU–FDP coalition in the 1950s and 1960s to a CDU–SPD coalition and then to an SPD–FDP coalition in the 1970s was more of a symbolic political process than a meaningful structural change. Indeed, important political-economic laws were put through by the party whose political philosophy was the opposite of what one would expect if any great conservative–liberal ideological difference existed between the CDU and the SPD. For example, the Act against the Restriction of Competition, or "Cartel Act," was enacted by CDU Economics Minister Ludwig Erhard and a CDU government in 1957, representing the liberal economic conception of the 1950s. On the other hand, the Act for the Promotion of Stability and Economic Growth was passed in 1967 under a CDU–SPD coalition with SPD Economic Minister Karl Schiller as its architect, marking a shift from a "social-market economy" to a more conservative "enlightened market economy."

In the late twentieth century this paradoxical phenomenon of conservative parties instituting liberal changes and vice versa has often led to the cynical conclusion that postindustrial societies eliminate major party differences to the point of making the parties themselves indistinguishable from one another. But it is more useful to view this convergence process as a collective learning experience within a larger psychocultural framework or mode governed by the "conservative impulse" of the winning party to turn to the mainstream and coopt the opposition to shore up its political base. Legitimacy in Western democratic states, after all, depends on compromise with other influential groups and on constant efforts to win the support of the uncommitted. The strong communal aspect of the German psychocultural heritage reinforces this process of democratic consensus, partially owing to the German people's desire to avoid the extremes of fascism, communism, or runaway inflation that threatened them in the recent past. So the normal psychological conservatism of parties taking power in postindustrial democracies becomes manifested in a more general ideological conservatism, or the West German form of nationalism.[19]

Officially, this conservative democratic ideology is symbolized by the Basic Law, the constitutional and legal basis of the West German state. The psychological "conservative impulse," in reacting against disruptive changes of the past, is reflected in the four basic objectives of this constitutional framework: (1) to exclude provisions of the post-World War I Weimar constitution that led to its breakdown, (2) to provide for individual civil rights through both federal and state (or *Land)* governments, (3) to establish a federal structure of government as insurance against the revival of authoritarianism of the Nazi type, and (4) to make sure that the federal political system would not result in a central government too weak to govern or cope with social change. Following their defeat in World War II and the resulting division and occupation of their country by the Allies, the West Germans had little but their conservative impulse to fall back on. Guided by Adenauer's strong conservative hand, they applied themselves as efficiently as possible to learning how to restructure the upper layers of German society according to acceptable democratic and capitalistic modes in order to gain badly needed political and economic support from abroad.*

The "penetrated" West German state quickly became stabilized around a democratic capitalistic consensus at home, allowing German entrepreneurs to focus their attention on markets abroad, particularly in other Western European countries, where the competition was still preoccupied with domestic splits, thus giving the Germans a hidden advantage. As Wilhelm Hankel, Schiller's assistant, has noted, the strong West German market position following the war was due in part to the German division itself, which consolidated the heavy concentration of industries in West Germany and forced the West Germans

---

*Even the few attempts to nationalize German industry after 1945 (vetoed by the Americans and the reluctant British) can be seen as psychologically "conservative" (or dogmatic) reactions, although they are politically socialist.

beyond their own limited domestic market. Not only were West German markets protected from East German competition; they also drew a large labor force from the East until the Berlin Wall was built in 1961. Hankel points out that the West German inability to create a political blueprint for foreign economic policy in the chaos following the war became a great strength. The main economic responsibility was therefore allotted to private industry rather than the federal government, and this established the industrial basis of West Germany's aggressive export market expansion. West Germany's "nonpolitical" economic foreign policy allowed the nation to cope with outside changes more successfully than other Western countries, an advantage that could be undermined in the future by any West German unwillingness to cooperate in European integration.[20]

Given this historical background, the structural* elements of West Germany's social-market economy, as guided by Economics Minister Ludwig Erhard and expressed in "the German economic miracle," were private ownership of the means of production, free-enterprise initiatives for the entrepreneur, unrestricted competition, and a guaranteed degree of social stability. Philosophically, the ideas behind the social-market economy were a blend of neoliberal and Keynesian economics, liberal social and political theory, Catholic social teachings, and the tradition of local self-government. This school of economic thought reflected traditional German values to the extent that it argued that specific policies should be viewed in the context of the economic system as a whole, evaluating action on any one problem in terms of its impact on other problems. A social-market economy is a free-market economy developed on the basis of a centrally planned system for the satisfaction of critical social needs such as state education, standardized controls for fair competition and marketing, taxation, and unemployment and health insurance.

The social-market economy of West Germany was based on a sharp contrast between economic order (the state-stabilized "structure") and economic process (free-market entrepreneurship and consumer democracy). This distinction of Erhard's was further developed by Schiller, who referred to the state's rule-setting role in the economic order as "influencing the market" (Marktbeeinflussungen). Such "influence" refers to state intervention in the market as contrasted with state control of the market. Economist Graham Hallett summed up this important distinction of Schiller's as follows:

> When the state intervenes in the market, it alters the data on which the participants work, and so changes the outcome, without altering the process:

*Here referring to the infrastructure.

for example, a (moderate) tariff on imports will reduce imports, while still leaving buyers free to buy them. Regulation of the market, on the other hand, refers to methods such as price controls, rationing or quotas, which prevent the normal working of the market; except as temporary measures they necessitate the introduction of further controls, and eventually the substitution of a centrally planned system. A similar useful distinction is that between procedures which are consistent with the market system (*marktkonform*) and those that are not. For example, if it is desired to lower the cost of housing for poor people, the payment of a housing allowance is consistent with a free market in housing, whereas rent control is not.[21]

The most critical element in West Germany's economic recovery and strong export position is the fact that the social and political structures continue to be taken for granted. The stability provided by an "apolitical base" (i.e., the passive acceptance of technocratic elites and the class system by the population) allowed industrial entrepreneurs and technocratic government managers to coordinate the effects of the German economic miracle without much populist interference. But social and economic changes in the 1960s began to undermine this acceptance of existing structures. After 1960, unanticipated price increases caused socioeconomic uneasiness. In 1963, the government had to modify its earlier goal of absolute price stability, owing partly to a growing scarcity of labor. This, in turn, politicized the normally docile trade unions, which could not take such price rises for granted without losing membership support, and escalated their wage demands. Government anti-inflationary measures then contributed to a decline in the growth rate and the economic recession of 1966–1967, which led to economic stagnation and government crises.[22]

The economic dislocations of the 1960s in West Germany and elsewhere were complemented in the late 1960s by the rise of New Left movements and student radicalism, which broke out simultaneously in most of the advanced Western industrial democracies. "Apolitical" ground rules became politicized as critics began to point out the inequitable distribution of opportunities and rewards in capitalist democratic structures and to theorize about the breakdown of capitalism itself. Worldwide inflation became commonplace. Throughout Europe, and in Germany in particular, government came increasingly to be seen as a form of crisis management. And with the threat of scarcity and instability in the air, mass publics that had learned by paying began to become more politically involved in the economic benefits and costs of certain policies for particular interest groups. Taken-for-granted social and political structures became politicized into symbols of a bargaining process.

POLITICAL-ECONOMIC CODES: WEST GERMAN
BARGAINING BEHAVIOR

Politics is social action that seeks to resolve the tension between psychocultural needs and values on the one hand and restrictive social facts or structures on the other. In times that are perceived to be "normal" because of their relative stability, politics is usually carried on behind the scenes—a back-room bargaining process among elites who divide existing benefits and opportunities and make their blueprints for production and the distribution of opportunities in the future. But as rapid social change and crisis break down the legitimacy of "normal times" in the eyes of the masses, the distrust of political and economic elites often comes to the surface: as conditions become more uncertain and desperate, many people begin to fight for their life chances more vigorously while others take what comes and passively accept their diminishing share of the economic pie. In *Loss and Change* Marris describes the dynamic motivations that can come from the frustrations of needs in times of rapid change and falling status:

> Most people learn to see themselves in terms of the opportunities familiar to their situation—even at the cost of gross self-disparagement. The harshest function of education is to prepare children realistically for their life-chances. . . . But for some, self-image and opportunity are at odds. A social class whose power and privileges are declining may transmit to its children a revised sense of their chances only after a lag even of generations. Race or religion may debar people from jobs or political status, without incorporating these handicaps, in the sense in which society intends them, in the way the victims of discrimination see themselves. Or the openness of an educational system may encourage higher aspirations than it can satisfy. Such disparities will provoke the symptoms of grief—apathy, withdrawal, random hostility and guilt. But it may also set people in search of unconventional ways to realise their self image, if they have access to resources. The source of their frustration can become a potential asset, once they turn aside from the established structure of opportunity.[23]

With the economic crises of the 1970s, individuals whose life chances were threatened, whose aspirations were frustrated, responded in diverse ways—apathy, violence, strikes, organization, entrepreneurship. Although their society was relatively stable compared to other Western countries, West Germans found themselves questioning the ground rules of formerly "apolitical" socioeconomic structures and institutions. Unions became militant. Workers went on wildcat strikes. Students rebelled and demanded reforms of the educational system. Business-people and taxpayers voiced discontent at the high cost of transfer payments, thus politicizing pension and health insurance issues.

People organized groups of citizens to mobilize support for grassroots issues. Politicians drafted legislation to keep out foreign workers, who would aggravate a labor market in which more than a million members of the work force were unemployed and many were being paid expensive welfare and security benefits. Another law prohibited communists and subversives from employment by the state. The calm before the storm gave way to turmoil as people turned right or left in political protest, depending on their background, their education, and most important, how their individual life chances were being threatened.

These conflicting political reactions were expressed symbolically in the parliamentary or *Bundestag* election of 1976—"an election without a vision,"[24] even though 91 percent of the eligible voters turned out—owing partly to the "politicization" of the West Germans in the economic crisis of the 1970s. The 1976 *Bundestag* election was notable for the *absence* of differences in the voting patterns of various professional groups. One might speculate, for example, that the "workers" would be more likely to vote for the SPD in such an election because of the party's socialist heritage. But in 1976 the SPD lost some votes in all professional groups, including the workers. In fact, the SPD suffered its greatest losses in many working-class districts.[25] What does this mean?

Normally, one might take it for granted that the absence of any great difference in how various professional groups voted is not very significant. But this is misleading. Taking the psychocultural context of West German values into account, we can hypothesize that the conservative psychological and ideological tendencies in the German population may well explain why there is so little difference among professional groups in terms of political-party identification: in Germany, national political orientations transcend class or professional loyalties. And this lack of major differences, reflected in SPD losses and symbolized particularly in the SPD decline among the working class, indicates that all groups and classes showed a measure of discontent with the governing coalition in power (the SPD–FDP coalition), reelecting it by a narrow margin. Indeed, many observers speculate that only the cool-headed, conservative, technocratic image of Chancellor Schmidt, clearly not beloved by the left wing of his party, kept the SPD from losing the election to the CDU, which gained votes throughout the country in impressive numbers compared to the elections of 1972. The vote in the 1976 elections reflected an ongoing conservatism rooted deeply in the past and reinforced by Germany's relative affluence and stability in a time of chaotic change in Europe. The Germans *knew* they could be worse off. The greatest threat to their life chances, regardless of class, seemed to be *change itself*. They were not totally happy with the boat, but they were not about to rock it.

A larger pattern becomes apparent in Western industrial democracies that are overwhelmed by change: throughout the Western world close electoral votes between the dominant parties have become commonplace, making it increasingly difficult for any one party or elected coalition to claim an effective mandate to govern the people. Democratic peoples do not seem to trust any one party or leader with too much power. They often opt for stability in an era of change rather than for risky, dynamic leadership. Political parties and government are no longer invested with decisive political power. We must look elsewhere—toward corporate management and the labor unions, for example.

The homogeneity of West German political attitudes is further reinforced when one looks at minority votes for extremist parties. The National Democratic Party (NPD)—the so-called Neo-Nazi party on the extreme right—received only 0.3 percent of the vote in 1976. And the West German Communist Party (DKP) received another 0.3 percent. In part this is explained by the law requiring a party to receive 5 percent of the vote to be in parliament: few wish to throw their votes away. But how unlike France or Italy, where deteriorating social and economic conditions have politicized millions of people who see their life chances as bound to benefit from change toward a better future rather than as threatened by change away from a comfortable present! Yet even here radical parties, such as the communists, must project an image of cool, efficient management and stability, even if their goal is redistribution rather than greater productivity.

In contrast with the French, the West Germans seem to identify their life chances and bargaining power with a collective code that seeks to resist or control change: the fear of losing their present security motivates them both to stabilize the existing order and to expand these patterns in new areas in order to create a surplus that they can fall back on when hard times strike again. This bargaining code explains why the Germans are so orderly, if not slow, in their innovations; why they are careful to balance redistribution of existing goods and opportunities with the productivity made possible by existing hierarchical and elitist structures; why they are so thorough in their analysis and planning before risking themselves in the social and economic markets of everyday life. Rather than collectively accepting change and then returning to a new equilibrium after change, as the French do, the Germans see change *through* their old equilibrium, as if it were a pair of glasses that must be preserved at all costs.

The reluctance of West Germans to change institutional structures that affect the distribution of life chances in society is illustrated by their slowness in reforming their educational system. In the late 1960s the educational situation in Germany was summed up as follows:

Important decisions about a pupil's future career are usually made when he is ten years old; not more than one out of every five pupils attempts secondary education, and the majority of these eventually fail; only five to six percent of secondary school graduates are children of workers; about two thirds of all boys and girls have practically completed general schooling at the age of 14 or 15.[26]

At the same time, Sweden was successfully reforming its secondary-school system and soon had all of its children in the same kinds of general schools, whereas by the mid-1970s West Germany enrolled only about 3 percent of its junior secondary-school pupils in *Gesamt-schulen* (comprehensive high schools). Although the 1970s were officially supposed to have been designated a decade of educational reform, in the final weeks of 1976 almost 300,000 students demonstrated in cities throughout West Germany in an era when students were being quietly absorbed into the mainstream of most other Western democracies. Why?

Apart from minor, specific grievances, students attempting to obtain a university education were faced with a set of generally depressing conditions throughout West Germany: their social position was deteriorating as thousands ceased to be eligible for government financial assistance; the uniform state university system was overcrowded, creating incredible competitive pressure at lower schooling levels and long waiting lists of eligible students for whom there were no openings (hundreds went to court to demand admittance); and nationwide legislation affecting university governance had the effect of eliminating the political rights of students and reducing their participation in the way their schools were run.[27] Many students sensed that their life chances were becoming increasingly restricted as some switched fields to find shorter waiting lines while others dropped out into an equally depressing job market. In Kiel in 1976 the University Students' Association expressed student discontent to Education Minister Walter Braun by presenting him with a piglet as a symbol of the "pitiable swine" that students are. The pig symbol seems to have been transplanted from capitalism to the police and then to the students themselves as they realized how they were being treated by the social structure.

Why were German educators so stubborn in their refusal to yield to demands for reform? Arnold Heidenheimer suggests that

paradoxically, their attitude can be explained partly in terms of preceding attempts to politicize the system, made mainly during the Nazi era but also during the Allied occupation, when "reeducation" policies were instituted. Schools and universities had been key objects of Nazi takeovers, and post-1949 changes were largely in the direction of a return to the patterns of the

Weimar era (1919–1933). Older pedagogical orthodoxies were reestablished in Germany just when they were being challenged in Sweden. In the face of such strong political pressures, many educational elites tended to regard a measure of *non*responsiveness to political direction as a prerequisite for the restoration of a liberal, pluralist society.[28]

After living through the Nazification and "de-Nazification" of their educational standards, the natural response of older educational elites in terms of their *own* freedom and life chances when threatened with change was to turn to an "apolitical" humanistic tradition. In defending the tripartite division of their secondary-school system against the "threat" of a comprehensive system on the Swedish model, German educators argued that "the school and its educational mission must not be subordinated altogether to the requirements of necessary social change. . . . The tripartite school system corresponds to the needs of the individual, and the differentiated demands of society."[29] Or, to put it another way, the socioeconomic framework must be preserved from social change so that it may structure life chances in the future as it has in the past: bargaining power must ultimately remain with authoritative elites at the top of the social hierarchy, who carefully—perhaps too carefully—distribute it to those below.

The German educational system not only illustrates the typical conservative ideology and bargaining codes of the German social system; it has direct implications for political-economic policy making as well. The thrust of the German educational system is to preserve the elitist hierarchy so as to maintain high standards of technological competence (which supposedly will be translated into greater economic productivity), as well as to preserve stability. But this overt intention of German educators, no matter how understandable from their own tragic perspective (i.e., that of an overly politicized past), prevents them from learning or coping effectively with present changes and future trends. This point of view blinds them to the present situation of students, who alone can prevent the recurrence of similar tragedies in the future. West Germany already has a marked need for middle-level managers in many of its business sectors, but instead of being adjusted to permit the educational system to cope simultaneously with this need and with the need for business-oriented students, university entrance requirements are being tightened and curriculum reform is incremental at best. The structures of the old German culture are getting in the way of the needs of the new German society, and the resulting economic bottleneck may affect more than just the life chances of students. Germany's "hidden culture" of the past is interfering with its people's ability to cope creatively with change in the present and to project themselves "beyond culture" toward self-actualization in the future.[30]

DOMESTIC AND FOREIGN POLICY: COLLECTIVE DECISION MAKING

In addition to education, which highlights the socioeconomic structuring of life chances, other areas of social action illustrate West German bargaining behavior more explicitly. These include social and industrial policy making both at home and abroad. An individual's life chances depend on his or her bargaining power as it is structured by given social facts: existing social values, powerful personalities, social and political institutions (including education, religion, socioeconomic class, and one's place in the social and political system), and rules of the game (such as bargaining codes). The distribution of life chances in a society at any given moment is revealed by analyzing its collective decision making or public policy. Such policies are created not only by German policy makers or elites but by forces and conditions beyond their control. Most conspicuously in the West German case, postwar policy makers from victorious nations imposed some of the basic ground rules, desiring to lobotomize West German political aggression by ensuring that West Germany would remain a split and interpenetrated system forever. A general postwar objective of West German policy makers was to renegotiate these restrictions to give the West Germans more flexibility—an aim that stimulated West German participation in the creation of the European Coal and Steel Community (with the French) as well as the EEC or Common Market.

Following their defeat in the war, the West Germans were forced to withdraw and to create a social order different from the Nazi past that had become a part of themselves.[31] To do so, they broke apart the most superficial structures of the Nazi system and were forced by the victorious Allies to "de-Nazify" themselves, to create an alternative collective personality and set of institutions. Some have argued that the roots of the German economic miracle lie here—in the "clean slate" with which the West Germans were forced to begin their recovery, causing them to cast off obsolete patterns and physical plants to create an effective modern infrastructure from scratch. But this *tabula rasa* theory of economic miracles (which has also been applied to Japan and Italy) neglects the substructures and infrastructures that *were* inherited from the past, giving stability to the present West German system. Today West Germany's superstructures and policies reflect antithetical democratic institutions erected on a system of classes and institutions that was not totally destroyed. This "antithetical restoration" of German society is awkward, if not unsatisfying, for the German people, since the democratic and free-market superstructure was initially not of their own making but was imposed upon them by victors and occupation forces. But the deeper, interconnected substructural and infrastructural elements that have so much to do with West German stability and productivity today were very much reconstitutions of the past accomplished by the Germans themselves, just as their social policies can be seen as a reconstruction in modern form of Bismarckian policies and of socialist ideas that were later modified by the SPD.

Giambattista Vico pointed out over two centuries ago that we truly know and understand only what we create, what we fashion consciously in our own mind and actions. After the war West Germans were not given the personal satisfaction of recreating their own political system without interference. Not unexpectedly, their hearts were not fully in it and they were considered "apolitical" or less politically interested than other people in Western democracies.[32] The occupying Allies also blocked their creative force from being channeled into the military field. Hence, their whole authentic creative drive was directed elsewhere, into economic recovery at home and expansion of export trade abroad. Taking politics and military security for granted (not being allowed to do otherwise), they were free to recreate themselves and to restore German pride through the economic miracle.

Industrial policy, therefore, became the chief priority of West Germans after the war, and its aim was to maximize productivity. But the Germans concerned themselves with social policy as well. German cities were devastated, people hungry and jobless, the entire social system in need of restoration. Some have argued that the West Germans gained a great competitive advantage in the industrial sector by having their old factories and technologies destroyed in the war, so that they were forced to create new ones and to begin with the most modern machinery and techniques (in contrast to the English, who saved themselves from being destroyed by bombs only to discover later that they had to live with their outmoded structures and habits, which reduced productivity). But the West Germans had a similar advantage in social policy: when starting from scratch it makes common sense to pool and share limited resources; to provide for the hungry, homeless, and jobless; to create new social structures to cope with these modern problems immediately and practically. Redistribution was therefore seen not as radical or socialist but as a commonsense way of surviving and preparing for later productivity. Because of the Germans' experience of catastrophic change, which made both productivity and redistribution necessary, the tensions between these objectives of the right (productivity) and the left (redistribution), or the industrial and social sectors, were more muted and accepted than in countries without similar experiences, such as the United States.

However, even the wealthy and stable society of West Germany has not found a way to resolve the basic dilemma of Western industrial democracies in our era: the disequilibrium between increasing private wealth and the impoverishment of the public or social sector. Free-market incentives encourage private gains; private transportation; private health, pension, and security systems; private clubs; and people who are more concerned with their privacy than with the general welfare. Economist John Kenneth Galbraith demonstrated long ago that the capitalist industrial system tends to stimulate the increase of private wealth simultaneously with the impoverishment of the public sector. As West Germany is better off than many countries in terms of the disequilibrium between private productivity and social poverty, the degree to which it experiences this tension symbolizes the inevitable problems that exist in more extreme forms elsewhere.

Public Goods vs. Private Gains

Perhaps the most useful way of measuring the extent to which a society is collectively deciding to support the public or social sector (parks, defense, hospitals, transportation, etc.) as opposed to the private or industrial sector is the share of the society's gross national product (GNP) that is allocated to public-sector investment or gross fixed capital-asset formation. This concrete indicator of money spent on social versus industrial needs also happens to be the only useful aggregate that has been statistically standardized within the Common Market, making it possible to compare Western European nations in terms of public-policy spending.* This macroeconomic indicator of public investment refers only to public funds controlled exclusively by state or local authorities.

Official government forecasts and results for 1965–1970 and forecasts for 1970–1975 of major Common Market nations have been compared regarding the rate of growth in their gross national product and the four basic ways in which that product is used—public and private consumption and gross capital-asset formation in the direct-production and public sectors. For the 1965–1970 period, two observations are striking: (1) all of the Common Market countries except Germany reflected a policy aimed at limiting consumption in order to increase capital investment, giving priority to investment in the public sector, and (2) all of these nations except Belgium failed to achieve their projected aim in public-sector investment, even though all of them achieved higher increases in the total gross national product growth

---

*Accordingly, it has its drawbacks: it reflects inputs but not total stock or the real value of the resources the inputs represent, nor does it include all public investments (such as postal and telecommunications services undertaken for everyone). In contrast, much more is known about private-sector resources—52 percent of Dutch households have an electric hair dryer; 23 percent of Italian households have at least one cat and 13 percent of German families have at least one bird; and so on.

rate than had been projected![33] The data, in short, confirm that, despite the intentions of democratic European governments to reduce the disequilibrium between the private and public sectors, the imbalance became worse even when general economic conditions improved.

The fact that Germany alone did not limit the rate of expansion in private consumption is most intriguing. Unlike leaders in all the other nations, West German policy makers intended to push the private consumption growth rate to the point of *equaling* the projected GNP growth rate. Could not the motivation for this bold policy (apart from vote-getting) be the hidden advantage it promised in terms of increased productivity? Was not the hidden cost of this policy actually a harmful effect on certain economic sectors, which helped create the grave structural unemployment that the West Germans experienced throughout the 1970s? Short-term industrial gains may have been paid for with long-term unemployment, which became so severe that the Germans passed laws to keep out foreign workers, who had been badly needed since the war to meet industrial demand. Moreover, the infrastructural costs of paying unemployment insurance benefits to the thousands who were laid off were heavy in the fairly liberal social-benefit system established in better times.

On the positive side, it is comforting to note that the Germans apparently learned from experience. In their projections for 1975 they aimed for a private consumption growth rate lower than the overall projected GNP growth rate. This adjustment was made despite the fact that the growth rate in private consumption greatly exceeded the earlier projection. The *learning* ability of West German policy makers is demonstrated by these adjustments and has much to do with the West German ability to maintain relatively low levels of inflation and unemployment at home in the 1970s compared with other Western European economies. Because they view social and economic change in a managerial cultural context of equilibrium and conservatism, the West Germans are always ready to make practical adjustments based on whatever new evidence comes in.

The learning ability of West German policy makers is revealed in their determination to bridge the gap between public-sector consumption and public-sector investment growth rates by aiming for higher public-sector investment rates in the future while increasing public consumption rates. In contrast, the French, Italians, and Dutch reacted with a policy aimed toward inhibiting the increase in the public sector. The German situation is particularly significant given the overall failure of European governments to accurately project the public-sector capital growth rate. Clearly, forces beyond the control of government policy makers, such as the high worldwide inflation rate, unexpectedly increased public consumption rates. But the international atmosphere of economic uncertainty caused by inflation makes the German ability to control inflation and public consumption at home all the more remarkable. Effective government management, after all, can be defined as profitably coping with change. The West Germans appear to be successful at such management, despite the electoral pressures that lead politicians to temporarily ignore the advice of economic experts (illustrated by Finance Minister Schiller's futile attempt in 1970 to induce the coalition government to reduce its expenditures). In the long run the West Germans long for stability above all else—for a return to their conservative but dynamic equilibrium.

Labor–Management "Codetermination," or Industrial Democracy

While the growth of public investment and consumption compared to overall economic production provides an intriguing case of collective policy making at the "macro" governmental level, labor–management codetermination of industrial policy provides an equally stimulating "micro"-level example of the bargaining power of different groups throughout the social structure of postindustrial democracies. And the "macro" and "micro" levels are neatly linked by recent national legislation (or its absence) in Common Market countries, legislation that seeks to wed workers to capitalism by putting them in the board room and giving them a role in the management of industrial firms. In terms of ideology or political economy, the implications of the recent European drift toward "social corporatism," symbolized by codetermination legislation, could be far-reaching indeed.

The codetermination issue illustrates as few others can the significance of West Germany's tradition of social cooperation, which permits domestic economic growth to progress with few major disruptions. German management–labor participation schemes date back at least to the Weimar Republic and West Germany became one of the most progressive models of such schemes after World War II. In 1951, Chancellor Adenauer responded to the demands of the German national federation of labor, or DGB (Deutsche Gewerkschaftsbund), and supported legislation instituting parity representation between workers and shareholders on the supervisory councils of the larger coal and steel industries. Shortly thereafter, a second codetermination bill extended the principle of worker representation to other industrial firms, but here such representation was limited to one-third rather than half of the seats on the supervisory boards.[34]

In 1969, when the Social Democratic Party came to power, the SPD dissidents on the left, such as the radical young socialist Jusos, combined with the more radical unions, such as the Metalworkers, to better their life chances by pushing for a more comprehensive codetermination (or *Mitbestimmung*) plan. In 1976, following a number of union threats and strikes, the government SPD–FDP coalition finally moved compromise codetermination legislation through the *Bundestag*. This complex legislation provided apparent parity between workers and shareholders in all major industries employing 2,000 or more workers, each group electing half of the membership of the supervisory boards of the joint stock companies of these firms. One worker representative on each advisory board must be a salaried employee, while another must be a senior employee (these are concessions to the FDP, which traditionally favors the position of management more than the SDP does). Moreover, each supervisory board must choose its chairperson and the managing board by a two-thirds vote, giving the shareholders' representatives a de facto veto in both of these important decisions. Finally, no neutral member is provided to break potential ties, as is done in the coal and steel industry pact; the chairperson is allowed to vote twice in such cases. Together, these elements ensure that private economic interests will continue to exercise a decisive influence on West Germany's productive process, even though the scope of worker representation has been expanded substantially.[35] The often-cited "docility" of the German labor unions is obtained at the expense of management flexibility as the large majority of West Germans work to stabilize the interests of the whole community despite the compromises required of particular classes and groups. "Industrial democracy" is accepted as another necessary step in the "democratization" of post-Nazi German society.

Foreign Policy: Exports *über Alles*

Why do government elites and industrial managers give in to labor demands? Although the reasons are complex, the overwhelming rationale in terms of West Germany's political economy seems clear: domestic stability must be preserved at all costs in order to focus on exports, the lifeblood of West German prosperity. Foreign trade accounted for 35 percent of West Germany's gross national product in 1976 (compared to 11 percent for the United States), and one person in five owed his or her job to exports.[36] Export expansion has been the hallmark of the West German economy since the war: between 1950 and 1953 average annual German exports accounted for 4.6 percent of world exports, but this figure more than doubled, to 11.2 percent, between 1970 and 1973, making West Germany the second largest trading nation after the United States.[37]

A nation's bargaining power, both economic and political, often depends on its ability to amass export surpluses, a skill that West Germany, like Japan, has developed to a fine art. In the mid-1970s the West Germans used this export surplus to build up foreign-exchange reserves totaling more than $30 billion. This gives West Germany greater diplomatic leverage while simultaneously building up the hopes of needy allies for foreign aid. West Germany's heavy dependence on exports has given its people a critical stake in a liberal world economy. Economic growth and popular support for both democracy and capitalism depend on the preservation of advantageous trade relations around the world.

But from the international perspective the West German political economy raises difficulties. It depends on a philosophy of neomercantilism, a subtle form of economic nationalism that benefits well-to-do industrial countries with modern infrastructures and great absorptive and productive capacities more than the majority of nations that are less developed. Mercantilism is based on increasing a nation's exports, reducing its imports, and increasing employment at home, regardless of the consequences of these policies for other countries. Although the West Germans have been sensitive to this problem in prosperous times, economic recession puts pressure on their government to put domestic priorities before global ones.

The mercantilist style of political economy means that the costs of adjustment to a nation's decisions are borne by other countries, that political and economic problems arising within the nation are exported to someone else. In terms of balance-of-payments deficits, for example, rich nations often export their deficits to poor countries, which can afford them least. Another example of the impact of domestic West German politics on other countries has to do with employment. While more than a million Germans who seek work are unemployed, more than a million Turks, not to speak of other Southern Europeans, are waiting to enter West Germany to seek work. For not only did West Germany have a tradition of using Mediterranean labor in good times, but according to the Common Market treaty of association agreed to by both West Germany and Turkey, the Turks should be permitted to move freely within the Common Market countries; 80–90 percent of them desire to go to West Germany. But this regional agreement is contradicted by West German legislation, put through during the recession of the 1970s, restricting the recruitment and entrance of foreign labor. Ironically, this leaves the hotel and catering business with thousands of unfilled jobs, since "West Germans, it seems, would rather be out of work together than serve their fellow countrymen coffee, cake or drinks."[38]

Moreover, although dependents of foreign workers are allowed to live with their families once they have been admitted to West Germany, they are not issued work permits (which might stimulate thousands of other dependents from Turkey to join their parents). This means that there are 15,000 or more young foreigners living in industrial cities with no job prospects, increasing the probability of crime. And the *Gastarbeiter* (foreign worker) families are concentrated in ghettos and socially isolated from the mainstream of German society by linguistic, racial, and physical distance. West Germany, in short, is caught in a double bind and is bound to lose either domestically or internationally. Wolfgang Bodenbender, the Employment Ministry official responsible for foreign-labor affairs commented that "our attitude is not one of narrow-minded nationalism but of genuine social concern. The unemployment problem facing millions of people in the world today cannot be solved on West German soil. This would simply plunge the Federal Republic into social and political chaos."[39] While this is undoubtedly true, West German policy makers should have thought of these consequences years ago, when cheap imported labor was viewed as beneficial to West Germany's export-oriented economic growth.

REGIONAL AND GLOBAL CONSTRAINTS

Common Market treaty agreements are not the only regional constraints that West German foreign policy makers must face. Global economic and political conditions and treaties with non-Western European states are important parameters as well. For example, the West German structural-unemployment problem may become worse as the West German–Polish agreements take effect and sixty to seventy thousand working-age Germans leave Poland to settle in the Federal Republic of Germany. This brings to mind a remark made by former Chancellor Ludwig Erhard in 1968: he said he believed that the West German *Ostpolitik* (political initiatives toward Eastern Europe and the USSR) was *"zu lautstark,"* or too blatant.[40] Time may prove him right as West Germans begin to pay domestically for their expansive foreign policies.

West Germany's *Ostpolitik* reflected at least three kinds of policy objectives that may become important in the future to the extent that they differ from those of other Common Market nations. At the most obvious, "superstructural" level *Ostpolitik* was designed to create better relations with Eastern Europe and the Soviet Union in order to reduce the Soviet threat to West German security and to ease the tensions between East and West Germany and the isolation of West Berlin. Superficially, these objectives appear to be consistent with those of other Western European states. But the division of Germany, the location of West Berlin deep in East German territory, and the official West

German policy of eventual "reunification" of East and West Germany give the West Germans a stake in the East that is different from that of other countries. Ever since the marked Soviet gains at the Yalta Conference and the resulting division of Germany and Berlin, the basic aim of Soviet policy in Europe has been to cement the status quo, whereas the thrust of West German policy has been to change the status quo to West German advantage.[41] West Germans are more deeply motivated to use political change to recover from past losses and restore the integrity of the German nation than people of other nations may be. West Germany's official recognition of the post-World War II European boundaries in 1970, reconfirmed in the all-European Helsinki accords of 1975, represents an attempt to steer this repressed motivation into economic and political affairs and to stay away from the military realm, where West Germany is so clearly vulnerable and dependent on the good will of the Soviet and American superpowers. After all, in terms of security against attack from the East, first-line defense and the immediate use of tactical nuclear weapons are clearly more in West Germany's interest than in that of the United States, on whom the Germans must rely.

The heavier export dependency of the West German economy compared with other Western European countries gives the West Germans a second distinctive reason for looking eastward more intensely than others: export markets. Export trade to Eastern Europe from West Germany was up 50 percent in 1974 alone, although even if this expansion were to continue it would still be too small to compensate for losses in trade to the United States and the Common Market. (West Germany exports three-quarters of its overseas sales goods to Western industrial countries.)[42] The country's dependence on American nuclear power and trade, for example, stimulated the West German government to revise slightly a $1 billion contract with Brazil that would bring the Brazilians a nuclear-reprocessing plant that was adamantly opposed by President Carter. It is clear that the West Germans consider it in their interest to push their aggressive export market drive to whatever limits they can while learning to quickly change their policies and behavior when they overreach regional and global constraints that could upset their cherished stability. Chancellor Schmidt's successful effort to initiate the European monetary system is an example of this "defensive" strategy to maximize stability.

Last but not least, the West Germans have a deep-seated motivation to overcome their legacy of humiliation and guilt from World War II and to recover their self-esteem, a drive that other nations can perceive but not understand, since they have not had the same catastrophic experience. To the extent that West Germany's security and economic needs are satisfied, the West German people will strive for national self-esteem and self-actualization, trying to perfect their social-market economy and capitalist democracy into a model for the rest of the world. They are likely to be generous in their foreign aid in order to create a positive German image and secure new allies and export markets. They will also bend over backwards to become "Europeans" and internationalists in order to blot out the memory of their nationalist past and preserve the security of their prosperous present.

NOTES

1. Herbert Arnold's definition in his translator's forward to Eberhard Jäckel, *Hitler's Weltanschauung: A Blueprint for Power* (Middletown, Conn.: Wesleyan University Press, 1972).
2. This view is spelled out in R. Isaak, "Power, Racism and Total War—Hitler," in *Individuals and World Politics*, 2nd ed. (North Scituate, Mass.: Duxbury Press, 1980). For the history of German ideology, see George Mosse, *The Nationalization of the Masses* (New York: Howard Fertig, 1975); Fritz Stern, *The Politics of Cultural Despair* (Garden City, N.Y.: Doubleday Anchor, 1965); and Klaus von See, *Deutsche Germanen-Ideologie* (Frankfurt: Athenäum, 1970).
3. See Harold Lasswell, "The Psychology of Hitlerism," *Political Quarterly*, 4 (1933), 374, and Seymour Martin Lipset, *Political Man: The Social Basis of Politics* (Garden City, N.Y.: Doubleday Anchor, 1963), p. 131.
4. Peter Marris, *Loss and Change* (New York: Pantheon Books, 1974), pp. 114–116. For the case of the Samurai of Japan, who turned to business to recover the purpose and status lost in the disintegration of their feudal society, see Everett Hagen, *On the Theory of Social Change* (London: Tavistock Publications, 1964), chap. 14; for similar entrepreneurial reactions on the part of the Balinese aristocracy, see Clifford Gertz, *Peddlers and Princes: Social Development and Economic Change in Two Indonesian Towns* (Chicago: University of Chicago Press, 1963).
5. Charles Higham, "Dietrich at 75–Her Life Has Been More Colorful Than Any Film," *New York Times*, December 26, 1976.
6. This extension of the Weberian patterns of authority from the "traditional" and "legal–rational" to the "technological" was first made in Isaak, *Individuals and World Politics*, 1st ed., pp. 98–99.
7. Jürgen Habermas, "Technology and Science as 'Ideology,' " in *Toward a Rational Society* (Boston: Beacon Press, 1970), pp. 81–122.
8. Marris, pp. 4ff.
9. Daniel Bell, *The Cultural Contradictions of Capitalism* (New York: Basic Books, 1976).
10. See Marc Howard Ross and Elizabeth Homer, "Galton's Problem in Cross-National Research," *World Politics*, 29, no. 1 (October 1976), 1–28.

11. Gebhard Ludwig Schweigler, *National Consciousness in Divided Germany* (Beverly Hills, Calif.: Sage Publications, 1975).
12. Craig R. Whitney, "West German Rich: Hard Work and a Bit of Luck," *New York Times*, November 13, 1976, pp. 25–26.
13. Silvan Tomkins, "Left and Right: A Basic Dimension of Ideology and Personality," in Robert White, ed., *The Study of Lives* (Chicago: Aldine-Atherton, 1969).
14. See R. Isaak, *American Democracy and World Power* (New York: St. Martin's Press, 1977), chaps. 4, 11.
15. Raymond Vernon, "Enterprise and Government in Western Europe," in *Big Business and the State: Changing Relations in Western Europe* (Cambridge, Mass.: Harvard University Press, 1974), p. 3.
16. Ralph P. Hummel, *The Bureaucratic Experience* (New York: St. Martin's Press, 1977), p. 198.
17. R. Isaak and R. Hummel, *Politics for Human Beings* (North Scituate, Mass.: Duxbury Press, 1975), pp. 103–107.
18. Georg H. Küster, "Germany," in Vernon, *Big Business and the State*, p. 65. See also Jörg Huffschmid, *Die Politik des Kapitals* (Frankfurt: Suhrkamp, 1969), p. 138, and Andrew Shonfield, *Modern Capitalism* (New York: Oxford University Press, 1965), p. 240.
19. See Schweigler, *National Consciousness in Divided Germany*, and Wolf-Dieter Narr and Frieder Naschold, *Theorie der Demokratie* (Stuttgart: W. Kohlhammer, 1971).
20. Wilhelm Hankel, a presentation to the Faculty Seminar in International Political Economy at Columbia University, fall 1975. See W. Hankel, *Währungspolitik* (Stuttgart: W. Kohlhammer, 1971).
21. Graham Hallett, *The Social Economy of West Germany* (New York: Macmillan, 1973), pp. 19–20.
22. Küster, p. 65.
23. Marris, p. 116.
24. Hans Heigert, "An Election Without a Vision," *Süddeutsche Zeitung*, October 4, 1976.
25. *Forschungsgruppe Wahlen E.V., Bundestagswahl 1976: Eine Analyse der Wahl zum 8. Deutschen Bundestag am 3. Oktober 1976* (Mannheim: *Institut für Wahlanalysen*, 1976). Based on a carefully selected sample of 496 people stung by the WASP system *(Wahlsimulationsprogramm)* of Carol Cassidy at the University of Mannheim (as adapted by Manfred Berger, Wolfgang Gibowski, and Dieter Roth).
26. Saul B. Robinsohn and J. C. Kuhlmann, "Two Decades of Non-Reform in West German Education," *Comparative Education Review*, 11, no. 3 (1967), 319. See also "Secondary School Reform: Why Sweden? Why Not West Germany?" in Arnold Heidenheimer, Hugh Heclo, and Carolyn Adams, *Comparative Public Policy* (New York: St. Martin's Press, 1975), pp. 44–65.
27. Hayo Matthiesen, "Student Protests May Become More Drastic, Authorities Fear," *Die Zeit*, December 10, 1976, as translated in *The German Tribune*, December, 26, 1976, pp. 13–14.
28. Heidenheimer, p. 49.

29. Peter Nixdorff, "The Pace of West German Educational Reform as Affected by *Land* Politics," Ph.D. dissertation, University of Florida, 1969, as cited by Heidenheimer, p. 49.
30. See Edward Hall, *Beyond Culture* (Garden City, N.Y.: Doubleday Anchor, 1976).
31. This interpretation was inspired by the Lurianic theory of creation. For the application of this theory in another context, see Harold Bloom, *A Map of Misreading* (New York: Oxford University Press, 1975).
32. See Gabriel Almond and Sidney Verba, *The Civic Culture* (Princeton, N.J.: Princeton University Press, 1963).
33. Michel Albert, "The Rising Cost of Public Sector Infrastructure and Resources and the Problem of Their Financing with a View to Harmonious Development in the Community," report submitted at the Venice Conference of the European Communities, April 1972.
34. See Erich Potthoff, Otto Blume, and Helmut Duvernell, *Zwischenbilanz der Mitbestimmung* (Tübingen: J. C. B. Mohr, 1962), and Abraham Schuchman, *Codetermination, Labor's Middle Way in Germany* (Washington, D.C.: Public Affairs Press, 1957).
35. M. Donald Hancock, "Productivity, Welfare and Participation in Sweden and West Germany," paper presented at the American Political Science Association Convention, Chicago, 1976, p. 16.
36. Deutsches Institut für Wirtschaftsforschung, *Wochenbericht 22/76*, p. 224.
37. W. Glastetter, as cited in Michael Kreile, "West Germany: The Dynamics of Expansion," paper presented at the Conference on Domestic Structures and the Foreign Policy of Advanced Industrial States, Harvard University, October 28–30, 1976.
38. Wolfgang Hoffman, "Free Movement of Labour Clause in EEC Association Treaty with Turkey Embarrasses Bonn," *Die Zeit*, August 27, 1976, as translated in *The German Tribune*, September 12, 1976, p. 5.
39. Ibid.
40. Personal interview with Ludwig Erhard at his summer home on Tegernsee on August 21, 1968.
41. The implications of West Germany's *Ostpolitik* are elaborated in R. Isaak, "West German Foreign Policy and European Integration: A Phenomenological Analysis," paper presented at the International Studies Association meeting in Toronto, February 1976.
42. Rainer Frenkel in *The German Tribune*, February 27, 1975.

Chapter 3

France:
An Administrative Economy
of Cultural Supremacy

To Frenchmen, their civilization is something permanent, something unique, and not to be equalled by other cultures. They feel themselves to be the direct descendants of classical Greek and Roman civilization, as the culmination of an historical duty to preserve and hand down a very precious heritage. . . . In fact there seems to be some doubt among Frenchmen that anyone can ever be a true member of French civilization who is not born and brought up in it.
—David C. McClelland, "French National Character and the Life and Works of André Gide"

France* is an enigmatic nation with one of the greatest gaps between rich and poor among Western industrial countries. This acute division of life chances has stimulated many French people to move to the left to support the Socialist and Communist parties. But this leftward movement can be interpreted as a deep-seated conservative consolidation in terms of French culture and national political economy, a struggle to prevent downward mobility in a highly class-conscious society. For the French exist for their own sake above all else. Those who push for redistribution are pushing for redistribution *within* the French national family; those outside the family circle are often perceived as second-rate citizens and appropriate targets for self-serving economic policies that benefit those at home regardless of the consequences for other nations. The government intervenes like a father figure, subsidizing agriculture and weak industries at home while coldly negotiating abroad for French business. Such behavior may explain why the French are often respected more than they are liked, no matter how much one might love their culture. For it does not seem fair for a Latin country with a sensuous life style to also have an industrial economy and a high standard of technological competence.

*See appendix, p. 213, for political-economic events of France.

63

The need to be born French in order to be permitted to participate fully in this pleasant set of circumstances is a social rule that adds insult to injury as far as foreigners are concerned.

But underlying French chauvinism, which understandably irritates more internationally minded Westerners, lies a disturbing possibility with profound political and economic implications: the possibility that the French approach may be the most effective one. Could it be that France's reputation for brilliant diplomacy is due in part to the French focus on nationalistic realism in the short term? Is it possible that the intervention of the French state for the sake of French business may make more sense for the national interest than countervailing power and antagonism between the state, big business, labor unions, and others—a pattern that is characteristic of the United States? Might not the pre-1978 movement to the left in France be merely a superstructural phenomenon that in the long run will merely mean a change in ideological clothing for a conservative administration dating back to Napoleon and destined to go on as long as France exists? Internationally, did not de Gaulle demonstrate that a nation gains the most in any "inevitable" process of regional integration if it holds out longest at the bargaining table for its short-term national interests? These are the nasty questions that the French case poses in terms of political economy and coping collectively with social change.

FRENCH POLITICAL CULTURE: MOTIVATIONS

The French, no doubt, find their culture more civilized than American culture partly because theirs is older. They trace their culture back to classical Greek and Roman culture and imply that all rational, modern people who are clear-headed in the Western tradition will come to the same conclusion if they stop to think about it. The chief artifact of this old Latin culture is language, the roadsign to French conservatism. Even avant-garde writer Alain Robbe-Grillet observes that

> the raw material—the French language—has undergone only very slight modifications for three hundred years; and, while society has transformed itself little by little, while industrial techniques have made considerable progress, our intellectual civilization has remained precisely the same. We live according to essentially the same habits and prohibitions—moral, alimentary, religious, sexual, hygienic, familial, etc.[1]

In an ultimate sense France may be merely its language—its writers and poets (particularly its poets) and the light, sounds, and senses they embody. Intellectuals count, but poets are the symbol of French life, especially as it is expressed in the *chanson*, the popular French art song.

Love may be what French life is supposed to be about, but its expression in poetic song is more lasting. In "high cultures" everyday human life becomes most meaningful in the concrete symbols it produces.

Such symbols allow the French to achieve the virtue of *distantiation*, a concept of balance and control that anthropologists have identified in the French culture. Distantiation permits the individual to avoid excess or extreme emotional involvement, to contain emotional impulses before they get out of hand by keeping such desires half-satiated, neither indulging them wholly nor suppressing them completely. Like the classical notion of the golden mean, the standard of distantiation allows the French to keep some distance from emotional problems in order to avoid destroying themselves or, more important, their families with too much passion. For the pride of French civilization is to combine the reasonableness and clarity of classical thought with the primacy of the *foyer*, or family circle, in which personal relationships between all the family members are carefully defined. The father has a split image, being the picture of reasonableness, protectiveness, and devotion (though always from a slight distance) within the family and a mysterious symbol of aggression and cool calculation outside the family, giving the children a sense of awe and respect. The mother is viewed as the carrier of the French cultural tradition.[2] The challenge for the head of the household appears to be to use his reason and wits to maximize his material advantages outside the family and outside the nation for the sake of his family and his countrymen, avoiding entangling alliances or emotional extremes that could undermine his will and make him vulnerable. This standard may explain why the French empathize so much with the person who commits a *crime passionel*, the person whose distantiation and balance are overcome by his raging animal instincts—a fate that could easily confront any Frenchman.[3]

These psychocultural values can be expressed in an "ideal type" of value formula relating individual obligations to self and society: "I will control my emotions through traditional forms of French civilization and reason to maintain the coherence of my family and my people." The traditional and conservative bias of this formula is striking. French people may rebel or form "illegitimate" emotional liaisons outside the family circle, and these may invigorate the culture and update it, as long as such rebellion stays within reasonable limits and does not become so passionate as to undermine the family or cultural tradition. The French saying "The more things change, the more things stay the same" now takes on deeper significance: the French view change as inevitable and do not fight it, as the Germans might, but flow with it in order to eventually turn it in their direction, to incorporate it into the past, present, and future of their civilization or, more specifically, their national interests. There seems to be an assumption that no matter what social changes occur, things will eventually settle back to "normal" and reconfirm French values. And there is a further assumption that all reasonable human beings who have experienced the classical French culture would come to the same conclusion: that this civilization is permanent, unique, and superior to others.

The final psychocultural theme, which complements other French values, is the desire to do as much as possible by oneself, to become as self-sufficient as possible. André Gide, for example, was preoccupied with the "pure gratuitous act," the act without antecedents. One interpreter of his work has noted that "the main theme of Gide's story of Theseus's life seems to be a consideration of what a man can do by himself, by his own unaided efforts, if he has a strong enough will and avoids 'entangling alliances.' "[4] Love women, but know when to leave them. Know that self-realization is often in conflict with family duty, and therefore be conservative in founding families. "Go ahead, but don't get stuck." All of these themes come together in Gide's *Theseus* and in conventional French wisdom. They are concrete maxims growing naturally out of the principle of distantiation. They are classically Western in their stress on individual self-determination and will power as the meaning of freedom. Should we then be surprised if French national leaders act for their nation as they would for their families— maximizing national self-determination and self-sufficiency at all costs, protecting the national *foyer* and fighting for its interests abroad with cool, nationalistic self-control and romantic independence for its own sake? Glory for oneself, one's family, and one's nation is the name of the game. This is why the novelist François Mauriac could write,

> What I found, in that first meeting with General de Gaulle, was not the disdain of all other men that his enemies attribute to him, but the narrow, unbridgeable gulf between them and himself, created not by the pride of self-conscious greatness, but by the calm certainty that he is the State and, it is not too much to say, France herself.[5]

The classic Western emphasis on self-sufficiency and self-determination in French culture is perhaps best symbolized by the French attitude toward authority. The French conceive of authority as absolute. In their authority system each stratum is isolated from other strata. Each is governed by the impersonal rules of a superior authority that is empowered to set such rules, but each is also limited in its powers. This conception of authority makes it difficult for the French to bargain as equals, since anyone who holds a share of authority tends to view his or her share as absolute and not subject to compromise or limitation through bargaining.[6] As a consequence of this psychocultural attitude toward authority, not only do the French draw a strict distinction between private life and public life, but French political history becomes a constant alternation between abstract, insensitive "routine authority" or bureaucracy and vengeful "crisis leadership" that initiates change through personal heroism in order to restore equilibrium and maintain continuity.[7]

Complementing the French attitude toward authority is the way the French traditionally view change itself—a view that Stanley Hoffmann has called *homeorhesis*. In contrast to *homeostasis*, which implies a return to the *status quo ante* after each crisis, homeorhesis implies accepting change *and* returning to equilibrium afterwards. In defining this term Hoffmann writes:

> It [homeorhesis] therefore better fits the French polity, where there is a pervasive dislike for change that disturbs the existing hierarchy of ranks and statuses and the existing hierarchy within each stratum, a willingness instead to tolerate either the *status quo* or, if it is untenable and provokes excessive strains, change that affects the whole society yet preserves the delicate harmony of hierarchy with equalitarianism. What is resisted is change at the end of which certain groups find themselves in a situation more disadvantageous than the one they held before or than the one they had been led to expect as the outcome of the change. Homeorhesis means, to be precise, a refusal to retrogress or a resentment at failing to progress during a process of change that improves the lots of others; it is the rejection of absolute or relative *déclassement*. It is based on the fear of insecurity.[8]

The French, in short, are very clear-minded about where their own concrete interests lie, and they evaluate and incorporate changes accordingly. Existing social and political structures are used in bargaining games colored by the traditional psychocultural attitudes of the French toward authority, change, and the primacy of home and nation.

FRENCH SOCIAL AND POLITICAL INSTITUTIONS: STRUCTURES

The French language has no equivalents for the words *statecraft* and *leadership*; it makes do with abstractions such as *le pouvoir* and *l'état*. It is common to refer to the government as *the regime*, implying a certain skepticism toward arbitrary power growing out of the traditional attitude toward authority. The French see the routine structures and bureaucracies of social and political life from a cool distance moderated by their own interests. As the structures of the status quo slip into decay or obsolescence, however, the French tend to turn to heroic personalities to lead them out of crisis and bring about the changes necessary to restore social equilibrium and tradition. From increasing distaste for detached, routine authority and bureaucracy, the French shift to a personal revenge symbolized by a strong leader like Charles de Gaulle, who restores the continuity of tradition by incorporating change and updating governmental structures to enable them to better cope with the times. The "all-or-nothing" view of authority seems to make incremental changes ineffective in "learning-by-paying" institutional structures in the long run: power resides either in a stodgy administrative bureaucracy or in a charismatic leader who momentarily becomes the state until the crisis can be resolved and equilibrium recovered.

The alternation between routine authority and crisis leadership is perhaps best expressed by the relationship between France and General de Gaulle.[9] After leading the British-based resistance movement against the Nazi occupation of France, de Gaulle returned to France to form a provisional government in 1944, a time of fake ration and identity cards and total chaos. After two years he resigned from the position of prime minister, disgusted by a weak parliamentary system that seemed to undermine his authority to no purpose.

De Gaulle outlined the basis for the French constitution as early as July 16, 1946, in a speech at Bayeux, stressing that party rivalry subverts "superior" national interests and calling for more state authority, efficiency, and prestige. He argued that difficulties incurred by the state result in the inevitable alienation of the citizen from the institutions of the state and this, in turn, can create the preconditions for dictatorship.

There are historical reasons for de Gaulle's opposition to parliamentary factionalism, particularly given the traditional multiparty system in France, the dominance of parliament over the executive, and the ministerial instability that frequently results. For example, Norman Stamps argues that

> the major cause of executive impotence has been party deadlock in the legislature; for example there were 12 parties in the Italian Parliament before the Fascist Revolution and 15 in the German Reichstag in 1928. People lost faith in parliamentarianism due to hopeless inefficiency produced by such factionalism. Furthermore, by following obstructionist tactics, a party can paralyze the work of an assembly.[10]

De Gaulle formed the *Rassemblement du Peuple Français* (RPF), a party that symbolized these sentiments and exploited the fear of communism. Weak, factional governments attempted unsuccessfully to govern France. From de Gaulle's departure from government in 1946 until his return in 1958, the Fourth Republic of France experienced the coming and going of twenty-three premiers—not a recipe for stable government. When French army leaders openly defied the French government in Algeria in 1958, France was faced with a possible civil war. De Gaulle appeared on the horizon as the only figure who could apparently unite the country in a time of crisis. But before he would assume responsibility he demanded that he be given absolute power for two years and that he be allowed to send parliament into recess while he saw to the writing of a constitution and brought French affairs back to order. As one might expect, the constitution granted the executive widespread powers and assigned the parliament a subordinate role in the new governmental structure.

THE GOVERNMENT FRAMEWORK

Michel Debré, a loyal Gaullist from the Resistance period, drafted the constitution for the Fifth Republic. Like so many constitutions, this one worked out quite differently in practice than the drafter intended. Aiming for a stable balance between executive leadership and parliamentary controls, Debré thought he had created a blueprint on the model of the British parliamentary system, not the presidential government into which de Gaulle transformed his words. The problem was that the founders of the Fifth Republic *did* set out to make the presidency the critical function in the government, and a lesser personality than de Gaulle might have been satisfied with the role prescribed as it was. The president was to be chosen by an electoral college made up of members of parliament, members of all of the ninety elected departmental councils and assemblies of Overseas Territories, and elected representatives of municipal councils. Ideally, this would broaden the president's electoral base, which was one of de Gaulle's objectives. But since 1962, because of de Gaulle's influence, the president has been elected by a direct popular vote.

The constitution of the Fifth Republic reconstituted state authority under strong executive leadership and established a parliament whose powers are limited in several ways. The president is elected for a seven-year term. He or she nominates the prime minister and can fire that person without parliamentary approval. Independently of the parliament, the president can dissolve the Assembly, refer bills to a Constitutional Council for questions of constitutionality, call referenda, issue decrees with the force of law, nominate three of the nine members of the Constitutional Council, send messages to the legislature, and invoke a state of emergency in which rule is by decree.

The other structures of the French parliamentary system are perhaps more typical: a bicameral legislature and a prime minister and cabinet responsible for the direction of government policy and accountable to the lower chamber of the legislature, the National Assembly, which is given the right to censure and overthrow the prime minister and the cabinet. In addition to granting the president broad powers and limiting the power of the legislature, thereby avoiding the weaknesses of the Fourth Republic, the constitution provided for a number of democratic measures such as the tenure of judges, immunity of legislators from arrest and prosecution without prior permission from their own chamber, freedom of speech and press, the freedom to associate, and provisions to counter arbitrary detention.

The key to de Gaulle's domination of the Fifth Republic and his ability to enhance presidential power was his historic role as leader of the Resistance to the Nazis in World War II. When he came to power the French people were disenchanted with older parties and leaders and eager for a settlement to the Algerian War. By fostering an image of heroic leadership and constantly appealing to French nationalism, de Gaulle used a vigorous foreign policy to institutionalize strong executive leadership.

Officially, the prime minister is the leader of the government and is responsible for day-to-day policy and for the implementation of laws. But in practice the president sets policy, and discord between the two executives can cause trouble. The governmental leadership role was to reflect the collective nature of government, thus ensuring collective responsibility. The accent of the first phase of the Fifth Republic was therefore on "depoliticization"—a concept implying that the government should be above politics. There were a multitude of attempts to introduce more administrative practices and more administrators into government. Ministers, for example, may not belong to the legislature or must resign upon appointment. Initially, there was a tendency to appoint "technocrats" to the cabinet, but after 1962 the trend turned toward exclusive appointment of National Assembly members. The image of "apolitics" was slowly but surely repoliticized. Yet a cumbersome public administration remained.

The primary forum for policy discussion is the council of ministers, which must be consulted before bills are submitted to Parliament. This body is headed by the president and the prime minister (who handles day-to-day affairs). Since the president appoints all the ministers, the ministers and their staffs work closely with the president's office to formulate the presidential policy blueprint. Often the prime minister seems to be left out, serving basically as a buffer and propagandist for the president with the National Assembly and risking his own demise if a vote of no confidence should be passed by the Assembly. This does not mean that the prime minister does not have his own ideas or influence, which has clearly been the case with economist Raymond Barre in the government of Valéry Giscard d'Estaing. It merely means that in this presidential–parliamentary system the prime minister is the middleman and must fit in or eventually get out.

The Parliament is made up of the National Assembly (elected for five years by direct universal suffrage) and the Senate (elected for nine years, one-third retiring every three years). Whereas the electoral system of the National Assembly was meant to benefit the center, the electoral college of the Senate was biased in favor of small villages—the *département* system. The two-ballot system with small constituencies encourages variety, decentralization, and parochialism. For example, on the first ballot for each of the approximately 490 available seats in the National Assembly there may be more than six candidates in each district, with as many as ten candidates for every seat in Paris. On the second ballot all but two candidates are usually weeded out, but one often does not know after the first ballot which candidate will withdraw and in whose favor. This system stimulates interest to the end, helping to keep voter abstention low.

Voting is just voting; it does not indicate active citizen participation in politics between elections. As the philosopher Jean-Paul Sartre put it, "To vote is to vote for voting." In rural areas French voters are more interested in local elections than in national ones, sensing correctly that these are more important for their individual life chances. However, in metropolitan regions the voter perceives that local officials and city government cannot cope with the problems and change that confront them and so turns out more frequently for the national elections than for the local ones. Again, as people see the intensity of change overwhelming the system's ability to cope, they look to the top of the superstructure for solutions.

The National Assembly is the lower chamber of the Parliament and has somewhat less than twice as many deputies as the 283 who make up the Senate. Both houses have equal powers, except that the Assembly has the prerogative of examining the budget first and the cabinet is responsible only to the Assembly, which has the last word on legislation. However, if the government (cabinet members) and Senate agree, the veto of the Senate stands and can be overruled only if there is agreement between the cabinet and the Assembly.

In effect, Parliament exists to rubber-stamp the government's (more exactly, the president's) proposals; it has initiated only 10 percent of the legislation proposed during the Fifth Republic. Parliament can legislate only on matters defined by the Constitution, whereas the government can legislate on all other matters by simple decree. The budget is initiated by the government, and proposals from Parliament are not receivable if their adoption means either a diminution of public resources or an increase in public expenditures. And if Parliament does not decide within seventy days after the budget is introduced, a simple ordinance suffices to put the budget into effect. The government has the right to refuse amendments and put a bill in "take it or leave it" terms. Furthermore, the constitution's reduction of Assembly committees from nineteen to six makes them too big to be very effective, further diluting the power of the legislature. Parliament functions to provide public deliberation and advisory consultation in a basically presidential governmental framework. The third legislative body, the Economic and Social Council, provides a largely ignored forum for debate for representatives elected by business, union, social, and professional organizations.

The Fifth Republic aimed to restrict the power of the committee system, organizing the committees on the basis of specialized subjects and ensuring the committees did not redesign government bills and present them as their own. The six areas to which the committees are restricted include foreign affairs; finance; national defense; constitutional laws, legislation, and general administration; production and trade; and cultural, social, and family affairs. Committee members are nominated to represent political parties on a proportional basis. Bills therefore are unlikely to die in committee.

The Constitutional Council of the Judiciary was created as an independent body to decide jurisdictional disputes between government and Parliament or, more bluntly, to enforce the restrictions placed upon Parliament by the 1958 constitution.* In terms of votes of censure, the government has the upper hand. There are such restrictions on the mode of censure that broad issues are rarely debated. In addition to the Constitutional Council, in descending order of importance, the judiciary consists of the High Court of Justice, the High Council of the Judiciary, the ordinary courts, and the administrative court.

The French have developed one of the most powerful and largest of bureaucracies. Indeed, the civil service can directly and indirectly lead the economy. The status of technicians is high, and many of the civil services are self-contained units run by technicians. This has reduced the role of elected government, which has limited control over the administration of the bureaucracy.

The bureaucracy has involved the state in continual economic policy making as an agent for both entrepreneurship and protectionism. Indeed, the rapid growth of the French economy since World War II was guided by a series of plans, the seventh taking effect in 1976. Such plans set social objectives as well as production targets and are spelled out by planning commissions under the supervision of the *Commissariat Général du Plan*. With such clear-cut structures for governmental stability, at least in theory, the change and apparent instability in actual political practice may seem surprising.

---

*The Constitutional Council is made up of nine justices and all ex-presidents of the Republic. The president, Senate, and Assembly appoint three justices each.

Yet the ministerial instability in France can be interpreted as being largely on the superstructural level. For the more deep-seated French infrastructure and substructure are grounded in the tradition of a strong, centralized state. Although the French Revolution bequeathed to France a rebellious, antiauthoritarian democratic ideology, the more significant inheritance may be the centralized state system and bureaucratic civil service and the expectation of strong executive leadership characteristic of Napoleon's rule. The loud rhetoric of rebellion often heard in France may just be another traditional ritual that helps conserve French civilization, particularly since such superstructural behavior may serve more to strengthen state authority and to refurbish nationalism than to weaken traditional ties or to lead to truly revolutionary changes on the substructural level. Again, the more things change, the more things stay the same; therefore, *Vive le changement!*

The traditional substructure of the French political system reveals that the elements of centralized state authority exist regardless of superstructural diversity if political leaders are astute enough to bring them together in executive power and policy making. De Gaulle clearly sensed this in 1958 when he was framing the constitution of the Fifth Republic, which, as noted earlier, not only gave primary authority for government to the executive—the president, the premier, and the ministers—but loaded the dice within the executive toward presidential power. And although this presidential power could have been interpreted moderately, as if the president were merely an arbitrator among the executive, the parliament, and the people, de Gaulle used all existing constitutional authority (and some that has been claimed not to exist in the constitution) to make the Fifth Republic a thoroughly presidential government: he made it clear to all that he was the chief policy maker; he held national referenda to gather direct support and popularity from the people (e.g., on whether Algeria should become independent from France); he dissolved the National Assembly when it suited his purposes; he exercised emergency powers. By pulling together the threads of central state authority and the desire of the French for strong leadership, de Gaulle made himself an indispensable instrument of change. He institutionalized himself and left a heritage of concentrated presidential power for his successors when students and workers rebelled against the Gaullist regime in 1968, the changed superstructure represented by de Gaulle only reconfirmed French traditions and statist authority, forcing it to adapt to the problems of the times.

De Gaulle's presidential successors made good use of the dominance of the presidency in the French system and continued the basic governmental policy of de Gaulle's Fifth Republic: to use the powers of the executive branch to bring together domestic factions, on the one hand,

and, on the other, to use all foreign relations with other countries as opportunities to further national domestic objectives, particularly economic ones. Although the *dirigisme* of de Gaulle was eventually replaced by the supposed liberalism of Giscard d'Estaing, the two approaches shared the substructural purpose of using the state in neomercantilist fashion as the agent of national society and French economic interests. Foreign relations were managed and directed in such a way as to turn the terms of interdependence to the advantage of French business and agriculture in both the short and long terms. Giscard's diplomacy focuses on getting business contracts and obtaining the best terms of exchange for France in the existing world order. The president has become a father figure for French society, leaving the *foyer* at home in order to protect its interests in bargaining abroad, using the structures of the state to maintain the values and infrastructure of the French culture.

Structurally, some observers view France as a "stalemate society":

> This halfway house between France's feudal and rural past and the dreaded industrial future, this haven for an undynamic bourgeoisie driven by acquisitiveness rather than profitability, *patrimoine* and property rather than market expansion, security rather than risk-taking.[11]

In the past few decades the old feudal and traditional logic of patronage has been reluctantly giving way to the new logic of modernization, industrialization, and management expertise. Whereas the old logic caused groups and clienteles to view the state as a political process useful for preserving their privileges and spheres of authority, the new logic has made the state the agent of transformation and modernization, the industrialization of agriculture, the management of the social security and "social transfers" policies, the instrument of a policy of regional balance and an updated telecommunications system. As Professor Stanley Hoffmann put it, when the watchdog state became a greyhound, those who were holding the leash had to learn to run.

But this learning process has been slow, painful, and erratic. Fearing losses due to change and the undermining of their authority, many people fought to view the new state according to the old logic, turning to state organizations and bureaucracies to help preserve the status quo. Many failed to support the social and industrial transformations that alone would make France competitive in world markets and satisfy the needs of the French people more equitably. Outmoded agricultural practices and ailing industries have been subsidized and cushioned by the state, which has let in competitive air only to the extent that these older organizations could learn to cope with necessary changes.[12] Of course, in areas in which the centralized state bureaucracy had less than dominant authority changes sometimes came more quickly, since bargains had to be worked out with the private industrial sector and its competitive imperatives. Still, even some of the state organizations are learning fast and taking the lead in modernization. For example, one of the *grands corps* of the state bureaucracy, the engineers of the Ponts et Chaussées, has been totally reorganized to take over urban development.[13]

However, the bulk of the evidence indicates that French society has not been learning fast enough and that political structures are not adapting sufficiently to cope with domestic and international change. Despite Herman Kahn's characteristically optimistic prediction that France would lead the way in Western industrial development in the late twentieth century, the overstress on industrial modernization and economic growth has caused French leaders to neglect the heavy social costs of such a policy. The gap between the rich and the poor in France has become one of the largest in the Western industrial world. And the resulting social problems have helped the socialists gain new strength while simultaneously splintering the conservative and moderate groups. The potential for political and economic crisis has reached proportions not anticipated since de Gaulle took power to lead France away from possible chaos in 1958.

POLITICAL-ECONOMIC CODES: FRENCH BARGAINING BEHAVIOR

Since World War II there have been two important shifts in bargaining behavior patterns in France as viewed from the overall perspective of political economy. First, there has been a shift in power from the regional notables and their clienteles characteristic of the old stalemated French society to a centralized administrative structure—the state. Second, since the goal of economic growth embraced by the state apparatus is specifically carried out by private industry, with or without state subsidy, the crucial bargaining arena in French society today is between the state and the large industrial concerns. While the first shift seemed to promise the French people greater equality of treatment by replacing regional privileges with the universal rules of a centralized authority, the second shift made it clear that, in effect, political-economic bargaining power was now doubly removed from most of the French people. Power was captured first by a state bureaucracy that was fated to be inefficient by having to cope with so many demands, and then seized by private industries, which had a monopoly on the means for satisfying the major goal of the bureaucracy: productivity. The politics of productivity so overwhelmed the politics of redistribution that deep-seated social inequities became even more extreme and the French state increasingly lost legitimacy with the people. This loss of legitimacy is perhaps the single most important factor in explaining the popularity of the Socialist and Communist parties in France in the 1970s.

The first power shift—that is, toward state centralization—is the most notorious. Not only does the Napoleonic apparatus of the state remain largely intact at the substructural level, but de Gaulle's consolidation of executive power following World War II made the state's domination of political-economic relations unquestionable. State officials have used this far-reaching administrative apparatus as a political tool to manage and direct economic relations toward the goal of increasing economic growth, thereby providing the prerequisites for increasing French independence and self-sufficiency. In part, the focus on economic growth was intended to make up for the slow pace of industrialization in France in the nineteenth century compared with industrialization in Germany and Great Britain. The French realized that the agricultural bias of their economy put them at a distinct bargaining disadvantage in the industrial–technological era. Many of France's current social problems are the unwitting result of this sudden shift to industrialization as the basic priority of the state. The politics of productivity so overwhelmed the politics of redistribution that hidden social costs were forgotten until they were exposed by social crises.

Perhaps the major institutional effect of de Gaulle's efforts in terms of bargaining power was that the bureaucracy acquired the power of initiative, a development that transformed ministers into legitimizers of the bureaucracy who try to further its objectives in a rapidly changing environment. The National Assembly is filled with former bureaucrats. And the transfer of power from the centralized state authority to the level of *départements* serves to further diffuse authority within the bureaucracy, allowing parliamentary members to pass the buck to regional civil servants who have time and red tape on their side and whose resistance is often well calculated.* French democracy thus becomes decreasingly representative as it becomes increasingly bureaucratic. Local *notables* or elites have lost meaning and power to regional *interlocuteurs* of the state bureaucracy.

> Yesterday, . . . the political *notables* were strongholds of the opposition to the regime and gained a certain influence through the local bargaining process. Today, such shelters have become ghettos. . . . The change from the past is symbolized by the reversal of old career patterns: yesterday, the local *notable* used his position to become a deputy, then a minister; today, among

*The 36,400 communes or local-government units of the French system are combined into the 95 departments created during the Revolution.

the Gaullists, civil servants become parliamentarians or ministers who then seek local office. The efficiency of the old *notables* is further limited by the ways local budgets are drawn up: many expenditures are compulsory, and others are at the charge of the national government—which also provides a growing amount of the local districts' resources.[14]

In contrast to the equilibrium and control orientation of the Germans, the French seek to maximize their life chances and bargaining power with a collective code that aims to use and incorporate change: fear of the loss of general social security seems to concern them less than fear of individual *déclassement* through changes that they are unable to incorporate to their advantage. Rather than being slow and orderly in their innovations, like the Germans, the French tend to watch where the wind is blowing and cast all their energies in that direction all at once. Equilibrium is not the concept through which change is steered or controlled, as the Germans would have it, but is the almost accidental and temporary result of countering one pole with another in thought or action. When the shift from an agricultural France to an industrial France finally came, for example, it came all at once with little moderation. But when the whole bureaucracy was focused on the goal of economic growth and industrialization, bargaining power was inadvertently shifted to the existing industrial and entrepreneurial class and to large business enterprises. The main goal of the state could not be accomplished without the resources of the business community, and as so often happens, the means became the ends.

This second shift in bargaining power, from the state bureaucracy to industrial interests, is subtle and complex, often displacing politics into management, which cloaks itself in apolitical technocratic expertise. The group consultation and bargaining that now takes place, mainly in Paris, has helped to weaken the separation between the public and the private. A large number of state-run enterprises stimulate this tendency. Mayors and local elites must negotiate in this centralized bargaining process not only with the state but also with the industrial partners and promoters on whom the state has become increasingly dependent. The loss of legitimacy in this process is clear, for although the official bargaining that goes on between state and industry officials is often acknowledged, it is far from open. For example, although the steel industry and the state signed a convention in 1966 indicating in general what the commitments of each side would be, how these negotiations were handled and exactly how much state aid was involved remain mysterious. As such economic dependencies become clearer in the politicized atmosphere of French society, the state loses legitimacy and the role of large industry becomes suspect, no matter how much the French people might want the benefits of economic growth.[15]

The interpenetration between civil servants and business and banking people in the bargaining process is particularly notable at the regional and local levels, where state bureaucracies are often weak and diffuse and where most of the important political "contracts" are made behind closed doors. Hoffmann notes that

> at the local level, particularly in cities, where the national services need local support to carry out development plans, the obsolescence or technical incompetence of the old functional *notables* often allows the administration to select its own correspondents, i.e., to choose among possible counterplayers. Since the natural tendency is to lean on supporters and to avoid politics—according to the conviction or myth that the state transcends political divisions and aims at the common good through "the best" technical means—this obviously becomes more a way of circumventing than of solving the problem of participation.[16]

The loss of legitimacy in the political-economic bargaining process is exacerbated by French psychocultural attitudes. In a classical culture that respects only clear-cut (if not absolute) authority, the present political system serves only to legitimize a bureaucracy that diffuses its powers and submits to the temptation of turning over influence to less incompetent managers in the private sector. Jean-Claude Morel, the Common Market's director for economic development, pointed out that in France *profit* has a negative connotation. This contrasts with Germany, where *profit* means that someone has worked very hard and deserves it. Accordingly, at times French conservatives are more to the left than the German socialists.[17] Since profit is usually the measure of economic growth (the government's main objective), French society is clearly in a double bind. The French want to become better off economically and more independent without being perceived as profitmongers. Even the broad social movement to the left that apparently peaked in the late 1970s does not eclipse the desire of the French to go on living well.

But whatever the deeper motivations or the final outcome of leftward movement and ideological polarization in France, the direction seems clear given the lopsided priorities of the recent past. There is a growing desire to reduce the many inequities in French society. Not only did the recession of the 1970s hit older civil servants and the unemployed hardest, but studies indicate that the great disparities between wages have not changed significantly in the past twenty years.[18] In contrast to the situation in Germany, the lack of separation in France between the political and economic spheres, combined with the radical tradition in France, politicizes such problems to explosive proportions in an atmosphere of fading legitimacy.[19] And wage differentials in France are notable. Whereas more than one-third of French workers earned less than

1,200 francs per month in 1973, more than one-third of the top executives earned more than 6,000. Not only are hourly wages in France below those in Germany and Italy, but among the original six nations of the Common Market France assigns the smallest share of its national income to remuneration of wage earners and has the highest level of undistributed corporate income.[20]

The French accepted a rather rigid class or "caste" system in the past because it provided a certain sense of security consistent with their attitude toward clear-cut authority. The worker had a stake in the hierarchy and sensed the promise that his son or daughter might get farther up the ladder through hard work and education. But this promise of security, with which the old social system cushioned the reality of inequity, is gone. Social and technological change has swept over obsolete social structures. Future shock and insecurity are widespread at all levels of society. Few people know where they are going, much less where their society is headed. And this massive, collective insecurity has made structural inequities increasingly unbearable: people want their life chances bettered now, in the short run, while there is still time left.

Nietzsche observed long ago that democratic states give rise to a feeling of *ressentiment*—a bitter envy of the success of others stemming not from concrete jealousy over not having or being something in particular but, rather, from the guilt one feels at voluntarily accepting a role that limits the expression of one's full potential. This general feeling of bitterness, of being used, is particularly characteristic of those at the lower end of the social ladder. Today in France there is no trade-off in terms of security for staying at the bottom and swallowing such resentment or directing it inward toward oneself. The full, bitter anger of repressed life chances and lack of opportunity is being directed outward toward the social system itself, toward the obvious inequities that are being systematically exposed by the political opposition and the press.

As belief in the possibility of individual upward mobility declined, the demand increased for collective redistribution of life chances—for group mobility. Students at the lycées and universities demonstrated against any attempt to restrict admissions requirements or change their condition in such a way as to "declass" them further—a movement complemented by German students. In 1976 the French government issued an order for educational reform designed to steer students out of fields like social science and the humanities and into fields that are more relevant to the technological maintenance of society, such as business administration. University students were outraged and demonstrated accordingly. Any change that might be interpreted as decreasing student bargaining power or making student opportunities more unequal has been fought tooth and nail. Superficially, this might be viewed as "liberal collective action." But more likely it is explainable as a reactive return to a deep-seated conservative psychological impulse typical of French people who sense changes that will reduce their status and that they cannot somehow reconstitute to their advantage. This more or less universal conservative impulse is viewed positively in the case of students, for the student position is simultaneously at the bottom of the social ladder and the first step of individual ascent and opportunity. Perhaps the generous "liberal" interpretations of student motivations and talk of student power by those who are established in the social structure are actually psychocultural means of alleviating guilt and stabilizing social change as it occurs. If there is one place where equal opportunity should be real, it is the school system, and to admit not only that students are at the bottom of the social hierarchy but that their situation is becoming worse rather than better over time would be to confess to a tremendous infrastructural deficiency in the social system that, if fully exposed, could generate a revolution, as it nearly did in 1968. Recent efforts to increase equality of opportunity in the school system have not led to equality of results in terms of social advancement owing to noneducational factors necessary for upward mobility and success in France's "caste" system. It may well be that the "democraticization" of the school system has merely reduced the meaning of any educational degree, inflating the social currency needed for a person to be selected for a good job to the point at which noneducational criteria have become even more important than educational attainments. The more things change, the more they seem to stay the same in French society—a self-fulfilling prophecy.

Mass education ironically exposes the negative aspects of the existing class system in France by giving a competitive edge to the children of the wealthy and the privileged. This system of stratification provided the comfort of security in earlier times, but today it has become a symbol of widespread inequalities. For the majority of the people on the lower end of the social scale, life chances seem to be contracting rather than opening up with new opportunity. Resentment results on both sides: the disadvantaged are angry with a system that provides them with neither security nor the promise of meaningful equal opportunity in a tight job market, and the privileged react defensively to protect their competitive advantages while they last. This tension is ready-made for political exploitation by parties on both the left and the right.

This tension was expressed in the 1968 revolt of students and workers against the Gaullist government's authoritarian policies on education and information and against low wage rates and the lack of social reform. The revolt ended the period of relative tranquillity that began with de Gaulle's consolidation of conservative forces in France, and caused his resignation in April 1969 after being defeated in a referendum on regional reform. This shift from right-wing tranquillity to left-wing ferment can perhaps best be understood in the context of the postwar development of right- and left-wing parties in France.

THE PARTY SYSTEM

Parties on the right are characterized by acceptance of the status quo (or a "backwards" revision of it) and fear of downward mobility through social change. Traditionally, they have stood for a strong executive, an army independent of state interference, support for Catholicism, and defense of the capitalist system of private ownership of the means of production. The postwar development of the right can be summed up as a gradual consolidation of a number of diffuse right-wing parties and movements by de Gaulle and his party that peaked in the early 1960s, followed by a period of decline, diffusion, and uncertainty in the 1970s that was arrested in 1978 by the narrow victory of the moderate–conservative coalition of Giscard d'Estaing over the left.

Initially, notables, or people known for personal merits rather than ideological positions, predominated in rightist politics, helping to explain the diffuseness of the rightist organization compared with the more disciplined, mass parties of the left. After the right was discredited in the war by collaborating with the fascists in the Vichy regime, small right-wing parties emerged, some of them grouping into the National Center of Independents and Farmers (*Centre national des indépendents et paysans*, or CNIP). This group represented rural, small-town, and Catholic France and became adept at using the immobilized Fourth Republic to protect its socioeconomic interests and prevent others from taking away the privileges it held. The weak superstructure was exploited to defend the existing substructure and infrastructure. Although the CNIP's strength peaked in 1958, it was overwhelmed in that year by the Gaullist movement and later split into two factions, one joining the conservative Christian Democrats and the other becoming the Independent Republicans (RI), headed by Giscard d'Estaing, which aimed to gain access to as many ministerial posts as possible.

In 1947, after resigning as head of the tripartite government of Socialists, Communists, and Christian Democrats formed following the liberation of France, de Gaulle made an unsuccessful attempt at a comeback by founding the right-wing Rally of the French People (*Rassemblement du peuple français*, or RPF). This party disintegrated over a diversity of views. But in 1958, when the National Assembly could not cope with the Algerian rebellion, de Gaulle was brought back, becoming France's "savior" a second time. The Gaullist party (the UDR) was formed just before the fall 1958 elections and was successfully organized around de Gaulle's popularity, becoming the electoral tool for his amazingly effective consolidation of right-wing forces during the following decade. This ambiguous platform appealed to French people in all sectors, including left-leaning "social Gaullists" and the majority group of "big-business" Gaullists such as Georges Pompidou, who succeeded de Gaulle.

Outside of the mainstream right-wing movements, a right-wing extremist group also emerged in the 1950s, with fascist nuances and contemporary relevance. In 1954 a right-wing government passed a bill demanding more careful scrutiny of income tax returns. As French small businesses are notorious tax evaders, the bill threatened to lower their incomes to the point—their greatest fear—at which their socioeconomic identity would be merged with that of the working class. Pierre Poujade led a protest movement of "little people" capitalizing on this fear of small shopkeepers, artisans, and small farmers. The threat of downward mobility among the lower middle class is the best breeding ground for right-wing extremism, rallying the people to save their dwindling life chances while they can. Such movements, including this one, are best defined by what they are against rather than what they are for. The *Poujadisme* movement was against taxes, big business, politicians, civil servants, technocrats, bureaucrats, the rich, the state, the Jews, financiers, intellectuals, academics, and cosmopolitans. Its followers' most concrete fear was that the more modern big-business interests of the mainstream right would press them to the economic margins, declassing them on the way. Eventually this movement dissolved and was absorbed by both Gaullism and the reactionary *Algerie Française* ("Keep Algeria French") group.

The unity of the right under Gaullism stimulated both the center and left-wing parties to form coalitions for their electoral defense. The result was that in the legislative elections of the late 1960s and 1970s four major party groupings confronted each other on the first ballot, allying into two blocs (moderate/right vs. left) for the second ballot, in marked contrast to the diffuse, multiparty elections of former years. The Center of Social Democrats (*Centre des Democrats Sociaux*) consists of four or five centrist parties and groups that previously were unable to elect an adequate number of deputies to form a political group in the National Assembly. The only coherent centrist party that has had some electoral success in the postwar period is the liberal Catholic MRP, which at one point attracted more than 25 percent of the vote but has since declined in strength.

France has been ruled by a left-wing government for only 6 of the past 100 years. On the left, Gaullist strength stimulated the Socialist and Radical parties to form a federation called the Democratic and Socialist Federation of the Left (*Federation de Gauche Democrate et Socialiste*, or FGDS). Leftist parties in general support socioeconomic change as a means to undermine or ameliorate the capitalist form of political economy for the sake of community ownership and control of the means of production. Rather than supporting the principle of private profitability, which dominates capitalism, the socialist or left-wing orientation is toward public redistribution of wealth and opportunity. The Socialist party was founded at the turn of the century and in the postwar period has been marked by its split from organized labor, which was coopted by the communists. From 1946 onward the French Socialist Party (SFIO), led by Guy Mollet, became increasingly stodgy and closed until the party (now called the *Parti Socialiste*, or PS) was taken over by François Mitterand, the leader of the FGDS. In contrast to the concentration of the French Communist Party on the traditional working class of blue-collar workers, the PS has focused on the new working class of technological personnel—salaried lower- and middle-level white-collar workers and people working for government and industrial bureaucracies. The smaller French Radical Party (*Parti republicain et radical-socialiste*) appeals to many of the same constituents but is on the liberal center of the ideological spectrum compared with the Socialists.

The French Communist Party (PCF) was founded in 1920 on Leninist principles and was later influenced by Stalinism. It has consistently managed to capture the support of about one-fifth of the French population by simultaneously serving as the revolutionary vanguard, a countercommunity and set of institutions, a "people's tribune" for the cause of the underprivileged and alienated, and a government party both locally and nationally that has supported the international communist objectives of the Soviet Union.

In the 1970s the essentially Stalinist PCF modified its image in favor of parliamentary democracy to such an extent that it made possible a temporary coalition with the Socialist party before the spring 1978 parliamentary elections, although at the time many people doubted that this coalition would last long even if it was able to assume power.[21] The last-minute split between the communists and the socialists initiated by Georges Marchais, the Communist party leader, was undoubtedly a key reason for the narrow defeat of the leftist challenge by the incumbent government coalition.[22] Although many leftist tacticians in Europe regarded Marchais's move to assert communist autonomy as little less than a disaster, it did serve to revitalize socialist movements in France and Italy that focused on various interpretations of the concept of *autogestion*, or worker autonomy from the state. The electoral catastrophe for the left also served to revitalize the center–right forces of the coalition government of President Giscard d'Estaing and Prime

Minister Raymond Barre. In May 1978 the French government decided to take the "irreversible step" of freeing industrial prices, lifting the state-imposed blocks on profits in industries ranging from clock-making to jam-making, from railway workshops to dairies. By purging industry of state subsidies, Barre hoped to make French industry more competitive while Giscard d'Estaing focused on the need for full employment to balance Barre's politics of productivity with the image of a politics of redistribution. Party factionalism notwithstanding, on the productivity–redistribution issues there is almost a classic split between the "equality"-oriented left and the inflation/production-oriented right. Since in 1979 Barre's policies, for various reasons (including the oil price hike), had failed to reduce either unemployment or inflation, the possibility of a Socialist-Communist alliance was raised again. Communist Marchais quipped "Better the devil you know than Barre." Giscard, however, who could fire his Prime Minister were Barre to prove inconvenient just before elections, continued to hold the cards.

Yet the public bureaucracy is so extensive in France that the promises of any future coalition on the left are apt to become as bogged down in red tape as the realities of the moderate–right regime of Giscard d'Estaing and Barre. The large public-administration bureaucracy may prove to be one of the greatest obstacles to a more socialist concept in France. Early in the development of the French nation–state, the baronic networks of the feudal heritage were replaced by the centralized common rule, which established public administrations in all areas affecting the public interest. This centralization contrasts with the federal structures of West Germany and the United States. Modernization speeded the growth of public administration in both quantitative and qualitative terms. All aspects of social life from the central city to the smallest province are covered by administrative agencies, which themselves have come to define the political system in terms of infrastructure, making the top civil servants the dominant element of the system. This is a far cry from the Italian theorist Antonio Gramsci's call for a "civil society," in which some aspects of society have not been taken over by formal political or administrative systems (with heavy reliance on public voluntary associations). In France such civil-society organizations are very weak compared to the situation in Germany, Britain, Italy, and the United States. French political parties are equally underdeveloped in such comparisons, particularly in terms of finance, organization, management, and budget. The sociologist Jean-Pierre Worms sums it up in no uncertain terms: "France is an overadministered and undergoverned country."[23]

One of the major problems of the left is that socialism is usually identified with the growth of bureaucracy, and more bureaucracy is not exactly what the French need. Yet in France it was not socialism that built bureaucracy but the particular course that capitalism took in terms of state centralization. The French civil service became a dominant cultural model for the whole society. All social needs and problems became real insofar as they are articulated by an administrative structure. Giscard d'Estaing, for example, had to develop a ministry for women and a ministry for labor to meet perceived needs. And groups threatened with the elimination of their ministry (i.e., with "déclassement") rebel militantly and can create social unrest. Thus, the ministry of World War I could not be eliminated because of heavy protests by veterans who felt that their social existence was at stake. Such examples demonstrate the interconnections between psychocultural attitudes toward change and authority on the substructural level with the administrative structures on the infrastructural level, revealing themselves at the official, "political," superstructural level only at times of explicit conflict or administrative reform. To understand overt political issues one must probe their infrastructural and substructural bases. For instance, issues of employment (which are issues of redistribution or equality) must be understood as they are perceived in France—in bureaucratic terms, where sophisticated legal weapons have been developed to maintain the domination of society by public administration.

A coalition socialist government would be under pressure in France's "administrative political culture" to extend the state bureaucracy to create public jobs; to extend social services; and to cope with cultural, leisure, and training problems, where great inequities now exist. There would undoubtedly be demands that it steer money from private training schools for the privileged to the expansion of adult education. The great anticipation aroused by the possibility of a victory by the left in 1978—but then dashed—symbolizes the beginning of a widespread social movement that could be difficult to control, with escalating demands for social-need satisfaction, state intervention, and extension of the state bureaucracy. And left-wing governments are notoriously vulnerable to criticism of their bureaucratic management. To date, attempts to reform the French bureaucratic apparatus have failed because of clandestine privileges and because interest groups see their bargaining power in organization to protect "their own" civil servants, their own turf.

For this reason Worms claims that the strategy of administrative reform is a closed strategy that the left cannot afford to take. He suggests a risky alternative: the left should create a counterbureaucracy alongside the existing one, aiming to reconstruct a "civil society" to increase the capacity of the unions and voluntary associations. One could force employees to go to voluntary-association meetings by giving them a certain number of credit hours. Public financing of campaigns could revitalize the party system. The aim would be to create a countervailing power against the traditional public administration, to stimulate the shifting of public demands away from bureaucracy and toward autonomy through state financial incentives.

Noting that this countervailing strategy risks reinforcing old structures and privileges in times of crisis, Worms still believes that the risk is worth taking in order to make possible any kind of meaningful change in political-economic bargaining power for the disadvantaged in France.[24] Who would pay for the "civil war" that he would institutionalize remains to be seen. Business and private enterprise—the hidden governors in the French bargaining system—might be skeptical about a second bureaucracy that could counter their power as well as that of the existing governmental administration. Public deficits and inflation would be the results of government expenditures to create a new system in addition to the old one. And this could, in turn, have a negative impact on France's competitive position in foreign trade, which depends on keeping domestic costs down. Moreover, decentralization through a countervailing administration might be such a diffuse strategy that it would not really change the gap between the rich and the poor, the strong and the weak. Such "redecentralization" may be the direction that democratic industrial societies will take in the future. But the payoffs may not change that much in terms of redistributing bargaining power to less advantaged groups. A smaller piece of a more fragmented economic pie for everyone may be the result of this blueprint for a bifurcated politics of redistribution. Yet, given France's present administrative fix, some sort of "learning by paying" appears to be an inevitable experience for most of the French people in the near future.

DOMESTIC AND FOREIGN POLICY: COLLECTIVE DECISION MAKING

In France since World War II the political-economic bargaining process has led to extreme outcomes in industrial and social policy, profoundly affecting the trade-offs between productivity and redistribution issues. After the war the French used the European Coal and Steel Community to help control and share in West German coal and steel production. This institution, in turn, became a basis for the founding of the Common Market, which, in effect, conceded industrial primacy to the Germans while protecting agricultural primacy for the French. This sometimes extreme protection of French agricultural interests remains as perhaps the fundamental reason for French cooperation in the Common Market.[25]

Internationally, in the late twentieth century bargaining power and independence go not with agricultural economies but with industrial economies. Charles de Gaulle, Georges Pompidou, and Valéry Giscard d'Estaing were quick to perceive this once de Gaulle had skillfully maneuvered France back into the elite circle of great Western powers after its bitter humiliation in the war.[26] French policy makers switched agricultural and industrial priorities to such a point that between 1960 and 1972 France held second place among the industrialized Western European countries in terms of growth of industrial production (after the Netherlands) and fourth place in expansion of the volume of exports (after the Netherlands, the Belgium–Luxemburg Economic Union, and Italy). From 1968 to 1972 French industrial production grew by 35 percent and the total volume of exports by 65 percent.[27]

The focus of domestic policy on rapid industrial growth has been facilitated by direct state intervention to buffer French society against economic disturbances. The government put explicit limits on the operation of the market while simultaneously encouraging productivity. Meanwhile the state has cushioned agriculture and created what has been called "a hothouse environment for industry" by protecting it from competition. In establishing learning-by-paying incentives, the state's domestic structure and foreign role combine to allow a gradual increase in competition and to help industries adjust.[28] The French government has used domestic structures to bend the terms of international economic interdependence in France's favor through state intervention and the manipulation of domestic and international markets. As a result the balance of trade has moved into surplus, and the percentage of manufactures in French exports by 1974 was more than 50 percent of the total (compared to 68 percent for Germany and 61 percent for England). Furthermore, as much as one quarter of the gross national product is spent on investment, and specific expanding sectors of the economy, such as chemicals, have been restructured.[29] Both the government and the general public have become increasingly aware of the need to revitalize French industry to meet increasing competition in international markets and to create the resources to satisfy the aspirations of a growing population. This awareness is symbolized by the top priority that has been given to the needs of industry in national policy making.

State intervention in industrial policy at home and abroad brings together the substructural, infrastructural, and superstructural elements of French policy making in an epitome of sophisticated bargaining power. The French state alone does not set industrial policy, but the centralization of the public administrative bureaucracy makes it a powerful agent in the bargaining process. Substructurally, the French people approve of a strong central authority representing their interests, as is symbolized by the long survival of the *dirigisme* of de Gaulle and its subtle transformation into the more modest, and supposedly liberal, "presidential politics" of Giscard d'Estaing. Although de Gaulle's focus was always international, he was aware of the need for a strong industrial base to make French power effective, and he cultivated strategic industries accordingly. Giscard d'Estaing's superstructural moves, while more modest, have been more sharply focused on the industrial-policy aspect of French neomercantilism (meaning: increase exports, reduce imports, and reduce unemployment at home regardless of the implications for other nations).

But most interesting of all in terms of collective-bargaining power at home and abroad is the infrastructure that has made this possible, particularly in the industrial sector. In terms of infrastructure, France has a banking–state–business complex that resulted naturally from the development of industrial capitalism in France, particularly given its tradition of centralized public administration. During its merger drive in the 1960s, intended to concentrate critical industries, the state often worked in alliance with the *banques d'affaires* and nationalized deposit banks, which provided investment capital. At the top of the infrastructure, the school ties of the *grandes écoles* (the elitist schools) and *grands corps* (administrative units) and a "club system" weave through the upper echelons of the bureaucracy, often making agreement and support among government, banking, and business elites a taken-for-granted rule of the game. Therefore, the state can often intervene quietly to steer specific industries into particular markets and product lines without public knowledge (except after the fact), avoiding politicization of industrial policy making until a *fait accompli* makes a decision irreversible.

The French state is best seen as a sophisticated coordinator of the domestic infrastructure, not overtly dominating events when more subtle influences can be employed. But it should be noted that this state power is contingent on the support of banking and business communities, which, of course, is much more likely to be forthcoming when the government favors a politics of productivity over a politics of redistribution. The major crisis on the horizon in France may explode exactly if it becomes clear that these priorities have been reversed. Businesspeople and bankers may then flee the country with their capital investments, much as they have in Italy and England, where redistribution issues have come to center stage. This is one meaning of "learning by paying" at the level of national political economy.

Public Expenditures and Private Interests

The authoritarian statist tradition in France has been modernized and diffused in our era, but it still serves as the basis for state intervention in the economy. State planning and influence are demonstrated by the wide variety of economic instruments used by public policy makers to affect economic outcomes in the private sector.

Government officials use banking policy, for example; to counter inflation by increasing interest rates, which lowers the incentive for French entrepreneurs to invest. Price controls are also used to check inflation, preventing the high price of borrowed money from being recovered by increasing the market price of the resulting product. State officials also give financial aid to certain types of businesses. The *Compagnie Française d'Assurance pour le Commerce Extérieur* (COFACE) provides short- and medium-term loans to finance exports—a major objective of neomercantilist French policy. The government even makes guarantees against shipping and other risks. Firms that are interested in expanding within France are given special tax exemptions, capital grants, and interest rate subsidies. As for research and development in the private sector, about 35 percent of such expenses are covered by public assistance, as are to 50 percent of the costs of certain innovations. In addition, the state encouraged mergers by eliminating capital-gains exemptions; "marriage bureaus" were established to help restructure such industries and to. help out medium- and small-sized businesses. All in all, the private sector receives about one quarter of all investments financed through public moneys.[30]

The heavy stress on industrial revitalization as a government policy, despite the positive social benefits of increased economic growth, in some ways compounded the crucial dilemma of Western capitalist democracies: the disequilibrium between increasing private wealth and the impoverishment of the public or social sector. For not only do free-market incentives encourage private accumulation, but one quarter of public investment expenditures encourage private gains as well. In short, the payoffs for the interlocking of public investment and private interests seem to go to the "haves" in the class system with the capacity to produce, aiming to pull up public resources by the bootstraps of private profit. The balance is not tilted toward the satisfaction of non-productive social needs or toward redistributing the benefits and opportunities of French society more equitably. Meanwhile the left continues to find support.

The imbalance between public- and private-sector support is reflected in the French government's failure to achieve its projected aim in public-sector investment or to accurately project the public consumption growth rate between 1965 and 1975. When they saw that their projection of the public consumption growth rate for 1965–1970 was too high, French policy makers revised their projection downward for the 1970–1975 period to match what actually happened (one form of "learning by paying," if you will). But this form of "learning" seems regressive in that it indicates an intention not to dissuade private consumption or to encourage public consumption. Projections were merely adjusted backwards to fit an imbalanced status quo. Such a superstructural effort to make the new projection agree with the old growth rate represents superficial learning behavior that fails to lead to needed adjustments at the infrastructural or substructural levels. Long-term costs that accumulate with inflation owing to the failure to invest sufficiently in the public sector are the price that is now being paid for numerical conformities that merely reflect what happens rather than pointing French society in a direction that is more likely to satisfy its needs.

In the 1965–1970 period the French both underestimated the growth in gross capital-asset formation in the private sector and overestimated the growth in fixed capital assets in the public sector. This particular inaccuracy occurs with enough consistency to represent a bias against facing the increasing gap between private growth and public impoverishment. This failure to learn in the short run implies that all of French society will be forced to learn to pay at a much higher rate in the long run when unsatisfied social problems explode into crisis.

A sudden shift to a government by the left might aggravate the situation by frightening investors who could take their badly needed capital out of the country just when it is most needed to stimulate the economic growth required to pay for great increases in public-sector investment. This, in part, explains why the Communist parties of France and Italy hesitate to take responsibility for the government in an era of almost insoluble economic difficulties, particularly given the push for redistribution that would bring them to power and that they might not be able to control. Left-wing voters want social justice and benefits now, not sacrifices for the sake of future productivity and economic growth. In such circumstances the politics of redistribution could overwhelm the politics of productivity to such an extent that the society's ability to pay its own way could be undermined. The government's efforts, through the controversial Barre plan, to make industries more competitive were directed to counter this possibility, but they may have the effect of stimulating an even more extreme left-wing reaction in the 1980s.

Still, the French government bureaucracy has advantages in that it collects information on the relationship between the public and private sectors that is sometimes nonexistent in other Western democracies. Accordingly, it has been calculated that public expenditure affects hardly 1 percent of food consumption, whereas it accounts for 66 percent of expenditure on education, sports, and health.[31] These data exist as a result of attempts to measure "broad household consumption" ("consumption" as it is understood in national accounting principles)—

efforts that are so intriguing that they have prompted UNESCO to develop similar studies at the European Centre for the Co-ordination of Research in Social Science (ECCRSS) in Vienna. Such research uncovers interesting social facts: In 1965, inmates of psychiatric hospitals in France exceeded capacity by 19 percent, one patient in six having to use a stretcher instead of a bed; in 1967, the average Frenchman devoted 82 percent of his "transport" budget to private transport and only 18 percent to public transport—and from 1962 to 1967, the total cost of transport by public car rose 7 percent whereas the cost for public transport rose 25.3 percent.[32] But the trend of most of the data points in the direction of the 1968–1971 period, when unprecedented overall growth (20.4 percent by volume, and 6.4 percent annually) was accompanied by diminished public-sector investment in absolute terms. The French know almost more than they want to know about private wealth and public impoverishment, making a swing to an extreme politics of redistribution (from an extreme politics of productivity) a possibility not to be discounted despite the loss of the left in the 1978 election.

The *Déclassement* of Immigrant Workers

One of the most poignant cases of the need for redistribution of life chances in the societies of advanced Western democracies such as France is the status deprivation among immigrant workers. The disequilibrium between the productivity and redistribution motivations becomes clearest in the case of workers who are taken in as cheap labor when economic growth rates are high and then dumped on the streets or sent home when recession sets in and fiscal pressures on public-assistance funds become most acute. This phenomenon has international implications. Cross-cultural data indicate that the lower a country's level of development (measured by per capita GNP), the higher the level of emigration. One analyst argues that this is a result of the structure of national political economies and their modes of production:

> At first sight . . . emigration/immigration is simply a product of the uneven development inherent in the capitalist mode of production as it affects the labour force. It must be noted, however, that this is not equivalent to viewing migration simply as the product of a succession of economic conditions, and hence as capable of being absorbed into jobs created by economic growth within each country. For, on the contrary, uneven development is a structural tendency of the mode of production and the gaps between firms, sectors, trusts, regions or countries, tend to increase rather than diminish. For example, in recent years, despite having the highest growth rate in Western Europe, Spain has had a regularly increasing level of emigration,

with small movements around this trend caused much more by recessions in the countries receiving immigrants than by any drop in requests to emigrate. Similarly, there are over two million Italian workers in other European countries despite Italy's high growth rate and production level. The reasons for such a permanent emigrant labour force are clear from the point of view of the sending country: decomposition of backward productive structures— especially in agriculture; structural unemployment in certain sectors; and the much higher nominal and real wages available in the advanced capitalist countries.[33]

The long-term trend is for continued growth in immigrant labor in advanced Western countries, which represented at least 10 percent of the working population in 1972. In France, official statistics indicate that there were 1,800,000 immigrant workers at the beginning of 1973 (8 percent of the working population), a low figure since it does not take clandestine work into account. But note what happens to the percentages in terms of specific tasks: immigrants represent 27 percent of all workers in building and public works (rising to as much as 90 percent on building sites in the Paris area), 17 percent in metals industries and 16 percent in extractive industries. In comparison, in Germany in 1972, 10.8 percent of all wage earners were foreign workers (2,354,200), constituting 25 percent of workers in the building industry and 80 percent in certain public work sectors (11 percent in the metallurgical industry).[34] The economic growth in France and Germany has opened the borders for foreign workers in good times, allowing them in to establish their own subcultures and ghettos, and then shut down opportunities for them in hard times, creating grave structural-unemployment problems, social discontent, and the basis for violent crime. Perhaps nowhere else does the perception of "déclassement" or sinking socioeconomic status strike so hard as at the bottom of the social ladder in the French caste system. And such extreme cases of inequity are ready-made to become political symbols for mass movements against the regime in power.

Foreign Policy: The Culture Business and Presidential Contracts

In foreign policy the psychocultural, structural, and political-economic bargaining behavior patterns typical of France come together in a colorful synthesis. Since the war the French have successfully maintained cultural ties to their former colonies, for fun and profit. French cultural supremacy has been fashioned into a slick image for foreigners who buy products labeled "Made in France" at a healthy price. Such strategies have become the basis of France's foreign policy of neomercantilism: increasing French exports, reducing imports into France, and reducing unemployment within France—no matter what the costs and consequences for other countries.

One should not be unfair to the French since the trend in most Western European countries appears to be to solve domestic problems with export-oriented growth. Still, it is not inaccurate to note that the French have specialized in neomercantilism or economic nationalism, first with the authoritarian gusto of de Gaulle and more recently with the entrepreneurial modesty of Giscard d'Estaing. They believe they have a good thing going—a unique civilization and a voluptuous life style. So why shouldn't the father figure of the French family work to see how far others are willing to pick up the tab?

The export-oriented thrust of French foreign policy has moved the balance of trade into surplus, and over half of the manufactured goods in France are exports. Unlike federalized countries, where authority is more diffuse, in France the president himself becomes a vehicle of export growth, using his diplomatic stature to solicit business contracts for French firms and the state. The French–British supersonic plane, the Concorde, is a case in point. To persuade residents near New York's John F. Kennedy airport to allow the Concorde to land, President Giscard d'Estaing used every diplomatic, business, and legal instrument he could find. He even had French people write personal letters to American families. In such a dispute Americans appear to be outclassed—particularly given the diffusion of power in their federal system—and the resistance of the Port Authority of New York City collapsed under pressure from the federal court system.

The statist tradition in France, which unites the political and economic realms behind the cause of economic growth, is radically different from the checks-and-balances separation of economic and political power that is often typical of the American system. It is tough for American businesspeople to compete with the French state, particularly if American governmental officials tilt toward the French for the sake of warmer European–American relations. By being so explicit about his main diplomatic objective—the Concorde landing—Giscard d'Estaing put the United States in the awkward position of appearing to be protectionist and anti-French if the landing was refused. Meanwhile the French policy of economic mercantilism appears in the sheep's clothing of "free world enterprise." The French state, symbolized by Giscard d'Estaing, is the ultimate business contractor, whereas the American government is supposed to restrict itself to the role of artibrator between conflicting interest groups.

These structural political-economic differences were ignored, however, in the public debate on the Concorde. In an editorial for *The New York Times*, C. L. Sulzberger argued that the issue was one of America's good faith as perceived by the French and the ability of the plane to keep within the decibel noise range required by environmental-protection regulations. His solution was to have the American administration in Washington ask the governor of New York State and the mayor of New York City to pressure the Port Authority to allow the plane to land, offering an inferential quid pro quo of financial generosity through loans to the beleaguered metropolis. Sulzberger not only missed the economic argument entirely but went so far in pressing the French view as to extensively cite a personal interview with Prime Minister Barre, who made the foreign-policy linkage (and threat) explicit:

> It will be a very serious attack if the New York Port Authority blocks Concorde flights. I cannot really appreciate the U.S. attitude. People here are shocked to see a plane furnished with the proper navigation certificate excluded from an airport—the most important airport in the world. They cannot help believing this is an act of bad faith.
> They feel that a technologically advanced carrier is being eliminated from access to New York, and maybe the entire United States, when all other countries including France have willingly accepted U.S. aeronautical equipment. We are especially shocked to see this occur in an industry where all Europe has accepted American supremacy although naturally our own aircraft factories must keep their potential.
> It is difficult under existing circumstances to envision the desirable long-term cooperation between Europe and the United States on future development of aircraft. Beyond that, I am genuinely concerned about Franco–American cooperation on other bilateral or multilateral projects.[35]

This is French diplomacy at its best and one would think that an experienced diplomatic correspondent like Sulzberger would see through it: French pride, shock at their American friends, flattery aimed at the American airlines industry, modest understating of French technological achievement in aeronautics, and a threat that future French–American cooperation may become impossible if France does not get its way—a classic neomercantilist argument. On legal grounds the French no doubt have a strong case. But on foreign-policy and political-economic grounds American officials have an obligation to work out the implications. The French–British plane was then expected to monopolize the upper-class jet business, thus confirming the powerlessness of democracy in controlling the use of technology at the expense of the environment, and to invite alienation and anti-French nationalism among Americans in retaliation. The American administration's basic antiprotectionist policy was admirable, but such a policy must be a two-way street and the French appear adept at getting both lanes to go their way in the short term (indeed, a typical French neomercantilist argument is that the short term is all there is). Albert

Bressand gave a typical French interpretation: "The growing number of conflicts in high-technology fields between a relatively less powerful America and an increasingly self-confident Europe tend to be looked down on by the former as European attempts to replace competitiveness with politics—witness, for example, the label 'political plane' condescendingly applied to Concorde and Airbus. This attitude often reflects a fundamental misconception of the new position of Europe vis-à-vis America."[36] Neomercantilism appears to be a contemporary French strategy for steering international interdependence much as de Gaulle used French nationalism to steer European integration.

REGIONAL AND GLOBAL CONSTRAINTS

France has developed a reputation for ignoring regional or global constraints when they are not convenient or profitable. When the OPEC countries quadrupled their oil prices in 1973, rather than going along with an agreement for united Western action the French bolted and made their own private twenty-five-year deal with the Arabs to assure themselves a predictable oil supply. Still, this very behavior could be attributed to regional and global restraints, since Western Europe as a region had to import about 90 percent of its oil from abroad.

French behavior in terms of regional and global constraints can perhaps best be understood through the French philosophy of adapting to change: discern the trend of the future and seize the inevitable in order to incorporate it into French national interests as soon as possible. De Gaulle's vision of European integration as a process of coordinating sovereign nation–states that preserve their autonomy—perceived by many as reactionary nationalism at the time—was his way of acknowledging the inevitability of European integration while using it as a tool to further French national interests before all others. By holding out so long for his objectives, de Gaulle made certain that France would derive short-term benefits from inevitable long-term trends.

President Giscard d'Estaing, while more understated than de Gaulle, has also been quick to see which way the wind is blowing in order to cash in as soon as possible. When President Carter came to power on a program that opposed the sale of nuclear reactors to other countries by the industrial West, Giscard d'Estaing announced that France would henceforth make no nuclear-reactor sales until adequate safeguards could be worked out in the future. This announcement came the month before Carter was officially sworn in as president, giving the French a progressive world image and a positive position from which to start bargaining with their powerful American ally. Yet past nuclear-reactor sales were not affected by the statement, allowing the French to stabilize what they already had while simultaneously declaring themselves open to the inevitable changes on the horizon. The fact that the nuclear-reactor business has become a bone of diplomatic contention among the Americans, the French, and Germans since that time merely confirms that the French lost nothing at all in concrete terms by declaring their good intentions at a dramatic moment, and that they may even have been able to use the resulting American good will in other negotiations—such as the Concorde dispute, in which Carter's de facto policy supported the French position. Giscard d'Estaing also used the 1979 European monetary system (EMS) negotiations to promote France's position on Common Market agricultural policy before agreeing to join the EMS. And it seems to be no accident that the French delayed until the European Summit hosted by Paris, giving Giscard a concrete result to announce from the French capital.

On the superstructural level the French appear to be brilliant diplomatic artists at adapting to regional and global constraints that they cannot change more quickly than most nations for their own national advantage. But while the short-term national payoff is clear-cut and indisputable, given French mercantilist logic, the long-term consequences for the Common Market and the international community remain as outstanding costs or debts for "others" to pick up—including the French at a later date. In short, the French position fosters an atmosphere of international mercantilism and short-term national gains regardless of the damage this may do to the prospects for cooperation and peace in the long term. Of course, the French do cooperate in many areas in the Common Market, and nothing here should be interpreted as meaning that one cannot cooperate to do international business with them. But the French view of time seems to be a bit shorter than that of many other nations, which could lead to a self-fulfilling prophecy: their time may be running out.

NOTES

1. Alain Robbe-Grillet, "A Fresh Start for Fiction," trans. Richard Howard, *Evergreen Review*, 1, no. 3 (1957), 99–104.
2. David C. McClelland, "French National Character and the Life and Works of André Gide," in *The Roots of Consciousness* (New York: D. Van Nostrand, 1964), pp. 96ff.
3. R. Metraux et al., *Some Hypotheses About French Culture* (New York: Research in Contemporary Cultures, Columbia University, 1950).
4. McClelland, p. 106.

5. François Mauriac, *De Gaulle* (Garden City, N.Y.: Doubleday, 1966), p. 7.
6. Michel Crozier, *The Bureaucratic Phenomenon* (Chicago: University of Chicago Press, 1964).
7. Stanley Hoffmann, *Decline or Renewal?* (New York: Viking Press, 1974), pp. 72ff.
8. Ibid., p. 70.
9. See R. Isaak, "National Bargaining and Regional Integration—De Gaulle," in *Individuals and World Politics* (North Scituate, Mass.: Duxbury Press, 1975), pp. 177–199.
10. Norman Stamps, *Why Democracies Fail—A Critical Evaluation of the Causes for Modern Dictatorship* (Notre Dame, Ind.: University of Notre Dame Press, 1957).
11. Hoffmann, p. 449.
12. See John Zysman, *Political Strategies of Industrial Order: Industry, Market and State in France* (Berkeley: University of California Press, 1977).
13. Jean-Claude Theonig, *L'Ère des technocrates* (Paris, 1973).
14. Hoffmann, p. 456. See also Jean de Savigny, *L'État contre les communes?* (Paris, 1971), and Michel Longepierre, *Les Conseillers généraux dans le système administratif français* (Paris, 1971).
15. See Lucien Nizard, "Administration et Société," *Revue française de science politique*, 23, no. 2 (April 1973), 199–229.
16. Hoffmann, p. 459.
17. Jean-Claude Morel, presentation on "EEC Economic Development Policy" at the Institute on Western Europe, Columbia University, September 9, 1976.
18. CERC, *Dispersion et disparités de salaries en France en cours des vingt dernières années* (Paris, 1976).
19. See Gerhard Leithäuser, "Alternative wirtschaftspolitische Konzepte in Frankreich," in *Blätter für deutsche und internationale Politik*, July 1976, p. 771.
20. See Georges Spénate, "Expansion et équité," *Le Monde*, March 17, 1973, p. 19, and Hoffmann, p. 464.
21. This view of the French Communist party was expressed by Flora Lewis of *The New York Times* at a "European Roundtable" at the Institute on Western Europe, Columbia University, October 12, 1976.
22. See "Les Élections Législatives de Mars 1978: La défaite de la gauche," a special supplement printed by *Le Monde* in March 1978.
23. Jean-Pierre Worms, "The Administration, Politics and the Left in France," presentation at the Institute on Western Europe, Columbia University, September 30, 1976.
24. Ibid.
25. For this development see F. Roy Willis, *France, Germany and the New Europe, 1945–1967* (London: Oxford University Press, 1968).
26. This French bargaining strategy is analyzed in Isaak, pp. 177–199.
27. Organization for Economic Co-operation and Development (OECD), *The Industrial Policy of France*, Paris, 1974, p. 123.
28. John Zysman, "The French State in the International Economy," paper

presented at the Conference on Domestic Structures and the Foreign Policy of Advanced Industrial States, October 28–30, 1976, at Harvard University. See also John Zysman, *Political Strategies for Industrial Order: Industry, Market and State in France* (Berkeley: University of California Press, 1977).

29. OECD, p. 123.

30. Charles-Albert Michalet, "France," in Raymond Vernon, ed., *Big Business and the State* (Cambridge, Mass.: Harvard University Press, 1974), pp. 108–109.

31. Michel Albert, "The Rising Cost of Public Sector Infrastructure and Resources and the Problem of Their Financing with a View to Harmonious Development in the Community," report submitted at the Venice Conference of the European Communities, April 1972.

32. Ibid., p. 7.

33. Manuel Castells, "Immigrant Workers and Class Struggles in Advanced Capitalism: The Western European Experience," Centre d'Études des Mouvements Sociaux, École Pratique des Hautes Études, Paris, February 1974, p. 4 (mimeographed).

34. Ibid., p. 6.

35. C. L. Sulzberger, "Concordat on Concorde," *New York Times*, March 12, 1977.

36. A. Bressand, "The New European Economies," *Daedalus*, 108, no. 1 (1979), 55–56.

Chapter 4
Great Britain:
A Socialized Economy in Crisis

The English working class is deeply ingrained in its own curious way of life. . . . They haven't changed their way of life 1%. They eat the same things today that they used to. . . . They do not want to become middle-class in the sense workers in the United States want to. The class division is in many ways imposed by the working class itself.
—C. P. Snow, at Pace University, April 25, 1977

Great Britain,* the leader in the industrial revolution and model of Western parliamentary democracy, has gone from wealth to making do, from imperial strength to weakness, becoming to many a warning signal indicating what Western industrial democracies should avoid if it is not too late. Is "the British sickness" contagious, an inevitable stage of capitalist development, or is it unique?

Analyzing the British sickness is like describing a patient who appears to be dying from ten diseases at once: geographic insularity, imperial breakup, physical and spiritual devastation by World War II, class rigidity, indigestion caused by work, managerial tax bite, overnationalized arteries, suffocation due to parochial familyness, an increasing proclivity toward public spending matched only by a decreasing inclination toward industrial productivity. Yet despite all of these ailments, and perhaps because of them, Great Britain is perceived as a mature example of Western civilization, a sort of aristocratic model of behavior to aim for if you are a member of the new-rich German or American elite. How to ape the sophistication of British decadence and community spirit while avoiding the economic and social problems of British society, this seems to be the question. The fact that "civilization" and capitalist well-being may be contradictory is an uncomfortable possibility that remains repressed in the minds of many people. What has become much less controversial, however, is the proposition that an "oversocialized" political economy leads to economic stagna-

*See appendix, p. 217, for political-economic events of Great Britain.

tion and a decline in economic growth—at least in the case of Great Britain.

In *The Cultural Contradictions of Capitalism* Daniel Bell suggests that capitalism may succeed only to do itself in: the requirements of the capitalist economic system, such as increased rationality, organization, and efficiency, come into conflict with the direction of capitalist countercultures that spring from the resulting wealth and leisure—greater emphasis on feeling, personal gratification, and total self-fulfillment. Social and sexual abandon may tear apart the fabric of the capitalist work ethic, which provided the goods and freedom to make such satisfaction and abandon possible.[1] Is Great Britain an example *par excellence* of the cultural contradictions of capitalism? Or does the nation represent rather a case of the cultural contradictions of socialism—social benefits and equality spread out to the point of damping the productivity necessary to provide the goods that are to be redistributed? At the very least, the British situation provides a fascinating example of the trade-offs that sometimes exist between social services and economic growth, between the propriety of civilization and the aggressive egoism of the successful entrepreneur.

The political implications of the British case may be far-reaching for other Western industrial democracies with similar conflicts between the need for economic growth and the desire for more redistribution or social justice. For when one takes apart the British situation to analyze its problems and prospects, universal paradoxes of capitalism and democracy reveal themselves.

BRITISH POLITICAL CULTURE: MOTIVATIONS

The continuity and stability of the English culture go back to the successful invasion of Britain by the Normans in 1066—the last major violent disruption of British society if one excludes World War I. The legitimacy of the English tradition of law is rooted in the Magna Charta of 1215. But the stability of the British political culture is due not just to its long continuity but also to its tradition of pluralism—a diffusion of power within a centralized political system that makes it more adaptable to change. Political scientists Gabriel Almond and Sidney Verba argue that Britain's pluralistic culture was made possible by its island security, its separation from the Church of Rome, an aristocracy with a variety of power bases, and British tolerance for nonconformism within the traditional pattern.[2] But the question is whether this pluralism brought enough diversity with it or whether the "British sickness" might be the stale parochialism of too much continuity.

Another aspect of British culture that may contribute to the so-called "British sickness" is the collectivist ethos that pervades the ideologies and behavior of both major political parties. Members of the Conservative party, for example, are not rugged, laissez-faire individualists of the American type; instead, they adhere to an organic conception of the public good marked by strong government, paternalism, continuity, hierarchy, and leadership.* Political scientist Samuel Beer has noted that this collectivist ethos distinguishes both Tory (or the Conservatives') and social (or Labour's) democracy from nineteenth-century political individualism, as well as from the Liberal and Radical parties in Britain:

> The major theme of this Collectivist theory of representation is party government; its minor theme, functional representation. In this Collectivist guise, democratic thought legitimizes a far greater role for group and party than did Liberal and Radical thought. To put the matter negatively: both Tory and Socialist Democracy reject parliamentarianism. Both reject the notion that Members of Parliament should freely follow their own judgment when deciding how to vote and that the House of Commons is, or should be, in Bagehot's phrase, in "a state of perpetual choice." . . . Both demand that the M.P. should not be a "representative" but a "delegate" (. . . a party delegate, not a local delegate). . . . Both accept the great organized producer groups of a modern industrial society and attribute to them an important role in government and administration. Both, in short, depart in major respects from the political individualism of the nineteenth century.[3]

The strict party voting and discipline characteristic of the Conservatives and Labour members in Parliament, so unlike the independence of members of the U.S. Congress, epitomize a traditional collectivist ethos in Britain. This collectivism trades individual initiative for customary loyalty.

Another critical aspect of the British political-culture case is parochial familyness. Henry Fairlie argues that the British sickness is due to the inability of the English to think about vital social and intellectual issues in universal terms because of their habit of treating them as family affairs. He writes:

> When I read a report in a British newspaper of the "colour problem" in Britain, I think that it ought to be on the sports pages, because it might as well be an account of a cricket match with the West Indians or the Pakistanis. It is debated as a family affair, as if it is a local question of the preservation of English society, of no consequence to the world. "You look after your niggers, and we'll look after ours," was the reply which Walter Lippmann told me Randolph Churchill had once given him, when he raised the ques-

---

*Although Margaret Thatcher's leadership of the Conservative party in the 1970s has been far more laissez-faire oriented than that of the previous generation, she constitutes the exception that proves the rule.

tion of Britain's relations with its colonies in Africa. And there is still something "colonial" in precisely this way about the British handling and discussion of its own "colour problem."[4]

The British political culture apparently contributes to an inability to conceptualize or discuss problems in terms that are relevant to the rest of the world, even when almost everyone else shares these problems. Only the restoration of intellectual rigor to the public debate of such issues can counterbalance this suffocating familyness.

A related aspect of culture that affects political thinking is British snobbism. Often snobbism and a residue of respect for aristocratic style are valued over expertise or efficiency. Another British journalist, Claude Cockburn, related the following story about his father, who had a first-class upbringing, just after World War I:

> A friend told him there was a good job going, a chief of some interallied financial mission to look after the finances of Hungary. Perhaps he would like that? My father asked whether the circumstances of knowing almost nothing about Hungary and absolutely nothing about finance would be a disadvantage. His friend said that was not the point. The point was that they had a man doing this job who knew all about Hungary and a lot about finance, but he had been seen picking his teeth with a tram-ticket in the lounge at the Hungaria Hotel and was regarded as socially impossible. My father said that if such were the situation he would be prepared to take over the job.[5]

One of the most disturbing explanations of "the British sickness" in terms of motivation or political culture is that the British have become so complacent because of the status accorded them for past successes that they are no longer moved to change their ways or to work hard for future benefits. Snobbism and deference to aristocratic standards undermine the possibility of innovation, productivity, and mere money-making. Sigmund Freud suggested in his essay *Civilization and Its Discontents* that civilization is possible only if the individualistic ego gives in to the superego, or the accepted norms and laws of society. But is not the motor of capitalistic economic growth exactly the entrepreneurial aggression that Freud would repress with civilized behavior? Has Britain perhaps become so much the civilized, self-appointed superego of the Western world that its people will never again be capable of vigorous production? The value formula explaining the individual and social code of behavior of the ideal–typical Englishman appears to be "I must act in such a way as not to violate the proper norms of traditional English society, regardless of the present and future consequences for myself and others." There are significant exceptions to this "propriety first" kind of thinking in Britain, but as often as not they tend to prove the rule in terms of the behavior of the British.

And the serious possibility remains that the British case is not an exceptional one but merely represents an overrefined stage of advanced industrial civilization that other Western capitalist countries, such as the United States, may slip into in the future. Norman Macrae, deputy editor of *The Economist*, has concluded that just as the British empire declined in the late nineteenth century because of growing disbelief in the importance of economic dynamism, entrepreneurship, and money-making, the American empire is likely to decline in its third century because of increasing upper-class snobbism, which looks down on the business culture, entrepreneurship, and economic growth.[6] If this projection is correct, all Western industrial democracies may be able to learn more than they would like to about their own future from the British case. In the motivations of a political culture, the more a nation succeeds in becoming a modern, industrial society, the more its status may make it incapable of recognizing its own limits and failures until it reaches a point of economic and social breakdown.

BRITISH SOCIAL AND POLITICAL INSTITUTIONS: STRUCTURES

Separating the motivations of political culture from social and political structures is like sorting doors from walls in the dark—the difference is there but is often not readily distinguishable. Since structures are actually past motivations and social relations that have developed into social institutions with age, they often stimulate political behavior as well as serving as the means and conduits for political action. One of the most subtle structures in this sense, particularly in Britain, is the class system.

Reporting about a conference on "The Future of Great Britain" held in Berlin by the Aspen Institute of Humanistic Studies in 1976, Stuart Maclure wrote,

It is obvious that what the Germans and the Americans admire (from a distance) are aspects of Britain which are breaking down; and more than this, aspects of Britain which many domestic critics blame for the larger breakdowns. In many cases, they are associated with a set of traditional social relationships—once marked by a shared understanding among the elite (who attend the same schools and universities, belong to the same clubs, go to the same tailors), and accepted with deference by the rest of society. Now deference is out. The old elite in the Civil Service, the older universities, the City, politics, is being challenged. The implicit assumptions about what isn't done no longer hold. They are being replaced by explicit rules and tribunals and appeal mechanisms, as government moves in with laws and lawyers to regulate areas of life formerly governed by custom and conviction—in fact by the class system.[7]

The stability of Britain has been due in part to the legitimacy of a rigid class system, which has now been thrown into question. Since the beginning of the nineteenth century, Britain has had a larger working class than the United States and France, with a high rate of manual labor. This has established a traditional sense of "working classness," of pride in being part of the working class, that led the English writer C. P. Snow to remark in 1977 that in many ways the working class imposes the class division on itself by stubbornly maintaining its old way of life and not striving for upward mobility into the middle class, as American workers do.[8] When it comes to politics, the British typically think in terms of an upper class and a middle class. They do not speak of a "lower class" but of the "working class" of which they are proud. But the working class has traditionally shown reluctance to assume power and responsibility: it supports management to run industry and the Labour party to run the country.[9]

After World War II, although the basic threefold class structure (upper, middle, and working) did not change a great deal, British attitudes toward the class structure did change. With the affluence and technological innovations of the 1960s, a nontraditional attitude toward class emerged alongside the traditional class structure. And in the economic crisis of the 1970s British standards of living decreased. Today, according to sociologist Frank Parkin, 40 percent of the children born into families of nonmanual workers can expect to become manual workers. Most of these people will maintain the attitudes of the higher class that they left, and they may actually become more right wing than the middle class in general. Parkin explains this in terms of the difficulty experienced by the downwardly mobile person in coping with change:

> It is not, of course, too surprising that the socially demoted should be somewhat more reluctant to jettison their former political identity than are the socially ascendant. Recruitment into the middle class entails a re-defining of the self in a more favourable light—as judged by prevailing standards of moral worth. Social descent, on the other hand, results in a potentially more damaging confrontation between self and social reality, a confrontation which people are likely to avoid, or at least to ease, whenever they can. One way of doing this is through the belief that the fall from grace is a temporary affair, and that one's former status will eventually be recaptured—if only through the success of one's children.[10]

A structural explanation of the British sickness might be that many British people have been unable to cope effectively with their collective downward mobility at home and abroad—they have been unwilling to adjust old attitudes to conform with the new objective reality of lower placement in the class structure. Even those who perceive themselves to be in the same class despite a drop in their standard of living in absolute terms, such as the managerial and professional classes, resist adjusting their attitudes to their new life situation.

Harold Lasswell and S. M. Lipset demonstrated that in the case of Germany such downward mobility among the lower middle class was among the factors leading to fascism.[11] And although the right-wing attitudes that often characterize social demotion are somewhat similar to prewar German attitudes in the human fear of insecurity and loss of status, the British case is different in important respects. Two-thirds of the British are working class, one-third middle class, and about 1 percent upper class.[12] With so many people at the bottom of the totem pole, there is less room for collective demotion and no place to go down to from the working class if you happen to be in the majority. And despite recent efforts to reform the class-bound British educational system, only about 2 percent of the children of unskilled and semi-skilled manual workers receive full-time higher education, compared to about 45 percent of the children of professional workers.[13] Expectations of higher status do not, therefore, run high in Britain, meaning that people may be less disappointed than in industrial cultures with higher rates of social mobility. The British have for the most part settled into their class structure, taking up the habits, dress, and language of their peers.

Moreover, there is a high correlation between social-class member-ship and voting behavior: the lower your class, the more likely you are to vote for the Labour party and the less likely you are to vote for the Conservatives. As a society that has peaked in power and influence, Britain reminds one of Tolstoy's description of Stepan Arkadyevitch Oblonsky in *Anna Karenina:*

> Stepan Arkadyevitch had not chosen his political opinions or his views; these political opinions and views had come to him of themselves, just as he did not choose the shapes of his hats or coats, but simply took those that were being worn. And for him, living in a certain society—owing to the need, ordinarily developed at years of discretion, for some degree of mental activity—to have views was just as indispensable as to have a hat. If there was a reason for his preferring liberal to conservative views, which were held also by many of his circle, it arose not from his considering liberalism more rational, but from its being in closer accord with his manner of life. . . . And so liberalism had become a habit of Stepan Arkadyevitch's, and he liked his newspaper, as he did his cigar after dinner, for the slight fog it diffused in his brain.

Of course, one should not underestimate the changing attitudes of some people in Britain, which contrast with this traditional class men-tality. A convergence of class attitudes is occurring in Western industrial societies, with those of the British moving toward the American model while Americans are becoming more class conscious—particularly in terms of attitudes toward racial minorities. But old habits die hard, and for many Britons class is a habit rather than a temporary position on an escalator, as many Americans see it. Recall the class attitudes portrayed in the BBC television series "Upstairs/Downstairs," which symbolized the pride of those downstairs in their own class and way of life between 1900 and 1930. The lack of interest in upward mobility on the part of not a few people, combined with the real expectation of downward mobility on the part of many, implies a social stalemate in British society and may help explain the lack of a strong desire to work or to become more efficient.

THE GOVERNMENT FRAMEWORK AND PARTY SYSTEM

Beyond class, another structural explanation of the British sickness lies in Britain's political institutions. A reason for the lack of dynamism in Britain is certainly to be found in the curious mix of Britain's centralized political system and stagnant pluralism. The British Constitution is largely an uncodified cumulative product of tradition dating back to the Middle Ages. Historically, it emerged in three phases marked by the primacy of the monarchy, the primacy of Parliament, and most recently, the primacy of interest groups.

The first monarchical phase ended with the "Settlement" of 1689, which established that Parliament and not the king would be primary in importance. But the Parliament of the seventeenth century was not very democratic, the upper House of Lords being made up of large landlords and the lower House of Commons consisting largely of members nominated by the Lords—wealthy men or political manipulators. A series of reforms in the nineteenth and twentieth centuries served to democratize Parliament and to extend suffrage—the last occurring in 1970, when the voting age of both men and women was reduced to 18. The unwritten and unsystematic nature of the Constitution has meant that British government has relied heavily on conventions developed over time, giving the system flexibility and stability. Britain is a unitary, not a federal state, making Parliament sovereign over all of the United Kingdom and reducing the comparative importance of local governments. However, recently some regional independence and administrative devolution of power have occurred, led by Scottish and Welsh political pressure for increasing leverage on local issues. Geographic pluralism and ethnicity are emerging as major political problems, symbolized by the Scottish nationalists' claim to most of the

North Sea oil and the violent rebellion in Northern Ireland. But the legal legislative supremacy of Parliament remains intact: the United Kingdom of Great Britain comprises England, Wales, Scotland, and Northern Ireland.

In the second historical phase, the primacy of Parliament, the two most important developments were the growth in importance of the cabinet, headed by the prime minister, and Parliament's increasing acceptance of responsibility to the electorate. The political position of the House of Lords has weakened compared to that of the House of Commons. Indeed, most everyday policy making is a question of interaction between the prime minister and the cabinet on one side and the opposition party in the House of Commons on the other. As the supreme legislative authority, Parliament may legislate in any area; the Queen reigns but does not govern.

The monarchy, of course, is hereditary. The sovereign is still the official head of state and the Commonwealth, with an important role as a symbol of the legitimacy of the political system. After the general election the monarch appoints as prime minister the leader of the majority party. The prime minister, in turn, appoints the heads of ministries such as the Foreign Office, who defend their policies in Parliament. Sixteen to twenty-three of these ministers make up the inner policy-making circle, or cabinet. In a very real sense the cabinet belongs to the prime minister, who calls it into session, makes up its agenda, and presides over its meetings. Usually there are two meetings a week, each lasting about two hours; the results are held in confidence.

The cabinet represents the executive power of the government. Legislative power resides with the 635 members of the House of Commons (elected for a maximum of five years) and the hereditary and appointed peers who make up the House of Lords. Either house can initiate legislation, but it usually originates in the House of Commons. Each bill is read three times in the House of Commons and then passed on to the House of Lords, which may make suggestions and amendments and return it to the Commons. However, once any bill is passed by the House of Commons the House of Lords cannot prevent it from becoming law after a maximum delay of one year.

The British cabinet is not just the executive focus of power, as the American cabinet is; it is also a steering committee of the legislature and a committee of the majority party, since virtually all of its ministers are members of Parliament (MPs). This not only gives the prime minister a great deal of power but ensures majority party solidarity. The House of Commons serves both to sustain the government (through the cabinet ministers and majority party members, who sit to the speaker's right in the chamber) and to criticize the government (through the opposition party or parties, whose members sit on the speaker's left). The speaker is elected by all MPs and traditionally is reelected until he or she expresses a desire to resign. The speaker's role is to remain a neutral interpreter of the laws and customs of Parliament; this requires that he or she shed all party ties upon taking office.

The opposition party is often underestimated in interpretations of the British parliamentary system. It is well organized, permanent, representative, and participant and constitutes an immediate successor government if the government falls. And it has an ultimate weapon: the opposition can ask for a vote of censure expressing lack of confidence in the government, a strong move that is usually used only when tactics of persuasion and delay through debate have failed at a critical political moment. The Conservative party, led by Margaret Thatcher, effectively used the vote of censure to force the governing Labour party to call a general election on May 3, 1979, which the Conservatives won. In that election there was an average swing of 5.2 percent from Labour to the Conservatives, giving the Conservatives a gain of 55 seats in Parliament for a total of 339, whereas Labour lost 40 seats, ending with a total of 268. The smaller parties won the remaining 28 seats (the Liberals, Plaid Cymru, Scottish Nationals, and others).

The limitations on its role in policy formation make Parliament more impressive in appearance than in effective power. Not only does the cabinet monitor its proceedings, but the leader of the opposition party may determine the topics for debate on particular days. Once the executive has prepared the budget (through the cabinet), its contents can be debated but it is not changed. The prime minister and his or her party draft legislation and control amendments. In contrast, the two houses of the U.S. Congress control their own proceedings and are independent of the executive branch as well as of each other. Furthermore, the American Congress has the power of the purse and is not constrained by the strict party discipline that characterizes the British governmental system.

British party discipline is so effective that a party can stay in power with a very small majority in the House of Commons. "Front benchers," or MPs with ministerial posts (or "shadow" ministers in certain fields in the opposition), look for support among the "back benchers," the regular MPs. Paradoxically, if the party majority in the House of Commons is large, back benchers may be more inclined to "rebel" (i.e., abstain or vote against the party position), since they can send a signal to their leadership in this way without defeating them. Each year both the government party and the opposition party suffer from several rebellions in which MPs abstain or vote against their party's position. MPs with strong electoral support who have little chance to become ministers are the best candidates for rebellion. But in almost all cases a party with diligent leadership can count on almost all its members to go along with it. Such discipline serves to consolidate the domination of the executive over the legislature in the British system. One source of friction afflicting all British governments in the 1970s was the pressure on them from back benchers to increase their salaries from a paltry £6,897 annually in 1979—a sum that serves to weaken party discipline.

Britain is run by a party government. Since World War II the Conservative and Labour parties have dominated the House of Commons and have won an average of almost 98 percent of all seats contested. By contrast, the Liberal party has averaged about 7 percent of the vote, just enough to give it the potential to become a wedge between the two major parties on certain issues. For example, in the May 3, 1979, election the Liberals announced that if the party that won the election wanted any cooperation from the Liberals thereafter it would have to support a proportional system of representation for Great Britain in the near future. Voters tend to vote for one of the two major parties, believing that only one of them has a chance of winning office, thus making an informal "two-party system" tradition a self-fulfilling prophecy.

Except in the extraordinary case of a vote of no confidence in Parliament, the prime minister determines when elections will be held, thereby biasing the electoral system in favor of the governing party. To be elected to Parliament a candidate does not have to receive an absolute majority of the votes, merely a plurality. Because of the way the system is set up, the strongest single party wins a disproportionate share of the votes. If a candidate does not receive at least one-eighth of the vote in his or her constituency, the £150 nomination deposit is forfeited. To be nominated one needs only ten elector signatures from the constituency in question.

The judicial system is narrowly defined in Great Britain, and judges practice the principle of self-denial. At one time the "rule of law" was advocated by the judiciary to check royal absolutism. But in the twentieth century the justices have argued that it is up to Parliament to determine what the government may or may not do. In contrast to American judges, the English do not want any part in the making or unmaking of the (unwritten) Constitution. The ultimate court of appeal is therefore political, not judicial. In fact, the highest court is a committee of the House of Lords—the Lords of Appeal in Ordinary. But there is an effective tradition of keeping the courts out of politics, at least most of the time. This may sound attractive unless you want to use the courts to rectify what you think is a government infringement on your rights; your chances of success are slim.

Politics in Britain tends to be national rather than regional or local, with everything centralized in London and officially monitored through a bureaucracy and a well-disciplined parliamentary system. But this dominant trend is countered by nationalist movements in Scotland, Wales, and Ulster. Functional and regional interest groups have become as important as the major parties in decisions on day-to-day policy issues. Trade unions and business groups lobby and demonstrate effectively for their short-term interests regardless of the long-term consequences for the country. Many observers have contrasted this bargaining dynamism with the decline in the significance of Parliament, which is filled with hardworking middle-class representatives who appear to be running in place—as is the case in other Western industrial democracies as well.

The most important functional interest groups in Britain today are the trade unions, which often seem to have the power to call the tune, particularly when the Labour party is "the government." One of the more moderate union leaders, Joe Gormley, president of the National Union of Miners, responded to a national appeal by Britain's Labour government in the 1970s for common sacrifices in the fight against inflation by saying, "The miners are going to be at the top of the tree, and if that hurts somebody, I am sorry." The short-term excesses of the labor union movement sometimes appear to be tolerated more readily than excesses of management or other groups would be, partially no doubt because Britain's background of upper-class privilege has fallen into disrepute. Take the case of the "Shrewsbury Two." Two union member pickets at a building site used violence against nonunion workers who refused to lay down their tools during an industrial dispute, and one of their victims lost an eye. But when the Shrewsbury Two were sent to prison there was a public furor and there were mass marches and demonstrations demanding their release, giving them a martyr status among fellow trade unionists. Even members of the Labour government were sufficiently intimidated by the public outcry to avoid denouncing this union-led agitation, although some have dissociated themselves from it. In the end, the Labour government refused to give way to pressure and release the Shrewsbury Two.

The power of the unions is also illustrated by the wage policies adopted by the government. From 1975 to 1977, in order to help control the runaway rate of inflation and save jobs, the unions agreed not to push for wage increases. But in return the government had to preserve employment by promising to subsidize British industries that might otherwise have gone bankrupt or been motivated to improve their efficiency and productivity. The short-term aim of the unions was to preserve jobs for their workers by helping out weak industries. The long-term effect may well be to make these industries less competitive internationally and to keep the cost of British labor and exports high.

Frustrated hopes that the labor unions would exercise wage restraint in support of "their" Labour government under Callaghan during the strike-ridden winter of 1978–1979 helped precipitate the swing away from Labour in the 1979 elections. If inflation continues at a high rate, as seems probable, the Conservative government will not be likely to enjoy much more success in constraining union demands or strikes. The mature working class of Britain can be expected to maximize their bargaining position in the market in what they see as a justifiable expression of citizenship rights in a decaying status order.

POLITICAL-ECONOMIC CODES: ENGLISH BARGAINING BEHAVIOR

The history of political-economic bargaining behavior in Great Britain has been one of a shift from the authority of the monarchy to the power of Parliament and then from Parliament to functional interest groups such as the labor unions. The prime minister has attempted to reestablish parliamentary and party power by appealing directly to the people—over the heads of functional interests—on economic issues. But such tactics have worked only in the short term and are more symbolic of the decreasing importance of Parliament than of its strength.

The dominant role played by the unions in the bargaining on day-to-day issues seems to derive from their self-righteous position representing the working class and from a decreasing sense of identity among countervailing power groups. The trade unions have managed to sell themselves as effective spokesmen for social justice for the underdog. Furthermore, in a culture that has always rewarded the "top dogs" of the aristocracy and the upper classes, the unions have managed to maintain their underdog image even when they are no longer weak in terms of economic and political power. The British journalist Peregrine Worsthorne has argued that

> just as the idea of the aristocracy as a kind of divinely ordained top-dog held sway over the imagination of Englishmen long after it had ceased to have any real basis in social or economic reality—long after, that is, aristocrats had ceased to fulfill their function from which their glamour originally sprang— so today the glamour of the trade unions, as a kind of divinely ordained defender of bottom-dogs, continues to hold a comparable place, although it, too, has no longer any basis in reality.[14]

Worsthorne notes that Labour leaders have a clear sense of their own value, an unshaken faith in their own function, unlike others, who are weighed down by a sense of guilt.

The power of unions in the political economy of Britain is revealed in the area of management–labor relations, which are so critical for British economic recovery and the ability of the country to produce the goods and opportunities that are to be more evenly redistributed when the Labour government is in power. Britain has dragged its feet in legislating an industrial-democracy policy that would give labor a meaningful voice in management policy making. The reason is simple: the codetermination proposals, such as the liberal Bullock Commission Report, recommend worker representation from the shop floor regardless of whether or not the workers are union members. Such liberal ideals of representation are seen as threats to union power and have therefore been successfully resisted so far in both Britain and Italy. Whether or not the militant British labor unions represent the long-term interests of the working class as a whole any longer is an uncomfortable question that must be answered by those seeking to cure "the British sickness."

The English writer John le Carré claims that the joke or "the Catch 22 of the whole so-called English social experiment" is that absolutely nothing has changed in his lifetime. The class-bound "feudal" structure of the British culture, a society so proud of its small discriminatory distinctions in education, title, dress, and accent, has changed images and attitudes more than the social realities in the life chances of most citizens. As le Carré puts it,

> In the minds of the movement that swept him triumphantly to office, the promises Clement Attlee made in 1945 have yet to be redeemed. We may have socialism, but we have no more "equality"—in any human or useful sense—than we had 32 years ago. Don't believe a word they tell you over there about our wicked Socialist trade unions either. Ever since I can remember, the unions have played the capitalist game to the letter. They are playing it still. It is not public wealth they are trying to secure for their members, but private wealth at the expense of public squalor. When did anyone strike (except the poor teachers) to improve the appalling staff–pupil ratio in state schools? When did anyone strike for better old-age pensions, better care for home invalids, better hospitals, more doctors and playing fields? To me, Britain's feudal instinct, so much admired by Anglophiles, is like the conspiracy between the prisoner and his captor.
> And the prison . . . is in our minds.[15]

What le Carré is getting at is that the socialist changes of the Labour party and Conservative counterproposals have changed the image more than the reality of the hierarchy in class and political culture in Britain. The children of the elite still go to the private, elitist schools— paradoxically called the "public schools" (for the 13–18 age bracket) and then on to Oxford or Cambridge University. Reforms have been aimed at the level below this, the state schools and "open" universities—reforms within "second-" or "third-class" institutions that do not really tamper with the first-class elitist schools. Rather than spreading out upward mobility more evenly, the promised effects of the reforms seem to have been stalemated in an increasingly sluggish civil-service bureaucracy.

Moreover, there is evidence that the strong relationship between the working class and the Labour party is under great strain, if not actually changing, in the late twentieth century. From the time the leadership of the Liberal party split in 1916, giving the Labour party the priceless opportunity to become the largest opposition party in a centralized system that greatly rewards that status, the Labour party has been identified with the working class. The long-run trend of the twentieth century is for manual workers to increasingly vote for Labour. World War II helped compound this trend. Since that time the Labour and Conservative parties have stabilized somewhat, giving the Labour party more of a status quo position in the bargaining system—particularly given the frequency of Labour governments since the war. In the 1960s Labour ministers actually initiated and carried through policies that increased unemployment and kept down workers' wages for the sake of bettering Britain's balance-of-payments position and controlling inflation.

More significant, perhaps, is the transformation of Labour party leadership at the highest level in terms of social identity: the percentage of university-educated Labour cabinet ministers rose from 30 percent in 1924 to 83 percent in 1969.[16] Only one member of the Labour cabinet at the beginning of 1969 had what could be called a manual occupational past. This awkward development within the Labour party has caused a polarization of its left and right wings, with a strong Marxist socialist minority pushing for greater identification with the working class, nationalization of more industries, more cuts in defense, and greater public spending.*

This split has led to the defection of some influential right-wing members of Parliament, who have quit Labour to join the Conservative party. In October 1977, Reg Prentice became the first Labour MP ever to join the Tories between elections. He switched because Labour "has been moving away from its traditional ideals. There has been a growing emphasis on class war and Marxist dogma."[17] According to Prentice, if Labour could have won a clear majority in the 1979 election (as opposed to having to share the majority with a minority party like the

*Many of the Marxist-oriented members of the Labour party came from the public-school, "Oxbridge" tradition—a paradox until one thinks about life chances and who can afford which attitudes most easily in an era of great change.

Liberals), left-wing elements could gain control of the government, swinging the country toward Marxism. The post-election struggle between Callaghan and the Marxist left wing of the party led by MP Anthony Wedgwood Benn seems to reinforce Prentice's prediction, since Benn's support for his democratic party reforms is mainly among the strategically placed regular party cadre. Benn won on two issues that will turn the framing of party policy over to the grass roots: the reselection of MPs by Labour constituencies and the stripping of the party leader of his veto power over the election platform. However, it remains to be seen whether this polarization will result in a radicalization of the Labour Party or its destruction should the disenchanted leave it for other parties.

Another member of the Conservative party, Dudley Fishburn, assistant editor of *The Economist*, confirmed the trend toward polarization and stalemate in Britain. He suggested that the British will be worse off the more the government is given the power to decide what to do with the wealth anticipated from the North Sea oil discoveries, which promise to make Britain independent in terms of energy by the early 1980s. Fishburn argued that the Labour party became too collectivist, working more and more with the civil service and less and less with the House of Commons, and that their policies often clogged up the works with bureaucracy rather than leaving productive people free to use existing resources effectively with more positive social and economic consequences for everyone.[18]

Yet the lack of a government program to use some of the North Sea wealth to both stimulate economic productivity and move a hierarchical society toward greater equality of opportunity would be likely to compound the present illness instead of reversing the downward mobility of many British people. Fishburn noted the popularity of the National Front—a working class (quasi-fascist) party that threatens to displace Liberals in the polls as the third-largest party in Britain by advocating restriction of immigration and white racism. But perhaps he does not recall that the downward mobility of the lower middle class was one of the main reasons for the rise of fascism in Germany. Not using government intervention to reverse this trend seems like an irresponsible policy on the part of the Conservatives—unless they have in mind coopting the National Front to ensure a majority in Parliament. For the National Front appears to do more political damage to the Labour party than the Conservatives, since the traditional Labour voter seems to switch to the National Front in areas of racial tension. And Britain's previous liberal immigration policy toward Commonwealth countries has made such racial tension widespread in an era when immigrants can compete for scarce jobs.

DOMESTIC AND FOREIGN POLICY: COLLECTIVE DECISION MAKING

The unpredictability of domestic and foreign policies in Britain today stems in part from the fact that the dominant bargaining patterns aimed only indirectly at maximizing the two basic goals of the British: economic growth and social justice. In policy making, government officials are caught in a vise. On one side, they are pressed domestically toward short-term gains for particular interest groups that are often detrimental to long-term national interests; on the other, they are dependent in foreign-policy decisions on the moves of wealthier, more powerful nations, as well as weaker nations that are supposed to buy British exports. In Britain, as in all nations today, it is no longer easy to separate domestic- and foreign-policy issues or regional and global problems. Three policy issues illustrate this relationship: industrial policy and the welfare state, Britain's dependence and balance-of-trade deficit, and Britain's ambiguity toward the Common Market and the world economy.

Industrial Policy and the Welfare State

If a political system undergoes more change than it can cope with, a conservative impulse often forces decision making up from the substructure and infrastructure to the superstructure—the most superficial level of governmental and political policy making—which alone is incapable of bringing about the changes necessary for effective national adaptation. "Learning by paying" becomes inevitable. This maladaptive reaction is particularly likely to occur in a democratic system like that of Great Britain, where Parliament is losing power and significance compared to functional interest groups like the unions or business. The problem is compounded when no one party by itself can count on a majority without forming a coalition with a small factional party (like the Liberals)—making the "democratic majority" inherently unpredictable. This unpredictability at the superstructural level creates loss of confidence in government and the future. Such uncertainty deters the business community from investing and expanding to stimulate the economic growth necessary to pay for government programs. Industrial policy therefore becomes the hidden key for projecting whether or not a political system with welfare state objectives will, when besieged by change, be able both to pay for itself and to expand in order to keep up with inflation and the threat of joblessness.

Looking at the British situation in these terms, we find that Britain may have locked itself into maladaptive structures in the twentieth century, thereby greatly politicizing economic- and industrial-policy issues. The sensitive relationship between the Labour party and the trade unions is a prominent example. Most of the British trade unions belong to a central labor organization—the Trades Union Congress (TUC). In 1975, 11 million of about 11.75 million union members belonged to the TUC, while the rest were split up into over 400 non-TUC-affiliated unions. This centralization can be traced to 1899, when the Labour party itself was created through TUC initiative. Individual TUC unions affiliate with the party at the local, regional, and national levels. This formal union hegemony masks a subtle flexibility.[19] Leaders of the TUC unions have usually separated their industrial and political roles in terms of behavior within the Labour party. Yet the unusual formal interconnection between the institutions and the leadership of political and industrial labor has important implications in industrial policy making and in the election of members of Parliament to represent the working class. When they are united, the unions can dominate the voting at the annual Labour party conference, where party policy is established. They can also steer the voting for the majority of seats on the National Executive Committee, the party's governmental and administrative organ, where the unions are guaranteed a number of seats.

In the late 1960s when the radical New Left movement emerged among some of the unions affiliated with the TUC, this caused an apparent split between left- and right-wing (redistribution vs. productivity) supporters of the Labour party. Nevertheless, both left- and right-wing trade union leaders shared a common pride in the unity of a union movement that is not divided by religious, political, or occupational distinctions, and this collectivist ethos helped the moderate majority leaders of the Labour party to muster restraint among the extreme factions to a degree that surprised many observers.[20] In part, this unity may well have been a natural response to the extreme economic dislocations with which Britain was faced in the 1970s. Even the most militant of unions realized that blindly pushing for wage increases was a meaningless gesture if the inflation rate stayed so high that the end result of such bargaining would be more unemployment for union workers and further economic decline for the country as a whole.

But this surprising moderation of the labor unions in their Labour party activities put them in somewhat of a double bind. By going along with wage restraints in the mid-1970s in order to keep unemployment of union workers down, unions were forced to support ailing British industries with government subsidies. Subsidies and worker participation schemes for sharing power within existing industries became the focus of industrial policy making. But Britain's problem economically is to raise industrial productivity, make industries more efficient, and increase the competitiveness of its exports on the world market. No matter how much restraint a union–Labour-party-dominated government exercised in terms of wage increases, the basic policy orientation seemed to be toward more equitable redistribution of a diminishing pie rather than toward creation of a larger pie. Structurally speaking, a politics of redistribution in Great Britain may have become so inbred in the political culture that a politics of productivity is no longer possible. And if union workers continue to see the real value of their wages decline, they may show much less restraint in the future when fighting for higher wages so that they can keep up with a double-digit rate of inflation.

Professor James Livingstone dramatized this shift away from productivity in the political culture by pointing out that British workers may not be greedy enough. That is, by demanding higher wages and becoming more entrepreneurial in order to better their standard of living, workers might help pressure the government into a politics of productivity. Such pressure would put inefficient employers out of business if they did not shape up, making Britain more competitive. As Livingstone put it, "If the pay-offs could reward the competent instead of making a sacred cow out of the lame duck, as has been typical in Britain recently, we might be able to turn the situation around."[21] No doubt this is also the hope of the Thatcher government, motivating its cuts of industrial subsidies and tax reforms.

Rather than fighting a seemingly inflexible structure that taxed managers and entrepreneurs quite severely, the enterprising ones often left the country (if they could find decent positions elsewhere) or cheated on their taxes or moonlighted (if they stayed on in Britain). A 1974 poll reported by Robert Ward of Stanford University indicated that 41 percent of the British would leave the country and become permanent residents elsewhere if they were personally free to do so, compared to 12 percent of the Americans. And at times repairmen offer discounts if customers pay in cash, which tax collectors cannot trace. Managers often choose to overlook suspiciously expensive business lunches, figuring that this is a way of rewarding employees whose salaries cannot be raised because of national pay restraint policies. In short, "the British are becoming a nation of fiddlers."[22] (Fiddling is slang for cheating in Britain.) As prices go up with inflation, the imaginative entrepreneurial activity that is on the rise in Britain seems to be the least taxable way of making money. Such productivity will not go toward the costs of the redistribution policies already legislated by the government. Instead, the short-term individual benefits of cheating on taxes will lead to significant collective costs for British society in the long run.

The international dimension of domestic industrial and economic policy becomes clear when one traces the "brain drain" and the "entrepreneurial drain" out of Britain into other countries where opportunities are greater. For example, in 1977, at the age of forty-one, James D. Wolfensohn resigned from the post of chief executive officer of Schroeders Ltd., a well-known British commercial and investment banking house, to join Salomon Brothers in New York. Many members of the British financial press speculated that this might just be one more indicator of London's decline as a financial center and the shift of the structure of international banking toward New York. Wolfensohn admitted that he saw Salomon as representing "the new wave in investment banking." He also observed that the players in the marketplace are changing as the heavily capitalized New York brokerage houses and huge European commercial banks (particularly German institutions) become more influential and London houses such as Schroeders lose their former position of dominance. He accepted a lower position in New York, pointing out that one important factor in his decision was that the heavy taxes levied on personal income in Britain made it worth his while to go to the United States, where taxes were substantially lower.[23] Entrepreneurial drain is another way in which nations "learn by paying." The efforts of the Conservative government, elected in 1979, to turn this situation may be too superficial and too late.

In order for a nation to maintain enough productivity to create the economic growth necessary to satisfy the needs of its citizens, it must provide profitable opportunities for aggressive native entrepreneurs. Otherwise, these most productive of individuals will gravitate to other countries where opportunities for enhancing their life chances are greater. Such individuals have been discouraged by the strikes, taxation, economic stagnation, and unpredictability which have characterized recent industrial and economic policies. Many see the United States as the last remaining capitalist stronghold for the entrepreneurial individual. To deter British people from investing abroad rather than at home, until the Conservative takeover in 1979 the British government felt it had to impose a 25 percent tax on foreign investment. Poor industrial relations have exacerbated Britain's problems:

> In the late '60's and early '70's, strikes rose dramatically. The government became directly involved in many of these disputes because key industries—coal, electricity, the railroads and steel—are nationalized. This injects an enormous amount of politics into bargaining and often leads to either capitulation or confrontation. The worst showdown was the miners' strike against the Conservative government of Edward Heath in late 1973 and early 1974 which put the country on a three-day work week.[24]

Public spending has further aggravated the problem of stimulating enough productivity to bring about economic recovery. Oxford economists Robert Bacon and Walter Eltis have demonstrated that during the past fifteen years British governments have increasingly shifted more workers into public-sector jobs at the expense of investment and exports. Although total employment remained basically steady at about 25 million between 1965 and 1975, employment in the private sector dropped from 19.2 million to 17.7 million while public-sector employment rose from 6 million to 7.3 million.[25] Half of the new jobs were in education. Old-age pension expenditures and other public spending also went up.

The public–private sector conflict in light of the tension between the politics of redistribution (including quality of life) and the politics of productivity is dramatically symbolized by the energy issue in advanced industrial democracies like Britain. The perception on the part of some people that modern democratic systems are overloaded with demands (for energy, etc.) with which they no longer have the capacity to cope may actually be an overreaction to future shock, a last-minute attempt to restore authority at the top of obsolete structures that are threatened on all sides by change. There are "sunk costs" perceived by threatened interests in any anticipated institutional change—tangible and intangible costs inhering in the old way of doing things as the only sure way of protecting individual security from relative *déclassement* (or downward mobility). Thus, the discovery of 500 million tons of coal reserves in an aristocratic rural area of northern England stimulated landowners to rise up to protect their fox hunts, farmers to demonstrate for their fields and food over energy priorities, and everyday residents to oppose changes in their environment and taken-for-granted life styles. No doubt the government's Coal Board is likely to predominate in the policy making at the top, but this does not mean that there will not be widely felt sunk costs in the region affected. The decision to mine coal there will clearly become another case of "learning by paying."

Ironically, the same civilized superego that keeps Britain going deters individuals from taking system-leaping actions to help turn things around for the sake of British economic growth. The British attitude toward change is to hang on to the past way of doing things as long as possible, to muddle through, accepting one's rough class station without much question. This passive resistance to change is perhaps best illustrated by the case of the civil-service job, created by the British in 1803, that called for someone to stand on the Cliffs of Dover with a spyglass. The man was supposed to ring a bell if he saw Napoleon coming. This job was not abolished until 1945.

Dependence on Trade; the Balance-of-Trade Deficit

The British, like most people, act politically not on the basis of the real "sunk costs" of old ways of doing things but on the basis of perceived sunk costs. They don't change if they think there is the slightest chance that they will be worse off—even when objective circumstances make it increasingly clear that they *will* be worse off if they don't change and adapt to new realities. Political culture, habit, laziness, and institutional inertia conspire to keep people doing things the same old way regardless of what goes on elsewhere. So when the British empire declined and British power collapsed, many British citizens continued to go on about their business as if nothing had happened, speaking and living as if they were still privileged members of a great power, the center of Western civilization. But international economic developments were not as faithful as the British people to the pomp and circumstance of historical tradition.

Since the nineteenth century the British have had a significant balance-of-trade deficit; that is, they have imported more than they have exported. For a long time Britain was able to make this up in its balance of payments with earnings on overseas investments and services, such as banking and insurance, and by encouraging foreign investments in Britain. This situation has not changed fundamentally: the country still imports 25 percent of what it consumes. But the British ability to offset the difference between imports and exports with these so-called "invisibles" has changed. The loss of its colonies, increasing difficulties in marketing its exports competitively, and the decline in investor confidence with the fluctuation of the British pound sterling are all factors that made Great Britain increasingly dependent on others to help in solving its economic problems. Yet although the illusion of great power and self-sufficiency faded with these changed conditions, British attitudes and behavior have not adapted to the changes.

For example, in the 1950s and 1960s British policy makers used what was called a stop–go economic policy, deflating to dampen consumer spending when the exchange rate got too high, then stimulating for growth when business slackened. The measures taken to protect the pound sterling also slowed inflation. In 1966, after promising modernization and increased social benefits in order to win the election in 1964, Labour Prime Minister Harold Wilson was faced with the worst balance-of-payments deficit in twenty years and introduced drastic measures to discourage imports, increase exports, and freeze wages. The economic crisis combined with these conservative measures lost the 1970 election for the Labour party and left a heritage of ill will and unsolved economic problems. Had "political-culture blindness" not prevented government policy makers from continuing to act as if Britain were a great power and defending the "status" of the pound sterling, avoiding devaluation at all costs, the British would have been better able to adapt to changing economic conditions.

For too long the British took it for granted that the pound sterling would remain an official international reserve currency; for too long they assumed that their government would assure prosperity, and they ceased to worry about the consequences of unrestrained selfishness, sectional interests, and declining industrial productivity. Demand stoked the furnace of inflation while the democratic government seemed to become increasingly incapable—psychologically, economically, and socially—of coping with these demands. Nationalized industries aggravated the problem, since the motive for increasing efficiency and productivity was undercut by assurances of government subsidies. Public spending outreached the capacity of the government to collect revenues without unduly taxing the managerial class, which alone could accelerate economic growth.

In the midst of this malaise, the clear-cut mismanagement of public policies in which the population was as guilty as the leadership, the British had one great stroke of luck: They struck oil. By 1980 the North Sea oil discoveries should satisfy all of Britain's energy needs and provide a surplus for export in the 1980s. By mid-1979 Britain was exporting 100,000 barrels of oil per day to the rest of the Common Market. This development could make a crucial positive difference in Britain's balance-of-payments deficit and permit it to begin to repay the massive overseas debts it has accumulated, perhaps restoring world confidence in the British economy. But there is a more subtle psychological and political danger posed by this oil bonanza: it may not stimulate the British to change their political culture or habits to adapt to the changing environment, to modernize British industrial structures, to streamline the social system. Being paid for not learning is not a good incentive for collective learning. The British may mistake their great good fortune for virtue.

Foreign Policy: Britain's Ambiguity toward Common Market Membership

Britain's precarious domestic situation has clearly spilled over into its foreign-policy objectives, where the British must learn from paying as well. After World War II, when Great Britain could have dominated the Common Market by joining and shaping it from the outset, the British opted for stronger economic ties with its former Commonwealth colonies and reliance on its "special relationship" with the United States. The insular parochialism of the British culture and its distrust of the continental Europeans undoubtedly contributed to this misjudgment. The British attitude rubbed General Charles de Gaulle the wrong way, and he continually vetoed Britain's attempts when it tried to join the Common Market. And since they finally joined, in 1973, the British, in turn, have often reacted negatively to the EEC, using it as a scapegoat for domestic economic and political problems. It is far easier for British politicians to blame the country's problems on the distrusted "Europeans" than to blame themselves. Once again, British attitudes seem to be resisting adaptation to change or to new realities. The Community's Social Fund has given Britain over £60 million in aid to date, but this fact has not been featured in the British press. Rather than inspiring community spirit, Britain's membership in the Common Market has created further antagonism among many citizens, who blame the EEC for higher food prices and their sinking standard of living. They are understandably upset by projections that Britain may be the largest net contributor to the EEC during the 1980s.

Other Common Market nations, for their part, have sometimes resented the British practice of "bargaining up" for a slightly sweeter deal on the basis of the same old circumstances. While de Gaulle made national bargaining the rule of the game of the European Community, the threat of actual withdrawal was rarely used. Britain's short-term independence in bargaining seems to have undermined its long-term credibility as a Common Market partner, since it has created a great deal of uncertainty as to whether or not it will eventually stay in the Common Market. This was particularly true in the EMS negotiations of 1978, in which Britain led the way in seeking a special deal for weaker currencies by asking for lower interest rates on debts caused by strong currencies that were forced by the EMS system to intervene for the sake of devaluation, and for transfer payments through a credit fund. British "exceptionalism" was again confirmed when of the nine Common Market countries Great Britain alone refused to join the EMS when it officially began to operate in March 1979.

It is in the long-term interest of Britain and the other eight members of the Common Market to cooperate and formulate united policies toward the outside world, since this gives them a stronger bargaining position as a unit in the international system. But what people perceive as their short-term domestic interests often prevail over the long-term interests of both nation and region, adding cumulative costs for largely transitory benefits.

REGIONAL AND GLOBAL CONSTRAINTS

British elites often find themselves in the awkward position of knowing that their nation must remain in the Common Market to maximize its national interests in the long run, yet feeling that they have to represent a critical attitude toward such membership to their skeptical voters if they want to be reelected in the short run. Again one finds a clear-cut cleavage between objective realities and subjective popular attitudes that symbolizes a resistance to learning on the part of both the elites and the masses. Rather than assuming a dynamic, if risky, leadership role in teaching the public about the advantages of Common Market membership for all concerned, politicians take the easy way out to get reelected on the basis of old attitudes, regardless of the headaches it will eventually bring them and the entire national community. The collective learning process in adaptive policy making is slow at best in democracies, and without dynamic leadership that constantly seeks to inform public opinion, policy making at the superstructural level can become stagnant, if not nonproductive. Paradoxically, in Western democratic societies individuals are motivated to seek powerful roles at the superstructural level of government policy making using any means possible, only to discover upon being elected that the means they used to get into office contradict the values they must work for if they are to be effective in helping to change the society at the deeper infrastructural and substructural levels. To get elected, politicians focus on domestic constraints. Once in office, they become obsessed with regional and international constraints, particularly in a society as dependent on the outside world as Great Britain is.

An example of international constraints is the South African dilemma. When the South African government locked up the leaders of all major black groups and newspapers in late 1977, British diplomats and officials worked behind the scenes to dilute the American response in the United Nations in order to head off full economic sanctions against South Africa. If economic sanctions were imposed on South Africa, Britain would lose more than South Africa and much more than the United States. South Africa counts for about 2 percent of British imports and 2.5 percent of its exports. If strict sanctions were imposed, the British would lose over $1 billion in exports, not to mention jobs, an oil source, diamonds, other minerals, and markets for their goods.[26] And if the South African domestic situation deteriorates badly in the future, as seems likely, many of the white South Africans and British living in South Africa might well decide to come to Britain to live—an influx of people that the British government would prefer to avoid. In short, international economic constraints militate against any desire British elites might have to support racial justice in South Africa. Although such constraints may not be determinants, they appear to be more accurate indicators of the probable future of British foreign policy than any abstract notion of social justice. Only a greater threat of economic loss—pressure from oil-rich Nigeria—has mitigated this trend.

Another instance of the importance of international factors in the British political economy is the partial economic recovery that took place in Britain in the late 1970s. In December 1976 the British balance of payments registered an annual deficit of about $2.4 billion, the inflation rate was over 17 percent annually, and the pound had slumped to less than 1.7 per dollar. One year later the balance of payments showed a small surplus, inflation was down to 12 percent annually, and the pound was up to 1.95 to the dollar. The Labour government had taken steps against the economic crisis with a tough incomes policy and tight control of the money supply. But two international factors made the turnabout possible: the discovery of North Sea oil, which cut oil imports in half in 1977 and improved the balance of payments, and a large loan from the International Monetary Fund, which had stiff conditions attached to it to lower the inflation rate and restrict government borrowing.[27] Without good luck, a brief period of good management by the government would not have sufficed to turn the tide. And there appears to be a lack of incentive to sustain the economic breathing space provided by North Sea oil by radically changing national political-economic behavior. The industrial and public-service strikes in early 1979 confirm this resistance to change, stimulating the vote of no confidence in the Labour government and the May 1979 election of the Conservatives.

In sum, "the British sickness" seems to be characterized by a gap between outdated subjective perceptions and new objective realities. The failure of particular groups to adapt flexibly to change—whether aristocrats or trade union leaders, politicians or voters, workers or managers—has cost the British a great deal collectively. Perhaps the hardest thing to accept has been the downward mobility, both domestic and international, that the British people have been forced to experience. Their reaction has been to stay put and cling to the past rather than learning to cope quickly and effectively. The British case may be a classic one of learning by paying.

NOTES

1. Daniel Bell, *The Cultural Contradictions of Capitalism* (New York: Basic Books, 1976).
2. Gabriel Almond and Sidney Verba, *The Civic Culture* (Boston: Little, Brown, 1965).
3. Samuel Beer, *British Politics in the Collectivist Age* (New York: Knopf, 1967), p. 70.
4. Henry Fairlie, "Transatlantic Letter to England," *Encounter*, 46, no. 1 (January 1976), 12.
5. *The Autobiography of Claude Cockburn* (Harmondsworth, Middlesex: Penguin, 1967), pp. 37–38.
6. Norman Macrae, "America's Third Century," *The Economist*, October 25, 1975.

7. Stuart Maclure, "The English Disease," *Encounter*, XLVII, no. 3, (March 1977) 66.
8. Conversation with C. P. Snow at Pace University, Pleasantville, N.Y., April 25, 1977.
9. Arthur Warwick, "Social Class in Great Britain 1930 to the Present," presentation at the Institute on Western Europe, Columbia University, November 10, 1976.
10. Frank Parkin, *Class Inequality and Political Order: Social Stratification in Capitalist and Communist Societies* (New York: Praeger, 1975), p. 54.
11. See Harold Lasswell, "The Psychology of Hitlerism," *Political Quarterly*, 4 (1933), 374, and Seymour Martin Lipset, *Political Man: The Social Bases of Politics* (Garden City, N.Y.: Doubleday Anchor, 1963), p. 131.
12. David Butler and Donald Stokes, *Political Change in Britain* (New York: St. Martin's, 1971), p. 49.
13. Robbins Committee Report; see *New Statesman* (London), January 29, 1971, p. 138.
14. Peregrine Worsthorne, "Of Strong Unions in Weak Societies," *Encounter*, 46, no. 1 (January 1976), 26.
15. John le Carré, "In England Now," *New York Times Magazine*, October 23, 1977, p. 86.
16. Butler and Stokes, pp. 129–130.
17. Philip Revzin, "Britain's Ideological Dances," *Wall Street Journal*, October 13, 1977.
18. Dudley Fishburn, "The Political and Economic Situation in Britain," talk given at the Research Institute on International Change, Columbia University, October 19, 1977.
19. Lewis Minkin, "New Left Unionism and the Tensions of British Labour Politics," paper delivered at a conference on "The European Left" held at the Graduate School and University Center of the City University of New York, November 1976.
20. Ibid.
21. James Livingstone, "Britain and the World Economy," lecture at Pace University, February 23, 1977.
22. Robert Prinsky, "Income-Tax Cheating Is on the Rise in Britain as Prices Outstrip Pay," *Wall Street Journal*, October 10, 1977.
23. Ann Crittenden, "A London Banker for Salomon," *New York Times*, September 11, 1977.
24. Robert Samuelson, "Britain's Plight: The Lion in Winter," *New Republic*, January 1 and 8, 1977.
25. Ibid.
26. CBS Television News, October 28, 1977.
27. See Victor Keegan, "Will Energy Resources Spark Economic Recovery in Britain?" *International Perspectives*, May–June 1978, pp. 14–17.

Chapter 5
Italy:
A Political Economy
of Disenchantment

What kind of life is that, they ask, in which a man must relentlessly fight for his position and not bask in the protection of powerful friends? This is one of the reasons why all kinds of rigid organization of economic life find favour in Italy. The people liked their guilds in the pre-industrial world, which regulated every trade and occupation from apprenticeship to the tomb; Fascism, before the war, which prevented all competition as dangerous to the State and surrounded the country with impassable tariff barriers; and any kind of Socialism today, as long as it allows ambitious men to get ahead as they have always done, using the protection of powerful relatives, personal charm, a facility for flattering people, and a keen eye for favourable openings.

—Luigi Barzini, The Italians

Italian disenchantment has such a fatal attraction about it that some of the people who are experiencing the breakdown of advanced industrial societies are tempted to do it "Italian style." Italy's* economic strategy has been compared to one version of the game of chicken: two drivers are headed for collision at breakneck speed wondering who will "chicken out" and swerve to avoid the other; Italy is like the car in which the driver rolls down the window and throws out the steering wheel in plain view of the other driver, Europe, which now knows that it must continue to swerve and adapt to the course of the vehicle that is out of control. By stubbornly refusing to adapt to change until the last possible moment, the Italians may offhandedly have conceived of one of the most subtle of political strategems for conserving their interests and present life style at the expense of others. "The good life" is expensive and the art of surviving effectively in the present is to get someone else to pay the bill as long as possible.

However, the recent concern of Westerners has been not Italy's po-

*See appendix, p. 221, for political-economic events of Italy.

litical culture, on which explanations of Italian behavior must be based, but the popularity of Italy's Communist party, which has threatened to become an official party in the government and not just an opposition party in parliament. Similarly, foreigners have worried about the possibility that Italy will go bankrupt because of its reliance upon loans from the International Monetary Fund and wealthier members of the Common Market (e.g., West Germany). And when the communist movement pressures government policy making and domestic economic conditions become more difficult, capital flows not into Italy but out of it at a time when the nation needs as much capital investment as it can muster to recover its economic strength. Actress Sophia Loren is raided as she crosses the border for the lira notes she is hiding on her body, and other well-to-do Italians sit up nights wondering how to smuggle most of their wealth into Switzerland, that paradise for refugee funds.

Historically, one must speak of two Italies—the North and the South—to understand the present Italian situation. The focus of the "Italian economic miracle" and capitalist development of industry has been in northern Italy largely at the neglect, if not expense, of southern Italy. To overstate the case only slightly, the politics of productivity goes north, the politics of redistribution south. Add to this traditional regional imbalance a historical antistate attitude on the part of Italians and a deep disbelief in the possibility of an effective, unified political economy, and the result is a political economy of disenchantment in which the Italians put their faith in their families and small groups of associates and clients. They typically ignore macrochanges in the Italian environment to concentrate on their own microsituations, preserving their traditions, values, and life styles through local deals and arrangements regardless of what the general consequences of such behavior might be for Italy if everyone acted this way. Italy, in this sense, is one of the most human cases of contemporary political economy in the West, illustrating the inevitable conflict between the developed and underdeveloped regions within the same country, and between the short-term payoffs for selfish behavior and the negative long-term consequences for the national community as a whole. Italians ignore change in order to cope with it in their daily lives, and they seduce others to help them out with their disarming style of disenchantment, which touches what is most human in people.

ITALIAN POLITICAL CULTURE: MOTIVATIONS

The disenchantment of Italians with their state and their economic structures has allowed them to perceive their country's weakness as a source of strength. There is great human appeal in arguing that you are particularly deserving of special help or favors from abroad because of inherent weaknesses and disadvantages that you are powerless to change. But the advantages that such a humanistic appeal from weakness and humility may have on an individual level become fatal national flaws on a collective level, throwing Italy from one crisis to another as unsatisified human needs break through and revolt against the "strategy of passivity" that the nation has been able to get away with so often in its history. Indeed, the Italian word for "crisis" derives from the Greek for "passage."

The sadness, fatalism, and desperation that underlie the Italian political culture are masked by colorful style, fascinating entertainments and distractions, a will to celebrate the present moment while it lasts— *la dolce vita*. Journalist Luigi Barzini strips the mask from Italian charm:

> Italian life is gay, effervescent, intoxicating. The *dolce vita* looks now more *dolce* than it ever was. Very few travellers see the ugliness underneath, the humiliation, the suffering. Not one in a hundred perceives the fundamental dreariness of everything under the glittering ormolu, the bitter fate of men who are condemned perennially to amuse themselves and the world, to hide their innermost feelings, to be *simpatici* at all costs in order to make a living. What do they know of the peculiar feeling of frustration and resigned discontent which paralyzes the best Italians?[1]

All political cultures may fate their members to a peculiar range of life chances and values, washing their motivations with different colors. But in Italy the dose of disenchantment seems particularly strong, especially when it comes to collective action. Italians are marvelous individuals in the art of living, but difficult group members when it comes to the organization of politics. They are brought up to fight for the survival of their families and themselves by making local private alliances with other individuals; by setting up clientele networks to satisfy their needs, often by playing with the ambiguities of the law; and by appealing to particular patrons who can give them something for their loyalty here and now. Short-term sacrifices for the sake of long-term community gains do not make any sense in this political culture; the ego drowns out the superego except, of course, when it comes to family or friends.

In the late 1970s the Christian Democratic government preached the need for sacrifice, wage controls, less tax evasion, less privilege, and a number of other austerity measures to cope with the economic crisis. But many Italians refused to feel the sting. They continued to eat imported steaks, drive cars, and spend as they had before. "The fat cats should pay, not us," said Mario Elsanino, a 38-year-old Roman who voted for the Communist party. "We are the ones who always worked. They should give up something."[2] The government suggested that those who worked for the Ministry of Transport should pay their way on the train. The response of the employees was to demonstrate by falling on the tracks, bringing all train traffic into the Rome station to a halt. In contrast to the tradition of sacrifice and saving typical of the German political culture, the Italians are used to spending, living for the day and getting someone else to pay for it.

The present Italian attitude dates back to the Renaissance, when educated Italians were taught to practice a certain *sprezzatura* or appearance of graceful effortlessness. At that time Baldesar Castiglione wrote in his influential *Book of the Courtier:*

> I have found quite a universal rule which . . . seems to me valid above all others, and in all human affairs whether in word or deed: and that is to avoid affectation in every way possible as though it were some very rough and dangerous reef; and to practice in all things a certain *sprezzatura* ["nonchalance"], so as to conceal all art and make whatever is done or said appear to be without effort and almost without any thought about it. And I believe much grace comes of this: because everyone knows the difficulty of things that are rare and well done; wherefore facility in such things causes the greatest wonder; whereas, on the other hand, to labor and, as we say, drag forth by the hair of the head, shows an extreme want of grace, and causes everything, no matter how great it may be, to be held in little account. Therefore we may call that art true art which does not seem to be art; nor must one be more careful of anything than of concealing it, because if it is discovered, this robs a man of all credit and causes him to be held in slight esteem.[3]

This graceful use of deception and the art of achieving results as if without effort appear to have been developed into a collective cultural style that masks actual Italian working habits and charms foreigners into aiding Italy. But charm hides not only what Italians *do* to increase their life chances individually and collectively; it also masks a certain desperation. In Italy, for even the modestly ambitious, opportunism is not the exception but a way of life. The rules are always changing. Opponents exist to be outwitted or destroyed. Laws exist to be gotten around or to be interpreted to one's advantage. The struggle is inevitable, the payoffs modest, and the risks great. In a chapter in *The Italians* entitled "How to Succeed," Luigi Barzini summarizes two basic rules:

> Rule One: choose the right companions. In order to succeed, a young man must not only join a large and powerful group but also, once in, worm his way to the top, become one of the influential elite, one of the leaders, or even the solitary chief, if he can, in order to use the whole group to serve his own purposes. It is clearly impossible for any man to do so alone. He must have an *entourage* of his own: he must choose a smaller group inside the

large group, join it, and eventually influence it. He must recognize, at the start, which of the various existing cliques presents the best chances.

Rule Two (perhaps the most important of all): choose the right protector. All inner cliques are usually dominated by a few influential men, sometimes by one leader. In all fields there are a few authorities. Any young man who wants to excel must attach himself to the proper mentor, become his aide-de-camp and use him for his own purposes. There are thousands of ways for a young man to seduce a more mature man, just as there are thousands of good ways to seduce women.[4]

As often as not, the Italian's success or failure depends at one point or another on the power of his or her family. At bottom, the political culture of Italy can be viewed as the interweaving of many family units or family-like groups of clients. This strong loyalty to one's family and group or organization refutes the myth that Italians are basically just opportunistic individualists. In one of his notebooks the founder of the Italian Communist party, Antonio Gramsci, had this to say:

Are Italians really individualists? Is it really individualism that makes the ordinary people ignore politics today and made them ignore the interests of the nation as a whole in the past? Is this the reason that made them repeat: "Let France come or let Spain [it is all the same], as long as we eat?" The fact that one does not participate in the life of the community or the State does not necessarily mean that he lives a lone life, the splendidly isolated life of the proud man who counts only on himself to create his own economic and moral world. It merely means that, rather than joining political parties and trade unions, Italians prefer joining organizations of a different type, like cliques, gangs, *camorras, mafias.* This tendency can be observed both among the lower and the higher classes.[5]

Of course, Gramsci idealistically believed that this tendency to form cliques was a result of capitalism and that when all private property became publicly owned Italians would be law-abiding citizens. But the inclination to use one's family and local groups as bases for protecting and furthering one's life chances is as deeply rooted in Italian culture as the distrust of the state and official laws and authorities. The value formula that seems best to describe the individual and social code of behavior of an ideal–typical Italian might be stated as follows: "I will look for my own best opportunities, regardless of change, helping my family and friends out as they help me." This value orientation makes the Italian political culture into one vast interconnected net of clien-teles, a disenchanted pluralism of group interest based on a worldly distrust of outsiders and authority combined with a longing for order and stability to hold the old culture and continuities together while sweetening the life chances of all Italians.

ITALIAN SOCIAL AND POLITICAL
INSTITUTIONS: STRUCTURES

In determining where the motivations of the Italian political culture come together with the structures of social and political institutions, it becomes clear that the Italians consciously perceive their weakness as a source of strength when it comes to bargaining for what they want. But the given structures of life chances or opportunities behind these bargains must be revealed if one is to assess their meaning. If the Italians are somewhat desperate, how much desperation is determined by the social and political system and how much by values or styles that are "freely" chosen? In short, what mix of choice, chance, and structure makes Italians Italians?

The ceaseless crisis of Italian society in the late twentieth century is very much a structural crisis within the social system. The capitalist development of the political economy since World War II split along geographic lines, with the cheap labor of the South providing the manpower for the development of the industrial North. As mentioned earlier, the underdeveloped South contrasts sharply with the "overdeveloped" North, with many intermediate sectors between them. It is difficult to split off different Italian social structures from the values of the soil on which they have been erected, region by region. The Italian social scientists Sabino Acquaviva and Mario Santuccio write:

> The power-system, the class-system and social stratification are based not simply on economic foundations, but on such ill-adaptive value-systems as Catholicism and Marxism, on a primitive religious attitude among the people as well as a widespread religious (and political) skepticism, on such mutually exclusive codes of conduct as the Mediterranean-type, male-dominated, family spirit of the South and the total lack of interest in moral considerations in the North (as in other advanced, industrial societies), on the startling inefficiency of the state bureaucracy in Central and Southern Italy and the comparative efficiency of the industrial bureaucracy in the North, and on considerable imbalances in matters of economics, science and technology.[6]

In short, values, knowledge, technology, money, jobs, and social structures all seem to follow the lines of the North–South split, almost as if an earthquake had torn Italy in half. To no small degree your life chances as an Italian depend on where you were born in relation to this split, how long you have been there, and what your family has done to better its situation over time.

The structural crisis in Italian society today was conditioned by the uneven phases of its modernization in the twentieth century. From a phase when Italy's economy existed at a mere subsistence level, there came a phase of slow development (1900–1948) when old social and economic conditions and the values underlying them were absorbed into the industrialization process, followed by a period of rapid development (1948–1973) leading to social dislocations and political upheaval marked by changes in value systems. This uneven modernization process undermined the old society, in which economic power was concentrated in a small number of hands, political power was centralized, and the male-dominated family group served as a stable structural reference point in society.

Industrial change brought with it the fragmentation of old economic and political power centers and a great increase in individual perceptions of insecurity. Old values existed alongside conflicting new values, rich alongside poor, slums alongside modern high-rise apartments and factories. The fragmentation of political and economic power, combined with the traditional Italian mode of clientelism and disenchantment, served to compound the unevenness in social development in various regions. Young workers moved north to seek jobs and to better their life chances as the percentage of the population actively employed in agriculture dropped from 42.2 percent to 17.3 percent.[7] The Communist party was well enough organized to meet migrant workers at the train upon arrival from the South, promising to help satisfy their needs in exchange for their political support. And Italians have been schooled from birth to take opportunity where they find it, whether it be from the fascists, the communists, the socialists, or whomever.

The structural development of Italy is comparable to that of France in that an old logic or "closed system" of values and underdevelopment exists alongside a new logic of technocracy and modernization leading to value conflict, bureaucratic stalemate, inefficiency, and further disbelief that any coherent national policy can be effective throughout the country. As in the French situation, people who perceive their interests in terms of the old logic, hanging onto old privileges or "arrangements" with local bureaucratic officials, resist the change and adaptation called for by technocratic modernization. But for the Italians this leads to self-contempt and a kind of "antipatriotism"—

> a resigned skepticism that makes most people believe that things . . . in Italy cannot go in any other way. . . . The true reason lies not so much in the weakness of patriotic feeling as in the rejection of all responsibility, whether individual or group. . . . People tend to exclude themselves from the general condemnation. A magic circle is drawn around oneself and around one's friends and colleagues.[8]

The closed, traditional system of a male-dominated, family-based, authoritarian society rooted in poverty and a fragmented rejection of the authority of the central state is being displaced. The new wave is a contemporary consumer society with national technocratic managers in which the prestige of the individual's life style depends on exactly what he or she consumes and the quality of life is almost transformed into a national religion.

THE GOVERNMENT FRAMEWORK AND PARTY SYSTEM

The conflicting values and traditions in the structure of Italian society are matched by an ambiguous attitude on the part of most Italians toward the political system and the state. Metternich is said to have remarked that Italy is not a country but "merely a geographical expression." Since the Italian state was unified only in the late nineteenth century, there is not a long tradition of national mobilization and loyalty as there is, for instance, in France or England.

The period preceding World War II was marked by strong church–state antagonisms, with Catholics initially not allowed to participate in politics. This resulted eventually in the confiscation of church lands by the state in reaction to church privileges. The failure to establish firm liberal institutions in this phase of Italian history was made clear by the rise of Mussolini's fascism during the war; fascism filled the gap between the left and the right, abolished labor unions, and popularized the notion of the "corporate state." In 1929 Mussolini signed a controversial concordat with the church, making the Vatican a sovereign state and granting the church significant control over education and divorce. In Italy as in France, the resistance movement toward the end of World War II provided the seeds for an extensive left-wing political reaction to right-wing politics in the postwar period.

An Italian republic was founded with the Constitution of 1948, which incorporated the church concordat, abolished the monarchy, and set up a two-house parliament, a prime minister, and a president. Italy's is a classical unitary parliamentary system, in contrast to the federal system of West Germany, but it does have twenty regions with limited local powers. The parliament elects the president, who has largely symbolic, figurehead status compared to the prime minister, who heads the government or cabinet—the central policy-making body, made up of ministers responsible to both chambers of the legislature.

Both houses of Parliament have equal powers; in fact, many critics believe they are redundant (like having two Houses of Representatives). The Senate or upper house has 315 members, compared with 630 in the Chamber of Deputies, the lower house. The decentralized system of proportional representation (in which voters cast ballots for party lists rather than for individuals) selects one deputy for every

80,000 votes cast and one senator for every 200,000 votes cast. Such a system encourages the development of disciplined mass parties. Both legislative chambers have five-year terms that coincide. But to vote for senators you need to be 25 years old, whereas you can vote for deputies at 18.

To become law, a bill must pass through both houses of the legislature and be signed by the president. The president can send back a bill that he or she does not like, but a simple majority vote can override this "veto." However, through the committee system bills can pass without coming before either full house *in sede deliberante*. According to this procedure, any one of the fourteen standing committees in the Chamber of Deputies or the eleven committees in the Senate can pass a bill unless one-tenth of the committee members (proportionally represented by party) insists that the matter be brought before the full house.

Once laws have gone into effect, however, they are as often avoided or "reinterpreted" as obeyed. A new law seems to announce that social reality is officially open for bargaining again. An Italian who always obeys the letter of the law is often called a *fesso*, a fool. Since tax evasion is so widespread, taxes are set higher than required on the assumption that people will cheat, and the honest person therefore pays more than is due.

An example of a "bargaining" law with widespread effects for the conflict between the politics of productivity and redistribution is the *Equo Canone* or complex-housing law that went into effect in 1978. According to this law, an apartment house owner is not allowed to take more than a 3.85 percent profit on his or her apartments annually, a small take if one considers that Italy has a double-digit inflation rate and that such an investor can get a return of up to 10 percent from a savings account or bond. Moreover, any written agreement with a tenant is automatically good for four years no matter what the original duration of the contract was, meaning it is hard for a landlord to get rid of a tenant. The price of the rent is carefully calculated by an equation related to the number of square meters of the apartment, its age, its modernity, and the area in which it is located. The law was a "redistributive" windfall for many tenants, who were suddenly able to negotiate their rents downward. But it stopped builders from building new apartments and investors from investing in old ones, bringing productivity to a halt in this sector of the economy. Since living space is already extremely scarce in many places in Italy, until the law is modified a festering social problem may well become malignant in the future. Laws in Italy are literally obstacles that one lives "between."

On paper, the Italian republic looks attractive, with its classical parliamentary system, proportional system of representation, and potential for adaptive flexibility. But major political problems arise when this governmental framework is combined with Italy's diffuse multiparty system. Italy has at least twelve political parties, not counting regional and extraparliamentary parties or violent extremist groups like the Red Brigades. They range from the extreme right to the extreme left: from the Popular South Tyrolian party (SVP) to the right of the Italian Social Movement (MSI), a neo-Fascist party, to the Proletarian Democrats (DP), who are to the left of the Italian Communist party (PCI).* This diffusion of political parties means that, in order to govern, a group must form a coalition between parties, a situation that complements the tradition of Italian clientelism and the tendency toward clique formation. The two predominant parties are, of course, the Christian Democrats (DS)—the Catholic party that has monopolized government power since World War II—and the Communist party (PCI)—the best organized party in Italy, whose success is due in no small part to the incompetence of the Socialist party and the lack of any serious competition as the main alternative to the ruling Christian Democrats.

Although the Christian Democrats have been able to maintain their position as the ruling government party in the postwar period, the Communist party has gradually gained ground peaking in the 1976 elections when it received 34.4 percent of the vote compared to the 38.4 percent won by the Christian Democrats. The Communists have proposed a "historical compromise" in the form of an official government alliance with the Christian Democrats. Thus far the latter have officially rejected the idea, preferring to keep the Communists out of the cabinet in order to avoid a further loss of electoral support.

The willingness of the Communist party to compromise, together with its efforts to create a more acceptable conservative and efficient image, helped provoke the radical Red Brigade terrorists into violence out of the feeling that "true" socialist revolutionary ideals had been sold out by a group of communists who had become part of the established order. The Communist party, on the other hand, has denounced the terrorist kidnapings, murders, and shootings, trying to dissociate itself from the Red Brigades, but it remains uncertain as to whether or how to attempt to gain majority control in the government in an economic and social situation that sometimes seems almost ungovernable.

In the 1979 elections, the Communist party (PCI) paid for its ambiguity in its first national electoral setback since World War II. The PCI's percentage of the popular vote dropped from 34.4 percent in 1976 to

---

*From right to left, these twelve parties are as follows: Popular South Tyrolian party (SVP), Italian Social Movement (MSI), National Democrats (DN), Radical party (PR), Italian Liberal party (PLI), Italian Republican party (PRI), Union of Valdôtaine (UV), Christian Democrats (DC), Italian Socialist Democratic party (PSDI), Italian Socialist party (PSI), Italian Communist party (PCI), and Proletarian Democrats (DP).

30.4 percent, giving the party a loss of 26 parliamentary seats. Party leader Enrico Berlinguer, whose historic compromise strategy of joining the government in an alliance with the centrist parties was repudiated by the vote, acknowledged what he termed an "appreciable variation with respect to our exceptional advances of 1976." The Christian Democrats slipped from 38.7 to 38.3 percent of the popular vote, losing one seat in the lower house. Italians appeared to be disenchanted with the cozy cooperation of the two major parties in parliament, which pretended to be total adversaries at election time.

The winners in the 1979 election were the small parties. The Radical party tripled its vote to 1.2 million, adding 14 new seats to the 4 it had before. This appeared to register a protest vote on the part of disenchanted leftists and individualists, also confirmed by the record 1.7 million blank ballots—the new so-called Abstentionist party. The Social Democrats increased their share of the popular vote from 3.4 to 3.8 percent, while the centrist Republicans hung on to their 3 percent despite the death of their party president, Ugo La Malfa. The support for the moderate-right Liberals increased from 1.3 to 1.9 percent. The third largest Italian party, the Socialists, was disappointed by its increase of only five new seats after all the erratic efforts of Socialist leader Bettino Craxi to give his party a new sense and image of direction. The election dealt another blow to Eurocommunism (following the 1978 defeat of the French left) and appeared to make future government coalitions even more difficult to form.

As things stand, the Communist party is still in a favorable position, being able to influence policy making through a "hidden veto" while it is not officially in the government and therefore is not officially as responsible as the cabinet. The worry in other Western countries that the Communist party might eliminate democracy and set up some form of Stalinist authoritarian one-party state should they achieve more electoral support than the Christian Democrats seems exaggerated when one considers that the Communists, like all other parties, know that they must form coalitions in order to govern at all in Italy, making democratic compromise more likely than any extremist gamble of authoritarianism.

The Italian Parliament is supreme but immobile, a virtual stalemate of coalitions and clientelism. The Italian political scientist Giuseppe Di Palma concludes that

> in the last analysis, social unrest, economic crisis, the very militancy of labor organizations, are not the result of objectively unmanageable problems but the product of government ineffectiveness. It is especially in this regard that Italy differs from other industrial countries faced with their share of social and economic problems, and it is mainly ineffectiveness that explains why in Italy the problems are so much greater than elsewhere.[9]

But Di Palma seems to unwittingly overestimate the abilities of government in the Italian situation, where the objective problems are perhaps more intractable than in other Western industrial democracies. Italy may be an overloaded government without a government, to overstate the case only slightly. That is, the Italian Parliament serves to maintain the existing ineffective system, the politics of clientelism, by offering incentives to induce both the majority and the opposition into good behavior. But social, economic, and political problems have outgrown the old organizational structures set up to cope with them. Whether or not these arrangements work or not may be academic, at least in terms of solving Italy's major social and economic problems. A case could be made that these structures do work and are maintained at the governmental level, making it impossible to cope with the larger social issues toward which governments are supposed to be aimed.

The stalemated parliamentarianism in Western democracies such as Italy, with more parties than they can cope with, can have grave political consequences. Recall Chapter 3, in which it was suggested that the major cause of executive importance has been party deadlock in the legislature. There were twelve parties in the Italian parliament before Mussolini's fascist takeover. People lost faith in parliamentarianism because of the hopeless inefficiency produced by factionalism. Norman Stamps suggests that two empirical causes of dictatorship are executive impotence (due to the supremacy of the legislature) and party stalemate (due to the existence of too many parties).[10] It may be that Italy is slowly moving toward a "two-party system" (the DC and the PCI). But if Stamps turns out to be right in this case, the Italians may soon have a feeling of déjà vu, sensing that in one form or another those factors have always been behind the traditional Italian political disenchantment.

POLITICAL-ECONOMIC CODES: ITALIAN BARGAINING BEHAVIOR

The bargaining process of the Italian political economy can be viewed as a socioeconomic pie cut into thin slices by many parties, government officials, businesspeople, and bureaucrats. Many people seem to get a small piece of what they want, thereby keeping the system going; but no one gets enough to be satisfied. On the extreme left, Red Brigade terrorists and Marxist ideologues believe that little is being done to aid the poor and the working class. On the right, business leaders argue that conditions have made privately owned free enterprise and productivity increasingly difficult in Italy as the debt-laden public corporation dominates the economic scene and redistributive laws deter new investment. And many Italians in the middle are frustrated by a political system that never produces an alternative governing coalition that allows them to "vote the rascals out." Wheeling and dealing in the politics of clientelism and coalition has allowed the Christian Democrats to monopolize government power since the war.

In Italy the conservative impulse to maintain old structures in reaction to drastic social and economic change pushes problems up to the superstructural governmental level, where superficial, ad hoc solutions merely paper over the difficulties in short-term political coalitions, leaving long-term infrastructural and substructural dislocations untouched. Thus, rather than trying to resolve deep-seated socioeconomic difficulties, the governing Christian Democratic party has tried to absorb and coopt opposition groups, widening its coalition, making more and more people responsible for the state of affairs. As a result the party has lost legitimacy and respect with each successive compromise. Traditionally representing big business as well as anticapitalist Catholic groups, the Christian Democrats have become further diluted as they seek the approval (or abstention from opposition) of the powerful Communist party for their legislation before they officially submit it to Parliament. Through incentives called *leggine* the Italian Parliament keeps the majority and opposition in line, and it is significant that the communists are not willing to give up these incentives to take the role of responsible opposition. Such cooptation buys time for the system and postpones meaningful structural reforms indefinitely. This *trasformismo,* or transformation of the adversary, has frustrated both the left and the right, and both neofascist and Red Brigade factions have not hesitated to use violence to express their protest—culminating in the Red Brigades' kidnaping and murder of former Prime Minister Aldo Moro, one of those most responsible for the cooperative agreements between the Christian Democrats and the Communists.

The Italian political economy is a vast spoils network in which clients and patrons scratch each other's backs and loyalty and selfish interests rather than efficiency or principle determine most of the payoffs. Of course, this is true to no small extent in all political systems. But in Italy the spoils system seems to have become the predominant feature of political alliances and economic behavior.

After the war businesspeople often saw their life chances maximized through the Christian Democratic party, whereas those who were out of such arrangements naturally interpreted this as corruption. The period of recovery led by big business and made possible by the capital investment of the Marshall Plan was characterized by an unabashed politics of productivity, setting the foundation for the economic boom of the 1950s.

The critical prerequisites for "the Italian economic miracle" of 1951–

1962 included low labor costs, a stable political structure, a steady currency, stable commodity prices, rising prices for finished products, and an aggressive, optimistic state of mind. These prerequisites were particularly important for a country like Italy, which lacked most natural resources and depended on converting inexpensive imported materials into finished products with a cheap labor force, products that could fetch a good price on an expanding world market. But success lays its own traps and often leads to its own undoing. Overemphasis on the politics of productivity led government officials and business leaders to neglect critical social problems as cheap labor from the South was exploited to build up the industrial sector in the North. Workers sensed that they were not getting their share of the expanding economy, and strong labor unions emerged, promising to increase the bargaining power of the worker.

The union movement splits the workers into two camps: full-time working union members who reap pension, health, and security benefits accordingly, and many more part-time and "underground" workers who do not belong to unions and receive neither the benefits nor the level of pay of full-time workers. Political economist G. Fuà has summarized this development as follows:

> Italy has achieved high salary levels compared with its level of income, and has achieved some goals more advanced than those accomplished by countries richer than Italy, regarding the salaries of women and old people, and—so far as can be determined—the overall rights of workers. These conquests obviously regard those people who are regularly employed . . . and, like the other side of the coin, to the fact that these are significant conquests there corresponds the relatively low quantity of regular employment, and the dimensions of underground work in Italy. It is emblematic that, while we are among those countries which seek excellent treatment of regularly-employed women and older workers, we are also among the countries which have very low levels of employment for these categories.[11]

In short, the politics of productivity led to a reaction in the form of a politics of redistribution, which helps explain the strong position of labor unions and the Communist party in Italy today. The critical preconditions for economic success disappeared accordingly: labor costs skyrocketed (increasing by an average of 15–20 percent annually since 1969); since 1969 Italians have had the shortest working year of all industrialized nations; in the same period unit production costs increased 137 percent; utilization of productive capacity dropped steadily; the political system, the Italian currency, and the price of commodity imports lost all stability in the 1970s, while the international market for finished Italian goods became unpredictable as their prices rose with labor costs and inflation.[12] From an economic miracle Italy was transformed into an economic disaster in need of being bailed out by the International Monetary Fund, the German government, and others.

Rather than finding any solution to the critical economic crisis, those in the governmental system sought ways of alleviating the frustration of Italian citizens in order to give them a feeling that their life chances were improving: the 1970s brought the legalization of divorce and abortion, despite strong Vatican protests, and a university reform admitting anyone who has completed secondary-school requirements, taking many young people off the job market and buying more time for the government. Progressive social policies often serve to obfuscate economic difficulties, further postponing the moment of reckoning. The counterpart to the Italian strategy of using weakness as a basis for strength is to postpone the consequences of weakness with the illusion of progress. In contrast to the equilibrium-and-control orientation of the Germans and the cooptation-through-change strategy of the French, the strategy of the Italians appears to be to ignore or postpone change as long as possible, sweetening life chances with surface shifts and distractions and leaving the bill to be paid another day if possible.

The popular panacea for problems in the Italian political economy has been to turn more and more private activity over to public enterprise. Paradoxically, this approach has had a profound impact on the Italian economy in an incremental way, basing industrial development on public enterprise to an extent almost unsurpassed in a nation that is presumably grounded on a market economy. But the social and economic crises have mounted since the 1960s, when macroeconomic efforts of the state to steer the economy failed and the relationship between the state and the business community became a selective set of privileged arrangements and a steady increase in public takeovers of private concerns. The initial power of the industrialists and financiers during the period of the economic miracle was weakened as the role of the market became increasingly restricted and social promises for redistribution were voiced more loudly throughout the land. Yet income and development differences in the *Mezzogiorno* (the South) remained; unemployment swelled; and disenchantment set in as many people began to doubt that the plethora of public enterprises could solve public, much less private, problems. Governor Baffi of the Bank of Italy, which has been forced to underwrite the Italian spoils system, observed that labor costs were growing at a much greater rate than in countries with which Italy had to compete on the world market, and that as the bank and the Italian system swelled their deficits for the sake of public enterprises, liquidity, flexibility, and choice were lost.[13] Redistribution occurs more in image than in reality; productivity wanes; and the Italians are further disenchanted with their prospects.

DOMESTIC AND FOREIGN POLICY: COLLECTIVE DECISION MAKING

The interlocking of Italian domestic and foreign policies is particularly acute in an era of crisis, when the economic means to solve social problems depend on effective political-economic management from the top and on cooperation and productivity from the majority below. Italians are caught between unfavorable domestic and international economic conditions, not all of which are of their own making. The recent reaction against the one-sided politics of the recovery and economic miracle phases in favor of a politics of redistribution has served to make the *Mezzogiorno* issue (i.e., the underdevelopment of the South) a central point in industrial policy, which, in turn, has caused Italy's political economy to develop in peculiar ways that often contradict the predominant concepts of the Common Market. And to the extent that these social and industrial issues have been recast in an effective electoral strategy on the part of the Italian Communist party, the national leaders of Western Alliance countries are concerned that Italy's foreign policy might become peculiar too, particulary if "Eurocommunism" (the belief that Western Communist parties will coalesce) proves successful, making Italy an awkward, if not unwelcome, participant in the strategic planning processes in the North Atlantic Treaty Organization (NATO).

Industrial and Social Policies

Italian industrial and social policies have become intricately intertwined as the public sector has expanded. Initially, public support was intended to help the ailing private sector regain self-sufficiency, but over time social aims overwhelmed industrial priorities. The response to the economic difficulties that Italy has experienced since the early 1960s has not taken the form of a comprehensive national plan but has consisted of a series of fragmented programs aimed to relieve certain depressed areas and shore up particular industries. As Italy's minister of industry, Romano Prodi, has written,

> The execution of the Italian government's policy of intervening to support firms in crisis has been almost exclusively in the hands of Italy's public enterprises. In the 1950s these rescue operations were a source of opposition and controversy in the private sector. In the early 1960s such practices came to be tolerated as a part of the legitimate strategy of large industrial groups. By the end of the 1960s and in the beginning of the 1970s, they were widely regarded as the only means of avoiding a chain of bankruptcies.[14]

A typical illustration of industrial policy taking the form of public financing is provided by the financial organization *Gestioni e Partecipazione Industriale* (GEPI), which was established in 1971 with $98 million, later increased to $268 million, to provide aid for businesses in difficult situations. GEPI has found support throughout the political system from entrepreneurs, trade unions, and political parties. But GEPI's stress on guaranteeing employment rather than on a coherent plan for industrial development is a crucial strategic choice. As Prodi notes, "The number of jobs has become the prime objective of industrial policy. Lacking any more general social policy, the country seeks to use GEPI's rescue activities in the industrial sector as a substitute."[15]

Although the initial purpose of GEPI was to help reorganize private companies so that they could survive as private enterprises on the model of the British Industrial Reorganisation Corporation, political pressures pushed the organization into the traditional Italian government business rescue, setting the stage for a public-sector takeover. Private managers have gone along with this search for security rather than taking entrepreneurial risks, and large-scale Italian industry appears to be losing its dynamism along with its productivity. The 1970s brought an increase in the importance of foreign-owned companies and of public enterprises and a marked decrease in the number of independent Italian firms, despite a small business mini-boom at the end of the decade.

Fiat, an exception to the rule, highlights the industrial situation in Italy. Gianni Agnelli, head of Fiat, is the largest private employer in Italy, representing the only major private enterprise that is not in debt. In 1977 Fiat had sales of $12 billion and a profit of $117 million, which is good by Italian standards. Only 40 percent of the profits of this conglomerate come from car sales. The rest are produced by *La Stampa* (Italy's second-largest newspaper), steel, tractors, car parts, production systems, airplane engines, trains, rails, buses, engineering, and construction in the Third World. Agnelli was not averse to using the cheap labor immigrating from the South in the 1950s and 1960s to stock his industrial plants in the North, a cause often cited for some of Italy's most frustrating social and economic problems. He felt that if they hadn't gone there they would have gone to Germany, Belgium, France, or somewhere else and that if he had started factories in the South they would probably have gone broke.

Two decisions have alienated many businesspeople and politicians from Agnelli: the Lama and Qaddafi deals. In 1975 Agnelli, then president of the Confindustria (an Italian federation of industrialists and manufacturers), met with Luciano Lama, the powerful leader of the Communist-dominated CGIL (Italian General Federation of Labor), to talk about what the ratio of cost-of-living increases for workers ought to be in relation to inflation. The deal resulted in an indexation* of over 100 percent in some cases, meaning that the more inflation Italy has, the more lower-paid workers increase the purchasing power of their wages—a deal that itself stimulated inflation to no small extent. Not accidentally, Agnelli gained a nice side benefit from the arrangement: the devaluation of the lira, which resulted directly from the Lama agreement, meaning that Fiat cars sold at a higher price abroad.

In addition, many people are upset by Agnelli's 1976 arrangement to sell 10 percent of Fiat to Colonel Qaddafi of Libya for $415 million, which allowed Agnelli to recapitalize his company but had far-reaching implications for the world political economy. Pro-Israeli circles in Washington were outraged. One implication of the deal was that it allowed Libya to underwrite expansion of the Fiat factory in the Soviet Union in return for the continuation of Soviet military aid and support for Libya's uncompromising anti-Israeli Middle Eastern policy.[16] Agnelli is undaunted by such criticism, referring to the Soviet Union as a "neutral country." From Fiat's viewpoint the Soviet Union has been neutral for the past thirty years—Fiat business with the Soviets has gone on that long (but Agnelli quickly added that he would not like to live in the Soviet Union, although he would recommend an extended stay for Enrico Berlinguer, head of the Italian Communist party).[17]

The contrast between the exceptional role of Agnelli and Fiat in the Italian political economy and the career of Eugenio Cefis, president of the chemical conglomerate Montedison, indicates the new direction that industrial policy has taken. Coming from the network of state-owned industries as president of *Ente nazionale Italcarburi* (ENI) in the 1960s, Cefis was able to negotiate the takeover of his chemical company, by ENI. This arrangement served to consolidate his hold on Montedison. He used government structures to liquidate unprofitable sectors of his conglomerate, reserving the profitable ones for himself. According to Italian analyst E. Scalfari, the worlds of Agnelli and Cefis are irremediably different, Agnelli representing the entrepreneurial bourgeoisie whereas Cefis symbolizes the bourgeoisie of the state—an entity no longer standing for "the general will" through an ethical–juridical arrangement but representing a massive power and profit structure that must expand in order to survive, even at the expense of the private sector.[18]

Combining the advantages of both the public and private sectors, Cefis was able to put himself in a position of great power by using his public-sector contacts. Despite the differences in their strategies, both Agnelli and Cefis epitomize the tradition of Italian bargaining behavior:

*Indexation refers to an automatic accounting system whereby worker wages or benefits are increased with every increase in inflation or prices.

Use your connections and institutional position to further your own short-term interests, regardless of the long-term consequences for the society and the state. Ironically, Montedison is now carrying big debts (typical of public corporations), leading political representatives among the Communists, Christian Democrats, Socialists, and trade unions to agree that Agnelli's ownership of Fiat is both necessary and good for Italy—and, hence, to oppose nationalization of Fiat. Luigi Macario, head of the Catholic-dominated Italian Confederation of Union Workers (CISL), summed up this feeling: "It's difficult enough to manage the already nationalized firms and I favor a mixed economy. I'm against private firms financed with public money—like Montedison."[19]

The general consensus on the part of most political, industrial, and labor leaders concerning the limits of public corporations as a means for solving Italy's social and economic problems has not, however, led to a reversal in this public expansion that might begin to contain labor costs, increase productivity, or attract new investment. Indeed, one of the most intriguing elements of the Italian political economy is the *scala mobile*, or indexation of the cost of living, which makes the direct tie between industrial and social policy clear. The indexation, which is calculated each trimester, provides automatic pay raises to keep pace with rises in living costs. Inflation in the cost of living is thus thrust back into the economic system almost immediately, making it extremely difficult for industries to increase productivity at a sufficient rate to make up for increases in production costs. Predictably, by late 1979 Luciano Lama was suggesting that while ". . . the escalator can't be touched now, it is no longer a taboo subject . . ." as far as his union (CGIL) was concerned. This position was seconded by officials in or close to the Communist party, such as Luigi Spaventa. The internal logic of the Italian political economy appears to be self-defeating in terms of both industrial and social policy as social demands cause wages and benefits to rise, which, in turn, cause productivity, investment, and employment to fall. As redistribution policies increase in number, the economic pie to be redistributed may be shrinking. Italians from almost all political parties fear that in the present economic circumstances and political climate multinational corporations may begin to pull up their stakes and leave at exactly the moment when Italy, like much of Europe, badly needs new capital investment to pick up its economy and cut down unemployment.[20]

Eurocommunism

With the reaction against the politics of productivity (which made the "Italian economic miracle" possible in the 1950s and early 1960s), a natural opening was provided for a left-wing movement based on the politics of redistribution. First, the Italian economy went from a focus on agriculture to a focus on industry. Then it shifted from a focus on manufacturing to an emphasis on the tertiary economic sector (dealing with social and other services). The split between the rural South and the industrial North became increasingly visible, and many people became more concerned with who was getting what of what there was to get than with how to keep the economy expanding. In the rush of Italian development, expectations were raised and extremes between the haves and have-nots became less tolerable. Astute tactical maneuvering on the part of Communist party leaders combined with incompetent leadership in the Socialist party allowed the Communist party to become the only well-organized opposition to the stale domination of the Christian Democrats in the Italian political system.

The French situation is somewhat similar in that the Communist party has formed temporary alliances with the socialists as the only viable alternative to the Gaullist-centrist domination of France since the war, but the communists by no means have the same predominance on the left that they do in Italy. For the Italian Communist party is a broad, loose coalition with a tightly organized core, unlike the French version, which often snaps back into its Stalinist mode like a steel trap, or the Spanish version with its proud, explicit anti-Soviet proclamations. But despite these and other differences, many Westerners have viewed the reinvigorated communist movements in Italy, France, and Spain in terms of their similarities, lumping them under the term "Eurocommunism," which is often viewed as something new, if not ominous.

There is one common theme to Eurocommunism that should not be underestimated by those who are unfamiliar with European ideological developments: the antifascist heritage and the inspiration provided by the Soviet Communist party in its earliest revolutionary phase. In this sense Eurocommunism, along with Western liberal democracy, is a natural outgrowth of the World War II resistance movement. When Western Europe was threatened by fascist totalitarianism (which was not accidentally allied with many big-business interests and a perverted form of the politics of productivity), revolutionary socialism on the Soviet model was the extreme opposite alternative, and an alternative capable of winning. It is hard for Americans, for example, to grasp how attractive the initial Marxist revolution executed by Lenin in 1917 must have been to many idealistic Europeans in the chaotic post-World War I era. Many of the same Europeans managed to overlook the cruel purges by Stalin in the post-Lenin era, although others saw this slaughter as a basis for a split of the ideal socialist movement into democratic versus nondemocratic camps. The violent verbal and physical attacks on the Soviet communists by the Western fascists served only to increase the relative attractiveness of the communist alternative for many repressed democrats in Western Europe. As the historian Louis Hartz pointed out so well in *The Liberal Tradition in America*, Americans cannot comprehend the real meaning of extreme left-wing and right-wing movements of the European variety. For America skipped the feudal stage of history and the revolutionary reaction to feudalism, meaning that Americans can never really understand the meaning of the socialist left's rebellion against feudalism or the reactionary right's opposition to socialism. Taught only to know what they themselves have experienced, many Americans tend only to see things in terms of their own dogmatic liberalism, making "Eurocommunism" just another incomprehensible anathema in their eyes.

European experience in the twentieth century provides a clue to the popularity of Eurocommunism. Although fascism was defeated on the battlefield, states such as Germany, Italy, and Spain inherited Fascist socioeconomic structures, namely an intertwining of political, economic, and social elites and institutions at the top of the policy-making apparatus, making an effectively managed politics of productivity possible in all of these countries, but at the cost of neglecting the politics of redistribution—more traditionally identified with the socialist camp. As the politics of productivity resulted in social affluence, there was a natural left-wing demand for more social equality, consolidated in the social-democratic movement, legislation, and coalitions in West Germany and in the socialist and communist movements in Italy, France, and Spain.

Following the liberation of Italy from the fascists in 1945, governments included representatives of all parties that had participated in the resistance movement, including the Socialists and Communists. For about a decade thereafter a Socialist–Communist alliance worked in opposition to Christian Democratic coalitions with the Social Democrats and Republicans. Then the Socialists began to develop a more independent line, making a center–left coalition possible when the Socialist party was brought into the government. Such a coalition, many felt, could steer Italy's potential for growth into areas of chronic social need, such as depression in the South, unemployment, emigration, education, health, and so forth. But this promise faded as it became clear that the previous high growth rate could not be maintained, that the unions would press for demands that were irrational from the perspective of the overall management of the economy, and that the Communists would maintain their pressure no matter what policies were adopted, and when the Italians followed the 1968 leftist revolt in Paris with a decade of strikes, demonstrations, and unceasing protest. The final breakdown in the center–left partnership occurred in the mid-1970s, when the Socialists demanded that the Communist party must be included in the government or they would not be part of it, figuring that this would force the Communists to accept some responsibility for Italy's problems and make the Socialists more attractive to voters in comparison to the Communists. The failure of this Socialist gambit served to virtually eliminate the Socialist party as an organized leftist alternative and opened the door for the Communists to monopolize the opposition role in the Italian political structure.[21]

Moreover, the incompetence of the Socialists was matched by the patience and shrewdness of Communist party tacticians. In 1964, when the policy of "frontism" (close cooperation with the Communist party) was abandoned by the Socialists in favor of joining the Christian Democrats in a series of majorities and governments, the Communists were depressed at first. The next decade was marked by indecision on the part of the party elite as to whether to return to the frontism policy or to go it alone and build up popular support for the PCI. The tactical brilliance of PCI leader Luigi Longo and his successor, Enrico Berlinguer, consisted in *not* choosing decisively between these two strategies, but rather keeping their options open by appearing officially to be frontist while preparing popular support for any eventuality. This tactic was complemented by a cooptative policy in which the PCI claimed to be *interclassista*—a synthesis of classes rather than exclusively proletarian—and that the solution to Italy's problems also had to be *interclassista:* "No one class can save Italy." The PCI became increasingly distrustful of the Socialists, and the downfall of Allende's socialist regime in Chile in 1973 settled the matter for the Italian Communists: they would focus on going it alone by building a large coalition capable of cooperating with any popular party, including the Christian Democrats. This, in turn, led them to advocate the *compromesso storico* ("the historic compromise"), the policy of offering to officially join the Christian Democrats in a government coalition.

But not all of those who consider themselves communists were happy with the historic-compromise policy. As early as 1968 some of the more revolutionary members published a newspaper, *Il Manifesto,* and pointed out that the PCI's cooptative strategy could lead to open anti-Sovietism, opportunism, and a dilution of the party's machine. In 1979 criticism of the party that had caused losses in the 1979 elections indirectly threatened Berlinguer's hold on the party leadership. Whereas in 1968 the dissidents were expelled from the party, in 1979 (reflecting the rank of the dissidents) they were either removed from their seats on the party's central committee or exiled to the "elephant's graveyard" of the European Parliament.

The 1970s were marked by the more extreme actions of the Red Brigades, who consider themselves true communists, as opposed to the "bourgeois" Italian Communist party. The strategy of the Red Brigades is to use blackmail, kidnaping, murder, and violence to force the government into taking such repressive measures that workers will rise up and overthrow the state. The nihilistic goal of West German terrorists is similar, and there is evidence that these and other terrorist groups communicate and coordinate their plans through international organizations such as Terror International. The brutal slaying of the bodyguards of West German industrialist Hans Martin Schleyer in order to kidnap and later murder him was certainly similar in style to the murder of the bodyguards of former Italian Prime Minister Aldo Moro by the Red Brigades in 1978, when the nation was kept in suspense for two months before Moro was killed.

One wonders to what extent, if at all, such terrorism might have been mitigated if the leftist opposition parties in Italy had been too strongly principled to make "historic compromises" or to go along with traditional clientelist party coalitions. Terrorism in Western Europe appears to be a transnational phenomenon stemming from the perception of "principleless" centrist politics in postindustrial societies. As Eurocommunist parties claim to be democratic even to the point of allowing themselves to be voted out of power should they ever succeed electorally in Italy, France, and Spain, the political corollary appears to be a spread of European terrorism led by leftist extremists who argue that such a dilution of communist and Marxist principles makes the Eurocommunist parties no different from the "bourgeois establishment" opponents whom they seek to replace.

The dramatic and traumatic murder of the consensus-building DC leader Aldo Moro and the subsequent "kneecappings" (crippling government and business elites by shooting them in the knees) and violence of the Red Brigades have produced a conservative reaction in Italy that resulted in an increase in local voting for the Christian Democrats and a decisive policy on the part of the PCI to dissociate itself as much as possible from the extremist "communist" terrorists by strongly denouncing their violent acts. Italian police appeared to be incapable of coping with the well-organized and well-financed terrorists, and the Italian secret police were disbanded in the early 1970s, when antifascist sentiment was running strong and Italian politicians bent with the wind, as usual. Later, as police began to succeed in controlling the Red Brigade, criminal groups adopted revolutionary tactics of extortion. Because of terrorism, the defeat of the socialist–communist alliance in the French elections of 1978, the PCI electoral losses in 1979, and the need of the Italian economy for more business confidence to lure foreign aid and investment, the future of Eurocommunism as an international movement appears to have faded somewhat. But individual communist parties in Mediterranean countries appear to be well enough organized, financed, and educated to be a dominant factor in their countries' political economies for the indefinite future as the battle between productivity and redistribution rages on.

REGIONAL AND GLOBAL CONSTRAINTS

Regional and global constraints are particularly important in Italy's present critical situation. For both security and economic prosperity the Italians are heavily dependent on other nations. The Eurocommunist movement has complicated the security issue from the perspective of both the United States and the Soviet Union. The American representatives of NATO are skeptical about the claims of the Italian Communist party that if it enters the government it will maintain democratic pluralism and support the anti-Soviet alliance. NATO's concern that if Italian Communists were officially in power they might push Italian foreign policy toward neutrality (in order to improve relations with the Soviets and increase Italy's political security) is so great that many Western military leaders do not believe Italian representatives should participate in nuclear secrets or weapons planning under such conditions. The Italian Communists argue, in contrast, that Italy should remain in NATO to protect Italy's independence from the Soviet Union—a credible, but untested, claim. The Soviet elite, for their part, are not enthusiastic about a third ideological wave of communism (after the Chinese and Yugoslav "heresies") so close to home, and have mixed feelings about a Eurocommunist movement that officially renounces the Leninist doctrine of the need for an authoritarian, elitist vanguard—the core of the legitimacy of the Soviet state.

Paradoxically, Italians may again be able to derive bargaining strength from strategic weakness. By playing on the fears of the superpowers with a carefully calculated policy of ambiguity toward NATO in the long run (perhaps on the French model), they may be able to gain more advantages than they expected. Certainly, this is one reason why the International Monetary Fund, West Germany, and the United States have continued to provide Italy with economic support despite the failure of the Italian government to put through meaningful economic reforms. The West wants to provide disincentives for the Italians to go socialist or to slip into neutrality or the Soviet bloc. International constraints can thus become a two-edged sword providing opportunities for shrewd statesmen who know how to use their limitations as levers. Machiavelli was not an accidental offspring of this land of political disenchantment, where power is often based on less than meets the eye.

NOTES

1. Luigi Barzini, *The Italians: A Full-Length Portrait Featuring Their Manners and Morals* (New York: Atheneum, 1964), p. 336. © 1964 by Luigi Barzini. Used by permission of Atheneum Publishers and Hamish Hamilton, Ltd.
2. Alvin Shuster, "For the Italians, Many Appeals, Few Sacrifices," *New York Times,* October 31, 1976.
3. Baldesar Castiglione, *The Book of the Courtier,* trans. Charles Singleton (Garden City, N.Y.: Doubleday Anchor, 1959; original published in 1528), p. 43.
4. Barzini, pp. 228–229.
5. Ibid., p. 218.
6. Sabino Acquaviva and Mario Santuccio, *Social Structure in Italy,* trans. Colin Hamer (Boulder, Colo.: Westview Press, 1976), p. 2.
7. Ibid., p. 28.
8. Domenico Bartoli, "Italy's Ailment *all' italiana,*" *Encounter,* 47, no. 2 (August 1972).
9. Giuseppe Di Palma, *Surviving Without Governing: The Italian Parties in Parliament* (Berkeley: University of California Press, 1977), p. 5.
10. Norman Stamps, *Why Democracies Fail—A Critical Evaluation of the Causes for Modern Dictatorship* (Notre Dame, Ind.: University of Notre Dame Press, 1957).
11. G. Fuà, *Occupazione e Capacità Produttive: La Realtà Italiana* (Bologna: Il Mulino, 1976), p. 77. As translated by Michael Ledeen, *Italy in Crisis* (Beverly Hills, Calif.: Sage Publications, 1977), p. 38.
12. M. Ledeen, p. 40.
13. P. Baffi, "Relazione del governatore della Banca d'Italia," *Il Mondo* (June 9, 1976), XII.
14. Romano Prodi, "Italy," in *Big Business and the State,* ed. Raymond Vernon (Cambridge, Mass.: Harvard University Press, 1974), pp. 48–49.
15. Ibid., p. 50.
16. Lally Weymouth, "On the Razor's Edge: A Portrait of Gianni Agnelli," *Esquire,* June 20, 1978, p. 35.
17. Gianni Agnelli, speech to the Foreign Policy Association, Hotel Pierre, New York City, February 24, 1977.
18. See E. Scalfari, *Razza Padrona* (Milan: Feltrinelli, 1974), p. 464.
19. Weymouth, p. 36.
20. See Joseph La Palombara and Stephen Blank, *Multinational Corporations in Comparative Perspective* (New York: The Conference Board, 1977), p. 8.
21. See Ugo La Malfa, "Communism and Democracy in Italy," *Foreign Affairs,* April 1978, pp. 476–488.

Chapter 6
The Common Market: Organizing for Collective-Bargaining Power

Common Market countries today [December 5] adopted a European Monetary System, but Britain decided not to participate actively and Italy and Ireland appeared on the verge of staying out because their demands for financial aid were not met.

The dispute about aid for poorer countries to enable them to keep up with the system threatened to confine the new system initially to six participating countries—West Germany, France, Denmark, the Netherlands, Belgium and Luxembourg.

French and German leaders had said they hoped the proposed system would reduce currency fluctuations and create a zone of monetary stability.

—The Herald Tribune, December 6, 1978

The creation of the European monetary system that went into operation in 1979 was only one of the most recent steps in the gradual integration of Western European political economies since World War II.* When they were recovering from the war, a core of European nations believed that the only way they could increase their bargaining power individually and collectively was to create a cohesive community, to drop all trade restrictions within "the club" and to discriminate against outsiders for the sake of the members. The European theory is that you can produce more and distribute it more fairly in a community that abides by rules and customs than you can if each nation maximizes its own short-term interests regardless of the long-term consequences for other nations in the same region. Nationalism was to be replaced by Europeanism. And if cooperative nations lost out competitively in the process, at least they would be subsidized for some of the short-term benefits they had sacrificed for the sake of long-term community interests.

*See appendix, p. 225, for political-economic events of the European community.

Until recently, the American view of the Common Market has been largely an idealistic one, a vision of a "United States of Europe." Such an integrated federal state would presumably provide a bulwark against the Soviet threat and supply America with a market and investment opportunities. Few observers anticipated that the Common Market would become as competitive with the United States as it is today while simultaneously remaining dependent on American security. The Common Market has become both more *and* less than many Americans would wish. Yet still the belief prevails that if Western Europe became even more integrated politically, if it became a state as well as a market, somehow this would be as good for the United States as it is for Europe. The possibility that the Common Market might represent a subtle political vehicle for eventual economic and strategic power, if not hegemony, is a viewpoint that has been long repressed, except perhaps in the business community, where a spade is called a spade.

Significantly, European businesspeople were among the leaders of the European-integration movement. Businesspeople generally act not out of altruism but out of self-interest. And indeed, the Common Market has been very good for European business. Whereas in 1958 only 29.6 percent of imports and 30.1 percent of exports by Common Market members came from other member nations, by 1970 imports reached 48.4 percent and exports 48.9 percent.[1] Common Market countries became more competitive in other parts of the world as well. While in 1959 an American company was the largest in the world in 11 out of 13 major economic sectors, by 1974 America dominated only 7 of those 13, having been displaced by foreign firms—two German, one French, one British–Dutch, one British, and one Japanese. During the same period America slipped from having 98 of the 156 largest firms in the 13 sectors to having 67, while Britain went from 15 to 17 and continental Europe from 25 to 40.[2] Within a decade after French writer Jean-Jacques Servan-Schreiber's warning in *The American Challenge* (1967) that American companies were about to sweep away weak European firms in Western Europe, a shift has occurred. Robert Heller and Norris Willatt's antithesis, *The European Revenge* (1975), observes that in 1967 the United States owned 27 percent of the world's financial reserves and Europe 58 percent, while by 1974 the American share had fallen to 13 percent and that of Europe (which had more than doubled in quantity) was 64 percent, or five times the American total.[3] Europe appeared to lose the war only to win the peace, with the United States providing capital, security, and support to nations that are now among its toughest competitors.

The success of the Common Market raises a number of political and economic questions with worldwide significance: If these nations continue to integrate economically and politically, will Europe's bargaining power lead to economic conflicts with the United States that have strategic implications? If the European movement disintegrates into nationalistic squabbles, will Europe's weakness cause more difficulties for Americans than its strengths would cause? What bargaining strategies do different nations use within the integration movement, and what are their implications? And is the European-integration movement imitable in other regions of the world as a way of organizing for greater bargaining power and cooperation, or is it a result of a unique historical situation and unusual prerequisites? Finally, does the trend toward redistributive politics that is built into Common Market structures imply that another stalemated European bureaucracy may be added to the existing red tape of Common Market members, making the politics of productivity increasingly difficult as the integration process continues?

THE COMMON MARKET'S POLITICAL CULTURE: MOTIVATIONS

The dream of European unity is an old one. The concept of European integration emerged twenty centuries ago with Julius Caesar's conquests of France, England, and the Lowlands, which were added to the Roman territories of Italy, Spain, and the Balkans.[4] Significantly, the Germanic tribes were not a part of this integrative process, the result being that much of modern Germany and most of the peoples settling there were never socialized by Roman law and did not absorb Roman culture.[5] The German *Weltanschauung* or world view was therefore distinctly different from neighboring "Latin" world views, contributing later to differences between these cultures' attitudes toward European integration and integrative strategies.

After the fall of the Roman Empire, the first person to attempt to reunite Europe politically was Charlemagne, the emperor of the Franks. Seven Germanic tribes, along with many other peoples, became incorporated into the Frankish Empire. Integrative experience was thus imposed upon the Germans from the outside. In 911, tired of outside manipulation and intrusion, the seven tribes made Conrad of Franconia their king.

For some time Europe remained hopelessly divided, with only the Roman Catholic Church, led by the popes, serving as a unifying force. One religion and a common civilization dominated the region, making disparate cultural and religious images more congruent. A common body of knowledge and the Latin language contributed to this integration of images. Moreover, the Mohammedan threat brought together many members of the European community for a series of military

expeditions, the Crusades. In the fifteenth century George of Podebrad, king of Bohemia, tried to stop the Turkish invasions by integrating Europe.*

The motivations for the European-integration movement and its regional (vs. national) political culture stemmed both from military and
economic threats outside Western Europe and from common cultural,
political, and economic traditions within the region. In his *Letters on a
Regicide Peace,* Edmund Burke noted the impressive cultural similarities
within Europe in comparison with non-European countries in the eigh-
teenth and early nineteenth centuries. These included autocracy (except Great Britain) and similar diplomatic customs; military and naval
organizations, strategy, and tactics; economic practices; and even ruling classes. Earlier, in *Perpetual Peace* (1794), philosopher Immanuel
Kant had made a complementary argument for homogeneity as a prerequisite for an optimum balance between stability and peace in the
European system, believing that such similarity would arise through a
prevalence of republican forms of government (i.e., separation of the
executive and legislative functions). Both Burke and Kant argued that
admitting dissimilar traditions (e.g., those of Turkey and the Ottoman
Empire) into the European system would be dangerous.

The history of Western European development thus provides the
tradition and rationale for a cultural, economic, and political integration movement on the one hand, while on the other it illustrates why
certain nations within Western Europe developed distinctly different
strategies for using the integration process for their own purposes.
National unity was consolidated much earlier in France and Britain
than it was in Germany and Italy, giving France and England distinct
"go-it-alone" tendencies based on their independent traditions. Paradoxically, the German and Italian failures to consolidate and go it
alone—in the early nineteenth century and in the Fascist fiascos of the
twentieth—made these nations more amenable to heavy involvement
in a regional bloc in which their "nationalist" needs could be met more
legitimately from the viewpoint of their neighbors. Historically, European integration is like a pair of scissors, coming together for mutual
interests and values in times of consensus only to spread apart again in
nationalistic traditions and bargaining patterns at opportunistic moments or in times of crisis.

The Germans, in particular, have never been forgiven for being late-
comers to the game of international colonizing: Bismarck was resented

*George of Podebrad derived this strategy from Pierre Dubois's *On the Reconquest of the
Holy Land,* the first book on European federation, which was published in 1306. Dubois
suggested that such integration could be accomplished by making the king of France the
chairman of a permanent council of princes, which, in turn, would nominate a supreme
court to mediate all European conflicts.

and Hitler justly hated. Stalin argued after World War II that Germany should be "broken up so that she could not reunite," for the Germans fight "like fierce beasts" and it was therefore necessary "to break up and scatter the German tribes."[6] Splitting Germany and Berlin in half after the war relieved part of the fear of German strength and efficiency felt by those who had fought against them. But some remained dissatisfied, and each nation had a different image of what it wanted in resolving "the German problem." The Russians and the French were interested primarily in being compensated for the damages and losses they had suffered, whereas the United States and Great Britain disliked the prospect of the heavy expenses implicit in long-term administration and economic support of their zones of occupation, and therefore wanted to create a self-sufficient German economy. The unofficial World War II settlement, and to some extent the Common Market, were largely positively flavored arrangements to dismember and coopt the Germans, disembodying them as much as possible militarily, politically, and psychologically and steering their energies into economics so that they could pay their war debts and stimulate European recovery. It is but a slight exaggeration to suggest that European integration and the Common Market are the direct results of a French strategy of diffusing the power of the coal- and steel-rich Ruhr district in northern Germany and letting West Germany develop into an industrial power on the condition that the Germans agree to subsidize French agriculture indefinitely.

Since its founding the European Community (EC—formerly the EEC) has raised the standard of living of the working class in member countries, and this has gained the support of the labor unions. Originally, of course, European businesspeople were at the forefront of the movement for European integration, meaning that support for the psycho-cultural values that the Common Market represents is spread throughout the social-class scale. Support for the EC among the mass publics of the original six members is overwhelming, whereas the populations of the three most recent members, Ireland, Britain, and Denmark, are largely opposed to further political integration in Western Europe.

In *The Silent Revolution*, Ronald Inglehart argues that the attitudes of people in the nine EEC members are not unhopeful, since they indicate broad-based support for further political integration among the original six members, a consensus spanning from left to right (from communists to Gaullists), and that with the passage of time and increasing prosperity one may expect an increasingly pro-European outlook among the skeptical publics of the new member nations. No one can doubt that the Common Market has already proved its ability to build a value consensus around a European political culture that transcends the mere sum of the political cultures of its members. Whether or not this value consensus is strong enough to persuade these nations to go against their political and economic interests on specific issues is another question.

THE COMMON MARKET'S SOCIAL AND POLITICAL INSTITUTIONS: STRUCTURES

The idealists maintain that the motivations behind the creation of the Common Market were basically cooperative, a process of nations giving up nationalism and short-term interests for supranationalism, or loyalty to symbols and organizations beyond the nation–state. Integration is a movement away from nationalism toward regionalism or internationalism, a shift away from the fragmentation of a region or the world of states and toward supranational unification. But the realists stress the national interests that motivate nations to join together in limited ways to maximize their own benefits more effectively than they could in isolation. Integration is not just an idealistic process but a strategic game.

In games of strategy, the best course of action for each player depends on what the other players do. Game theorists have identified two types of strategy game that are relevant to the Common Market: *zero-sum games*, in which one player gains exactly what the other player loses and cooperation is not rational (as in chess or checkers), and *variable-sum games*, in which there are options that pay off both players more for cooperating than either could gain by going it alone, at least in the long run (examples are the Strategic Arms Limitation Talks between the United States and USSR or the idealist's version of the Common Market). Whereas zero-sum games represent the struggle to get the biggest piece of the existing economic pie, variable-sum games suggest that it is more satisfying to cooperate and create more pie for everyone by using available means jointly rather than individually.[7] In these terms, the Common Market was based on France's "mixed" strategy of leaving the zero-sum game of war with the Germans behind and offering to play a variable-sum game, on the condition that France could play a subtle zero-sum game of its own within this cooperative framework in order to maximize French advantages.

The background that set the stage for the institutions of the European Community included two significant events that both occurred in 1948: the Convention for European Economic Cooperation, which established the Organization for European Economic Cooperation (OEEC) to distribute Marshall Plan funds, coordinate investment programs, and encourage intra-European trade; and the Hague Congress a month later, in which European federalists flocked together in a symbolic demonstration resulting in the establishment of the Council of Europe in Strasbourg, the first official political body of the hypothetical "united Europe." The cooperation manifested in the OEEC and the Council of Europe became the basis for the founding of the successful European Coal and Steel Community in 1952, much as the NATO alliance provided precedents of cooperation leading to the aborted plan for a European Defense Community during the same period.

Another decisive event for the process of European integration was the election of Konrad Adenauer as chancellor of the German Federal Republic in 1949. The uncontested leader of the Christian Democratic Union, Adenauer dominated German foreign policy with his advocacy of cooperation with the Western powers, anticommunism, and support of the "European idea" to replace a discredited nationalism, even if it meant sacrificing German reunification. But the German masses were more nationalistic than the elite group Adenauer represented, and in 1954 Adenauer noted that the pro-Europeanists among the German and French elites were also a minority:

> The French nationalists are just as ready as the German to repeat the old policies, in spite of past experience. They would rather have a Germany with a national army than a united Europe—so long as they can pursue their own policy with the Russians. And the German nationalists think exactly the same way; they are ready to go with the Russians. . . . Believe me, the danger of German nationalism is much greater than is realized. The crisis of European policy emboldens the nationalists, they are becoming self-confident, and winning supporters. . . . Make use of the time while I am still alive, because when I am no more it will be too late—my God, I do not know what my successors will do if they are left to themselves; if they are not obliged to follow along firmly preordained lines, if they are not bound to a united Europe.[8]

At the beginning of the Adenauer era, the Germans were concerned with reducing occupation restrictions (such as the dismantling of German industries, occupation costs, and regaining control of the International Ruhr Authority) and with improving Franco–German relations. Adenauer successfully cultivated public support for German membership in the Council of Europe and used interviews with foreign journalists to suggest foreign-policy initiatives that would stimulate European integration. In 1950 he used such an interview to advocate the desirability of a customs union between France and Germany as a step toward full political integration. French Foreign Minister Robert Schuman then proposed the "Schuman Plan" for pooling German and French coal and steel production, which would be open to other regional members as a first step toward a European federation. Coal and steel are important strategic industries, and Schuman was no doubt aware of the advantages of "controlling" the rich Ruhr resources of northern Germany through his "sharing" proposal.

The result was the pioneering European Coal and Steel Community (ECSC), founded in 1952. The six ECSC member states (later called "The Six" when they formed the Common Market) included West Germany, France, Italy, Holland, Belgium, and Luxemburg. The ECSC abolished customs duties and restrictions as well as dual pricing systems and transport rates for coal, coke, iron ore, steel, and scrap for all Community members. It was responsible for production targets and investment programs. Moreover, the organization became a model for "codetermination" (worker participation in management decision making) policies for West Germany and other European countries. In an effort to head off the dismantling and nationalization of German industries that had been tainted by Nazi leadership, Adenauer promised the unions that the workers would have a major voice in running private companies. In the ECSC coal and steel industries, this resulted in workers' being allowed to elect 50% of the membership of the supervisory boards compared to 33% of the seats in the rest of German industry.

The ECSC founded four institutions that were the precursors of similar Common Market institutions: the High Authority, the Council of Ministers, the Common Assembly, and a Court of Justice. The High Authority (corresponding to the Common Market or EEC's Commission) was an executive body made up of nine members representing the member countries (with two each for France and West Germany) that could legislate binding decisions and issue recommendations and opinions. For example, the High Authority had the power to make loans and dismantle cartels without the consent of the Council of Ministers, and it represented "supranationalism" insofar as it could levy taxes on business turnover of coal and steel. The Council of Ministers (similar to the EEC's Council of Ministers) represented the national interests of member nations through their ministers of trade, industry, or finance, providing a counterpoint to the High Authority. The Common Assembly (corresponding to the EEC's European Parliament) possessed only consultative powers. And the Court of Justice (similar to the EEC's Court of Justice) could make authoritative decisions on matters related to the treaty on which the ECSC was based; these cases were brought before it either by the High Authority or by individual business firms.

In strategic terms, the formation of the ECSC was based on a French–West German axis of power, allowing Germany to develop into an industrial power and giving France the right to share and partially control this development. This French–German axis became the linchpin for the creation of the Common Market through the Treaty of Rome in 1957. Other groups and individuals, such as Jean Monnet's

Action Committee for the United States of Europe and European feder-alist Paul-Henri Spaak, wanted a more idealistic, supranational Euro-pean federation, a true political integration as well as a functional eco-nomic arrangement. But de Gaulle later opposed this "Europeanist" vision, believing in a Europe of separate states, each of which pre-served its own sovereignty and cultural uniqueness:

> Europe can never be a living reality if it does not include France with its Frenchmen, Germany with its Germans, Italy with its Italians, etc. Dante, Goethe, Chateaubriand, belong to all Europe to the very extent that they are, respectively and eminently, Italian, German, and French. They would not have served Europe if they had been countryless, of if they had thought and written in some integrated "esperanto" or "volapük."[9]

De Gaulle went on to criticize regional organizations, claiming that they worked only in noncrisis situations and that vital conflicts were always a question of national, not supranational, policy. In the end, de Gaulle's strategy for France was as brilliant as it was subtle: if Euro-pean integration was inevitable in the postwar atmosphere, he would play the European game as much as possible by French rules, maximiz-ing French national interests in the short run even if that meant coop-erating in the long run. De Gaulle gambled that he could have his cake and eat it too, and history has yet to refute this controversial bargain-ing stance.[10]

In game theory terms, de Gaulle wanted as much of the existing economic pie as possible for France even if it meant zero-sum national conflicts, whereas the Europeanists, represented by the Germans try-ing to live down their nationalist past and the small northern countries whose leaders saw greater productive potential in group efforts than national programs, argued that variable-sum game thinking would lead to the creation of more economic pie. De Gaulle had astutely negoti-ated France into a position in which his nation won whether the Euro-peanists were right or wrong. Knowing that Adenauer's policy was based on French–German reconciliation, de Gaulle used this policy to the hilt to get Adenauer to go along with many of his "Europe of separate states" proposals. He proposed the formation of a permanent political secretariat for the six EEC members and of coordinating com-missions to harmonize policy in various ministries. The Europeanists responded by asking whether Europe was to become a French Europe or a European France. Despite Adenauer's support, the Belgians and the Dutch finally blocked Gaullist proposals, led by Paul-Henri Spaak. This frustrated de Gaulle but did not change his mind. His determina-tion became clear when he vetoed British membership in the Common Market in 1963, arguing that Britain's cultural, economic, and political traditions and viewpoints were too dissimilar from those of the continental "Six."

The basic aim of the Common Market was to progressively reduce all trade barriers between its members, abolishing them completely within a twelve- to fifteen-year period. It has succeeded in this objective, although it has been less successful with its other targets: harmonizing agricultural, transport, and social policies and creating a common currency. So effective was the EEC at reducing trade barriers that Europe became a formidable economic bloc, presenting a common tariff to those outside the Community and coordinating one of the most highly developed concentrations of agriculture, commerce, and industry in the world, with a population of about 200 million.

Nations that were not members of the Common Market were confronted with a significant political-economic problem when they came up against the collective bargaining clout and conditions made possible by EEC solidarity. In 1959, led by Reginald Maulding, the British paymaster-general, "The Seven" (Britain, Austria, Denmark, Norway, Portugal, Sweden, and Switzerland) worked out a European Free Trade Association (EFTA) to counter the EEC. However, EFTA's purposes were limited to reducing and eventually abolishing tariffs and other trade restrictions between EFTA members; it did not aim to establish a common policy toward the outside world.

EFTA, plagued by Britain's problems with its Commonwealth ties to its former colonies, was not nearly as successful as the EEC, and Britain soon applied for Common Market membership. The Benelux countries (Belgium, the Netherlands, and Luxemburg) were in favor of British membership, figuring that Britain would protect the smaller members against the Franco–German axis. The Germans supported British entry, thinking it might end the division of Europe into competing trade blocs and knowing that Germany would stand to gain greatly from trade with Britain and the Commonwealth. Significantly, at the time West German trade with the EFTA "Seven" amounted to more than three times the sum of French trade with the same countries. And French imports from EFTA totaled only slightly more than one quarter of Germany's.[11] The negative French position toward British membership may be understood not only in terms of the cultural and philosophical colors in which de Gaulle wrapped the issue but also in terms of political-economic payoffs: West Germany stood to gain much more than France from British membership, and this economic difference might dilute the French ability to influence EEC decision making through the French–German axis. Similar cost–benefit calculations were behind de Gaulle's reluctant participation in NATO: if the United States and NATO's protection of France was inevitable if the Soviets should attack, why should not France withdraw from NATO's military branches and costs, maximizing French benefits and independence while risking little in terms of real security? Postwar European politics have been dominated by this basic French strategy of maximizing short-term national gains while negotiating long-term payments to the community—an astute use of zero-sum tactics in a variable-sum game that tilts the rules toward the French position.*

In 1973 three more nations joined the Common Market after difficult negotiations: the United Kingdom, Ireland, and Denmark. "The Six" became "The Nine," a bargaining unit with great political and economic potential that is larger than the United States in a number of ways: area (square miles), population, civilian employment, exports, number of automobiles produced, and the size of the merchant marine. By increasing the size of the Common Market, the French may have anticipated that the organization's supranational powers may be diluted, particularly if Greece, Portugal, and Spain (currently "associate members") become full-fledged members in the next decade, as has politically already been decided. This dilution of central authority may also be a hidden reason for the United States' support of Common Market expansion, in addition to the positive goal of coopting an increasing number of countries into a permanent commitment to Western democracy and free-trade and market economy principles. A diluted economic bloc may appear less threatening to nations within it that are worried about their sovereignty and independence, as well as to nations outside it that are worried about its competitive clout on the world market.

A representative sample of some of the accomplishments of the Common Market to date may indicate its potential power as a united bloc in the political economy of the world. These accomplishments are the elimination of all tariffs among The Six and eventually among The Nine; a common external tariff; a common agricultural market with provision for outsiders importing agricultural goods to pay the difference between the EEC price and their own price to a Common Fund; free movement of workers within the community; positive discrimination for Community workers over non-Community workers; the slow harmonization of national social policies; freedom of capital to flow from one member to another for direct securities investments; movement toward harmonization of tax practices and the establishment of a central bank; harmonization of transportation rates and practices where possible; and the establishment of a Community Social Fund to help relocate and retrain workers.

More than the French, the Germans, the English, and the other national members might like to admit, the collective values and activi-

---

*Jean Monnet and Robert Schuman are short-term exceptions to this rule.

ties of the Common Market are slowly building up a "European" political culture that is more than the sum of its parts. In short, the functionalist thesis of European integration is at least partially accurate: the notion that if they cooperate on "nonpolitical" functional needs, such as economic conditions, European nations will find that there is an automatic "spillover" from functional to political cooperation that will prepare the way for political unification. The difficulty, of course, is that the economic and the political cannot easily be separated from one another in the first place and, as indicated earlier, economic cooperation has often been a result of political and strategic thinking. It makes more sense to view the integration process as political-economic learning behavior: the more my nation benefits in the short and long term from integration in both standard of living and political significance in the world, the more I will support the process; the converse is also true. Public and elite opinion poll data appear to confirm this hypothesis, indicating that the longer a nation has been a member of the Common Market, the more its people believe the unification of Europe should be either speeded up or continued at the present rate rather than slowed down.[12]

THE GOVERNMENT FRAMEWORK AND PARTY SYSTEM

The political culture of the European Community—the Common Market, the European Coal and Steel Community, and the European Atomic Energy Commission combined—is reflected in a number of institutional structures with increasing economic and political significance. More than 9,000 civil servants based in the Brussels headquarters work for the institutions of the Common Market alone. The most supranational institution of the Common Market framework is the European Commission, the executive or federal authority made up of thirteen members appointed by the nine member governments: two each from West Germany, France, Italy, and England, and one from each of the five smaller countries. A president and five vice presidents are appointed for two-year periods by the member governments. Each commissioner has a four-year term and is expected to represent the supranational interests of the European Community as a whole. The Commission and its staff are often referred to as "Eurocrats"—politically active bureaucrats who are expected to suppress their own national interests for the sake of the Community. The Commission initiates and executes policy decisions and oversees their enforcement.

However, the policy-making body of the Common Market is the Council of Ministers, made up of the ministers of the member states.

This represents the national arm of the international organization, and different ministers attend various Council meetings depending on the issue at hand (e.g., transportation ministers meet on transport problems). These ministers either accept or reject Commission proposals and can make amendments only through a unanimous vote. But in an increasing number of cases Commission propositions can be made binding on all Community members through a weighted-majority vote in the Council of Ministers. In the enlarged institution this weighting is broken down as follows: 10 votes for France, West Germany, England, and Italy; 5 for Holland and Belgium; 3 for Denmark and Ireland; and 2 for Luxemburg. Forty-one votes of the 58-vote total are required for a resolution to pass in this qualified-majority system. The shift from unanimous voting to weighted-majority voting for an increasing number of decisions may be viewed as a concrete measure of growing supranationalism or integration.

Another possible sign of spreading supranationalism is the direct election of the European Parliament in 1979, in contrast to the old system in which parliamentary representatives were appointed by member states, each according to its own national procedures. Again, the number of representatives for each country is weighted: West Germany, France, Britain, and Italy each have eighty-one members; Holland, twenty-five; Belgium, twenty-four; Denmark sixteen; Ireland, sixteen; and Luxemburg six. Although the Parliament has only consultative power, party loyalties cut across national lines and Socialists, Christian Democrats, Communists, Liberals, Conservatives, and Progressives cooperate to work out "party positions" on important issues. The election of national "political stars" to the Parliament brings it prestige. Furthermore, some national parties—such as the Socialists in Italy—have tried to increase their support at home through a strong "European" showing.

The first European parliamentary election served to consolidate the trend toward the center-right in European national elections of the late 1970s. The Christian Democrats registered significant gains in West Germany, the Netherlands, Belgium, and Luxemburg, while the French marked a victory for the centrist supporters of President Valéry Giscard d'Estaing.* The British Conservatives made sweeping gains, following the national election pattern of 1979 that resulted in the election of Tory Margaret Thatcher as British prime minister. However, the British result in the European elections must be taken somewhat with a grain of salt due to the winner-take-almost-all approach of assigning

*This victory was marred when the French election committee gave almost 100,000 votes and one seat received by the Socialists to Giscard's UDF, leading Mitterand to quit the seat he had won in protest.

seats used by only Great Britain and the Danish constituency of Greenland. Thus, with less than 50 percent of the popular vote, the Conservatives took three out of every four British seats in the European Assembly. Had the British used the prevailing system of proportional representation, the Liberals, with 12 percent of the vote, would have won nine to ten seats in the European Parliament rather than none. In Italy the trend of the national elections held ten days before the European contest was confirmed: both the Christian Democrats and Communists slipped in support, while the pro-European Socialists moved from 9.8 to 11 percent of the votes cast in the high Italian turnout for Europe—86 percent of the eligible voters (in contrast, less than one out of three eligible British electors bothered to vote). Officially, the Parliament has the power to censure the Commission and force it from office. But this power is more apparent than real, since it has never been used. The committee work, plenary sessions, and reports no doubt stimulate European integration through socialization if nothing else. But to the idealist's claim that the new, directly elected Parliament is the first real political step toward a United States of Europe the realist will answer that the Parliament—like most parliaments—is but a political smokescreen behind which national elites make the real decisions.

The other major institution of the Common Market is the European Court of Justice, which is responsible for settling disputes arising under the Treaty of Rome, the document that established the Common Market. The Court accepts cases from member states, business firms, the European Commission, and individuals. Nine justices make majority decisions on the cases that come to the Court, and can impose fines to enforce those decisions. A fundamental aim of the Court in terms of integration is to develop a body of "community law," of enforceable supranational principles that are accepted as legitimate norms to which all members adhere. Community law, in the Court's eyes, must take precedence over national law. The Court represents the superego of the European Community, and to the extent that its word is accepted by all Community members as sovereign authority, European integration and unity will be furthered by its existence.

POLITICAL-ECONOMIC CODES: COMMON MARKET BARGAINING BEHAVIOR

The promise of the European ideology of a United States of Europe and the legal and institutional steps toward making this supranational vision concrete have distracted many people from the tough bargaining and strategic implications hidden beneath the rhetoric and structures of the Common Market. The EEC was created through the strategies of national leaders and will have political and economic significance only to the extent that national leaders believe that the payoffs of more integration are greater than the benefits of going it alone on specific issues. The Gaullist thrust highlights a certain truth: national leaders ask themselves how the Common Market can be used to maximize specific advantages for their own people and what integrative steps should be opposed because they imply more costs than benefits for their national constituencies.

The Common Market represents a variable-sum game in which "mixed strategies" are most appropriate, a "prisoner's dilemma" that continually tests national philosophies of risk, trust, patience, time, and individual payoffs. The following oversimplified game, the "integration dilemma," serves as a metaphor illustrating the nuances of bargaining strategy in Common Market negotiations.*

Assume for a moment that in a particular Common Market negotiation two countries—say, France and Germany—each have two choices whose payoffs depend on what the other nation chooses. In the following situation the first payoff in each case is that of F and the second that of G.

	Go it alone G_1	Integrate G_2
Go it alone F_1	−5,−5	10,−10
Integrate F_2	−10, 10	5, 5

NOTE: F = France, G = Germany; amounts in billions.

Now let F_1 and G_1 stand for "go it alone" and F_2 and G_2 for "integrate" (or cooperate). If you represented France, what would you do? If you trusted Germany and believed that the Germans will always be consistent, you would probably select F_2, assuming that the Germans would do likewise, netting each of you 5 billion Eurodollars. Or would you? If Germany goes for broke, aiming at the maximum German payoff of 10 billion Eurodollars by choosing G_1, France loses 10 billion by aiming to integrate or cooperate (F_2). But if both nations "go it alone" on the issue, each will be sure to lose 5 billion Eurodollars (F_1,G_1) in every round of negotiations, rather than picking up 5 billion each by integrating or cooperating consistently over time (F_2,G_2).

If you divide people into two groups to play this game and do not let them communicate, you will probably discover that the most frequent outcome is F_1G_1, implying that neither group trusts the other not to take advantage of the integrative setup, even if each side repeatedly loses 5 billion. If you change the rules and let the groups communicate and negotiate with each other, the outcomes may be more varied as

*This is meant merely as an illustrative metaphor to represent kinds of thinking and their collective consequences: it is by no means a closed game of precise payoffs as in formal theory.

attempts are made to strike a deal. But it is still necessary to trust the other side. Rationality (i.e., aiming only for the greatest individual gain regardless of the other parties involved) always produces a less-than-optimum outcome for all concerned if everyone thinks this way.

The theory of European integration maintains that by cooperating over time nations will learn to trust each other and will provide sanctions for black-sheep members who go their own way on critical issues. Yet theory is often different from practice, as the 1973 oil embargo crisis illustrated: France decided to "go it alone" and negotiate its own deal for oil supplies, followed by Germany, Great Britain, and Italy. Each country selfishly negotiated for the best bilateral deal it could get with the Middle Eastern suppliers, regardless of the consequences for other member states or the Community as a whole. By negotiating as a bloc, Common Market countries may have been able to get a better deal or, at minimum, to create a stable basis for oil supply over time (a critical need, since the Community imports about 90 percent of its oil). But impatient nationalism aimed at the short-term needs of a particular group undermined a more cooperative strategy, tilting the game toward a zero-sum conflict of all against all rather than the variable-sum strategy that would have been more appropriate. The benefits of such cooperation were illustrated in the 1979 EEC commitment to limit daily oil imports from outside the Community to 9.4 million barrels per day (based on privileged access to Britain's North Sea oil, which led Britain to slow its growth for the sake of the EEC).

The "French tilt" is a variation on this go-it-alone strategy. By alternating at opportune moments between "go-it-alone" and "integration" strategies, the French have often managed to gain unusual short-term benefits without losing the long-term advantages of integration. De Gaulle used this approach, trading French acquiescence to integration for concessions to the French position in other issues, such as agricultural subsidies. If one experiments with the integration dilemma game just described, one finds that the first party to successfully achieve the maximum amount possible in a round can continue to maintain the advantage gained by simply sitting on the "go-it-alone" strategy. The French have effectively used a version of this strategy to "tilt" the game of European integration in their favor with little apparent material cost in the long run, no matter what kind of temporary animosity is stirred up.

Another example is France's shifting in and out of "the snake," a 1972 agreement by "The Six" to maintain a 2.25 percent margin restriction in the fluctuation of Community currencies.* Italy was the first

---

*This means that each member country to the agreement agrees to limit the change of the value of its currency to 2.25 percent either above or below the initial agreed-on par value by government intervention to stabilize the currency in question.

country to break this agreement: in 1973, challenged by an outflow of capital, it let the lira float. In 1974 the French government floated the franc and halted interventions on the exchange markets for six months. It returned to the snake in 1975 under certain conditions, but later it pulled out again.[13]

It is, of course, unfair to single out the French for using a nationalistic bargaining strategy in the European-integration game when in fact all the members of the EEC have used such mixed strategies. The British and the Irish refused to enter the snake in the first place; the Italians have been adept at getting the Community to subsidize their economy without reforming it; and the Germans have used the ideology of Europeanism as a front for their quiet build-up of economic and conventional military power. Yet the French have appeared to use this mixed strategy more consciously, if not more effectively, than the rest, justifying the label "the French tilt" for the natural outgrowth of the Gaullist vision of a Europe of loosely integrated (more loose than integrated) sovereign states. By using the mixed strategy first and consistently, the French have refurbished their reputation as shrewd diplomats and seem to have tilted the ground rules of the Common Market firmly in their direction.

Many other theories of Common Market integration strategies exist. The German scholar Hartmut Berg, for example, has identified three such strategies: integration-through-competition, the "Community method," and coordination of national economic policies.[14] The integration-through-competition strategy is flawed since, despite the elimination of protective tariffs, oligopolistic markets continue to prevent meaningful economic integration—these markets can be countered only by developing large corporations that are capable of competing with American firms. Stronger Common Market regulation of mergers could help this strategy along. The "Community method" strategy of relying on existing Common Market institutions is also faulty, for the Council of Ministers is apt to either settle for the lowest common denominator of agreement or not make any decision at all. Hence, this serves to preserve and maintain existing institutional structures and bureaucracies without forcing them to adapt effectively to change or breaking new ground toward integrative supranationality. As the 1975 report to the Trilateral Commission on "The Governability of Democracies" suggested, European integration may have served to reinforce national bureaucracies, making meaningful adaptation or unity impossible to achieve.[15] The third strategy, coordination of national economic policies, is the only effective one. Here integration is viewed as a learning process in which nations with successful international strategies will be imitated by those with less successful approaches. The only difficulty with this view of integration is that it might imply that other members should mimic the successful "French tilt," making all members less well off in the long run (with the French in the relatively best position for cashing in first on the tilt strategy).

Fortunately, however, not all the French people believe the French tilt is the optimum strategy for them. Jean-Claude Morel, director of economic structure and development at the European Community's Directorate General for Economic and Financial Affairs in Brussels, argues that Common Market nations should mimic the German model, not the French. Morel claims that the West German elite was destroyed in World War II, a social revolution that created a strong sense of unity and social consciousness. Spending in West Germany has therefore been directed toward social objectives, and social discipline, with the aid of a powerful central bank, has made it possible to control inflation. Inflation is as much a question of stability and a unified national social conscience as an economic question. Therefore, other Common Market countries should mimic West Germany's social-market economy and avoid the clientelism of Italy. The success of labor participation in management through the German codetermination policy (*Mitbestimmung*) is another sign of Germany's underlying social cohesion and its people's willingness to give in for the "social good," which helps keep inflation in check.

With skyrocketing energy costs, inflation has become the existential theme of the *fin de siècle*. In advanced industrial societies, technical debates about monetary and cost-push causes of rising prices have been overwhelmed by public protests and tax revolts. Meanwhile, national policy makers overload the economic system with liquidity by printing paper money and providing generous credit. Voters, unions, bureaucrats, and politicians all maximize their personal interests as much as they can, stimulating injections of money into the system. Inflation appears as an individualist scar in the superego of capitalist societies, resulting in part from the high expectations promised by quasi-free-market systems, and representing a cover for the social costs of the gap between the demands of individual maximizing behavior and the ability of democratic political economies to satisfy these demands. To go against the mainstream "redistribution ideology" of inflation is perceived as nondemocratic and technocratic, especially by formerly dominated interest groups, such as the working class, in a decaying status order. Anti-inflation policies will be unpopular in the short run and intolerable in the long run unless national governments can persuade their peoples that only social cohesion and sacrifice can guarantee their future economic prosperity. The German domestic model alone will not inspire such sacrifice without clear Community payoffs to stabilize energy consumption and double-digit inflation rates.

It is not just the West German conservative consciousness and propensity to save. The idealistic functionalist thesis of going from economic cooperation to political cooperation may become obsolete: without political union, monetary union means nothing, and without social consciousness and cohesion, political union is impossible. The primacy of the West German model helps explain why the snake initially became a "DMZ" (Deutschmark zone), a "private enterprise" made up basically of Germany, Denmark, and Austria rather than a fixed exchange rate system within the Common Market, as it was initially intended to be.[16] Perhaps the 1978 French–German plan for EEC monetary coordination, and a workable "snake" (the "European monetary system") is in part a French attempt to share in (i.e., partially control) the DMZ before it becomes too strong, much as the ECSC was a French means of sharing the rich German Ruhr area.

DOMESTIC AND FOREIGN POLICY: COLLECTIVE DECISION MAKING

One great advantage of the Common Market is its attempt to systematically collect uniform information about its member countries as a basis for efforts to harmonize their governmental and social policies. All of the members are advanced, industrialized Western democracies with many similarities, but their differences may be more striking. For example, although France, West Germany, England, and Italy are all counted as "large members" in terms of voting quotas, France and West Germany dominate the Community politically.

After its initial economic success the Common Market focused increasingly on the politics of redistribution, or "social policy," assuming perhaps that a certain amount of productivity could be taken for granted to pay for such redistribution. However, the economic crises of the 1970s put all such assumptions in doubt as economic growth stagnated, unemployment exploded into a major issue, and inflation seemed beyond the control of everyone but the Germans. In the late twentieth century advanced industrial democracies in the Western world seem to be fated to experience an endemic war between the politics of productivity and the politics of redistribution, between the profit, growth, and freedom motives and the welfare, equal-opportunity, and social-justice motives. And even if the Common Market resolves this tension in terms of some policy of dynamic equilibrium within the Community, the question remains of how much wealth and good will will be left over to distribute to less advantaged areas, when domestic social costs are skyrocketing and economic forecasts are gloomy. The Common Market, in short, is making foreign policy as well as domestic commitments when its members decide on certain trade-offs between productivity and redistribution, between industrial policy and social policy.

Social Policy in the Common Market: The Redistribution Motive

By the late 1970s total unemployment in the Common Market countries, primarily among young workers and migrant workers, reached 6 million, while consumer prices were rising about 10.7 percent per year on the average. Those from the least favored social strata, with inadequate vocational training or an educational background that is inappropriate for the job market, were hit hardest by unemployment. After two decades of using some 10 million foreign workers to supplement their labor forces, the Common Market countries began to send them home. Taking the initiative, West Germany passed labor legislation contradicting the free-labor-market principles of the Community. Unemployment continued to climb in the late 1970s as the Europeans entered a period that most economists believe will be characterized by slower economic growth. Between 1973 and 1976 alone, the number of people under 25 looking for jobs doubled, accounting for one-third of total unemployment in the nine EEC countries.[17] Such conditions do not serve to deter crime, violence, and extremist politics in advanced industrial democracies where the promise is often greater than the fulfillment. At a 1976 conference in Luxemburg, some 200 members of the European Community nations, employers' associations, and labor unions established a goal of full employment within "The Nine" by 1980. But again, the promise appears to have been greater than the reality. Full employment in the Common Market would require not merely an upturn in the European economic situation but new investments in member countries and a favorable climate for new private investment.[18] Social demands stimulated by frustrated life chances increase as the economic prerequisites for fulfilling them wither away.

Some idea of the comparative potential and social problems of the nine members of the Common Market can be derived from table 6-1.

Although the figures in table 6-1 give a general idea of the EEC's unemployment and inflation patterns, table 6-2 makes it easier to understand how the cost of living affects the life style of those who are fortunate enough to work.

The data make it clear that heavy drinkers should spend their time in the Benelux countries, where the work/consumption ratio is best. Those who must drive while drinking should stay in Denmark as much as possible, as gasoline costs are lowest there. The reputed Irish capacity for drinking remains mysterious until one realizes that it is, after all, demand that drives up prices for beer and whiskey. And steak eaters had best go Dutch and steer clear of Italy.

Table 6-1 Unemployment and Inflation in Common Market Countries

Country	Area (100 km²)	Population (millions)	Unemployed (August 1979)	Rise in Consumer Prices, 1975–1979	Rise in Wage Costs, 1975–1979
France	547.0	53.3	1.3 million	45.9%	60.3%
Italy	301.3	56.69	1.6 million	78.6%	102.8%
West Germany	248.6	61.3	799,000	17.1%	23.3%
Great Britain	244.0	55.88	1.45 million	71.4%	56.6%
Ireland	70.3	3.22	89,000	59.8%	56.9% (Sept. 1978)
Denmark	43.1	5.1	122,000	47.3%	47.3%
Holland	40.8	13.9	218,000	26.4%	35.6%
Belgium	30.5	9.8	381,000	27.9%	41.4%
Luxemburg	2.6	.358	9,000	26.4%	35.6% (Sept. 1978)
Common Market	1528.2	259.65	5.96 million	46.8%	42% (Sept. 1978)

Source: Eurostatistics Eurostat, Luxemburg (September, 1979).

Table 6-2 Number of Hours (h), Minutes ('), and Seconds (") of Work Needed to Purchase Various Items

	1 l Milk	1 l Beer (Gravity 1040/1049)	1 l Gas (Premium)	1 l Whiskey (Ordinary Brand)	1 kg Beef (Sirloin)	1 kg Salted Pasteurized Butter
West Germany	5'43"	18'11"	5'15"	2h19'22"	2h23'40"	57'8"
France	7'37"	13'47"	8'46"	3h53'18"	2h45'53"	1h20'11"
Italy	9'12"	21'5"	11'2"	3h21'39"	3h4'14"	1h49'20"
Netherlands	5'22"	9'16"	5'50"	1h 4'28"	1h40'0"	1h1'43"
Belgium	5'12"	10'53"	5'31"	2h8'2"	2h0'2"	54'23"
Luxemburg	6'13"	9'6"	4'23"	1h35'10"	1h47'31"	53'50"
United Kingdom	6'43"	24'5"	6'57"	3h29'18"	2h26'4"	35'20"
Ireland	5'44"	28'30"	7'55"	h6'11"	1h43'10"	43'39"
Denmark	4'11"	13'8"	4'13"	3h15'52"	2h16'33"	39'14"

Source: European Commission, reply to a question from a European member of Parliament in October 1975. *European Report,* as cited in *Economic and Monetary Affairs,* no. 421 (May 28, 1977).

In examining such comparative data the members of the Common Market concluded that the good things of everyday life should be spread out more and the bad things diluted—a politics of redistribution. Therefore, a European Social Fund was set up to better the conditions of workers, particularly in less advantaged regions; to ameliorate structural unemployment and retrain workers to adapt to changing market conditions; to improve opportunities for working women, and to harmonize health and welfare programs for people throughout the European Community.[19] The Social Fund was initially set up under the Treaty of Rome to help raise the standard of living and mobility of workers within the Community, drawing on the ECSC's experience with a similar fund (which anticipated job surpluses and paid workers for up to two years while they were waiting for jobs). In the Common Market's Social Fund Community members pay a fixed scale of contributions, the bigger and richer nations paying more (France and Germany each pay 32 percent, Italy 20 percent, and the Netherlands 7 percent.)[20] In the 1970s Italy has received much support from the fund for the retraining and resettlement of workers, particularly in its southern region. In addition to Italy's Mezzogiorno, the European Commission has singled out other regions with low living standards or underemployment problems for coordinated redistributive aid and national-policy harmonization. These are western France, the eastern frontier area of West Germany (*Zonenrandgebiete*), northern and western England, the whole of Ireland, the northwest and southeast of Denmark.[21]

The budget of the European Social Fund amounts only to about $250 million out of a general Common Market budget approaching $5 billion. Most of the budget goes for supporting farm prices, which is part of the policy of protecting European farmers from competition outside the Community (e.g., efficient American farmers). Such policies give French farmers a competitive edge in the Common Market, since they are the most efficient farmers in Europe. Over $400 million is allowed for the activities of the Commission, the Council of Ministers, the Parliament, the Court of Justice, and an atomic-research program. Therefore, most of the money under Common Market control goes toward administrative costs rather than the funding of policies initiated by the Common Market itself. However, the Social Fund and the EC's ability to give food aid to needy regions are redistributive patterns that are likely to take on increasing importance in the future in an egalitarian age. The Commission has recently been granted 1 percent of the value-added tax, a kind of sales tax collected by member nations. The Common Agricultural Policy (CAP) is another source of income. The Community now takes in over $9 billion annually, a concrete basis for optimism for many supranational Europeanists. But except for the amount going explicitly to the Commission and EEC organs for administrative costs and programs, all other moneys must be approved by the Council of Ministers before they may be spent. Still, since 1978 the European Community has had a budget financed entirely from sources of income belonging to the Community, and the right to raise taxes on the general public is seen by many people in Western Europe as a basic aspect of sovereignty.

Public expenditure by members of the Community in 1975, another indicator of redistributive politics, was about 45 percent of the gross product of the Common Market as a whole. In comparison, expenditure by all Community institutions is but 0.7 percent. Per capita incomes are as unequal among the nine member nations as they are among the various regions within them. Equalizing effects of public expenditure and taxation reduce regional inequalities by about 40 percent on the average in the European and Western industrial democracies, according to a Common Market study of public financing (comparing five federations—West Germany, the United States, Canada, Australia, Switzerland—and three unitary states—France, Italy, and the United Kingdom). The report concludes that

> the redistributive power between member-states of the Community's finances, by comparison, is—not surprisingly—very small indeed (1%); partly because the Community budget is relatively so small, partly because the expenditures and revenues of the Community have a weak geographical redistributive power per unit of account. . . . As well as redistributing income regionally on a continuing basis, public finance in existing economic unions plays a major role in cushioning short-term and cyclical fluctuations. For example, one-half to two-thirds of a short-term loss of primary income in a region due to a fall in its external sales may be automatically offset through lower payments of taxes and insurance contributions to the center, and higher receipts of unemployment and other benefits. If only because the Community budget is so relatively very small there is no such mechanism in operation on any significant scale as between member countries, and this is an important reason why in present circumstances monetary union is impracticable.[22]

One fascinating conclusion that could be drawn from this report on public financing in European integration is that government efforts toward redistribution in unitary states with strong central controls, such as France, Italy, and the United Kingdom, tend to go largely unnoticed, since they involve automatic deductions from taxes and more welfare payments. In federal systems, such as West Germany, on the other hand, government actions for redistribution are argued publicly all up and down the system at the federal, state, and local levels so that by the time the funds are allocated for specific projects the public has been made aware of them through the media.

This contrast suggests a hypothesis that would help explain why some southern European states had movements to the left in the 1970s whereas attitudes in some northern European states tended to move to the right: not being aware of the redistributive efforts actually made by unitary governments in the south (particularly in France and Italy), many people may have concluded that not enough was being done for redistribution and social justice. As a result they turned to the socialists and communists. On the other hand, seeing too much of the problems of redistribution and the costs of such programs to the taxpayer, people in federal systems like West Germany may have been stimulated to turn to the conservatives to monitor and cut public spending. Western Europeans want the benefits of public spending without paying the taxes to support them, as seems to be the case in the United States, where taxes are generally lower than in Europe. The average rate of sales taxes in Common Market countries is 15%, compared to 8% in the United States, and social security accounts for about 30 percent of total tax receipts in Europe (more than 40 percent in France and Italy) compared to 23 percent in the United States.[23] The governments of southern European countries with high percentages of self-employed people and farmers find that taxes are harder to collect; hence, they rely more on indirect taxes levied by employers. And tax evasion in northern Europe is rapidly becoming a national pastime as journalists ask to be paid in Scotch and handymen ask for cash, not traceable checks. In short, Europeans increasingly seem to perceive cradle-to-grave security provided by the state as a right, while resisting the taxes required to pay for such security.

Industrial Policy in the Common Market: The Productivity Motive

When people want more social benefits provided by the community without additional cost to themselves, inflation is stimulated, government bureaucracy is increased, and industrial productivity is dampened by taxes and red tape. While Europe has demonstrated that there *is* such a thing as a free lunch, the productive managers and entrepreneurs capable of producing all the extra lunches required have been emigrating out of Europe in increasing numbers, seeking new opportunities where business flexibility is greater and the tax bite less severe. Small wonder that the number and scope of European multinational corporations have increased greatly in the 1970s.

Common Market governments have increased their spending and taxing as a percentage of their gross national product. The primary cause of this increase has been the growth in transfer payments—pension and unemployment payments, subsidies for industries, and so forth. Such payments are actually made through the private sector and provide a growing portion of its income. Consumption makes up most of the gross domestic product of European countries, investment being the other major factor. But investments are made largely by the private sector and depend on investor confidence in domestic political economies where such investments are to be made, as well as on tax rates, worker fringe benefits, and other risks that threaten profits. The crucial question for Western political economies in the late twentieth century is, At what point does the growth of transfer payments overwhelm the conditions necessary for the economic growth and productivity required to pay for them?

In political-economic terms, advanced Western European societies are characterized by private consumption on the one hand and increasing public ownership of critical industries on the other.[24] One major difficulty with Europe's "mixed economies" is that increasing public ownership of industry does not appear to stimulate productivity. In the health and education fields, for example, which rank among the top in terms of government spending, services are labor intensive and are therefore without the same potential for improvements in productivity that is found in many private-sector activities. In Europe health and education are viewed largely as basic rights. To prevent "free riders" from dragging down school and medical services, governments have to increase taxes to cover rising costs. Such taxes, in turn, dampen productivity in more capital-intensive private businesses, becoming a drag on economic growth.

State ownership of assets, which often ties up entrepreneurs in red tape, is a complex phenomenon in European countries and does not permit simple comparisons. In Sweden, which is often thought of as a "socialist" political economy, the two largest banks are privately owned, whereas in "capitalist" France the three biggest banks are nationalized. Most of the central banks in Western European countries are publicly owned, and basic utilities (railroads, gas, postal service, etc.) form "natural monopolies" that operate under somewhat mysterious commercial principles that cannot easily be matched with a productivity index in the normal competitive sense. Such natural monopolies are usually transformed into public corporations, which, in turn, set targets that guide pricing policies. However, public corporations are often expected to raise capital on the open market, and this helps make them commercially viable.

Concerned about the impact of public corporations upon the supposedly free market within the Community, if not upon productivity, in late 1979 the EEC's Directorate-General for Competition began a crackdown on state-controlled companies in the EEC. The Rome Treaty (founding the EEC) prohibits the abuse of dominant market positions, price fixing, and the unwarranted use of subsidies and other forms of government aid. Violators can be asked to pay fines of up to 10 percent of a company's sales. In the decade following July, 1969, forty-two cases of fines imposed totalled $35 million for the EEC, much coming from multinational corporations such as BASF, Continental Can, Philips, Hoffman-La Roche, and Kawasaki. In the 1980s the focus will shift to state-controlled companies such as Italy's Istituto per la Ricostruzione Industriale (IRI), the Common Market's largest single industrial employer with a payroll of about 600,000. The Italian state subsidizes IRI to the tune of about $1 billion annually, leading EEC investigators to the conclusion that this may have allowed some of IRI's 600 subsidiaries to operate below production costs, which might be considered unfair in terms of competition with private companies. But whether or not more EEC regulation from Brussels leads to more or less overall economic growth and productivity for the Community in the future is another question.

In the postwar period there have been five cycles of European economic growth (from trough to peak): 1945–1950, 1952–1955, 1958–1960, 1967–1969, and 1971–1973. As the Common Market brought the Western European countries closer together in their policies, their business cycles became increasingly synchronized. From 1974 to 1976 they all synchronized downward into the worst recession since the 1930s. In the 1970s the strong rates of growth on which the liberal redistribution policies of European countries had been posited could no longer be taken for granted. The structural shift of these economies away from agriculture and into the industrial and service sectors not only created widespread social and unemployment dislocations but led to an apparent point of diminishing returns at which more investment appears to become progressively less able to deliver more economic output.

Consider, for example, the incremental capital-output ratio (Icor), which measures how many extra units of capital are required to produce one extra unit of output. The Icor for industrial Western Europe went from 3.4 in the 1950s to 4.1 in the 1960s, falling to slightly over 1.0 in the early 1970s and then rising to almost 5.0.[25] Such variation in the efficacy of investment in advanced capitalist economies has led Marxist theorists to argue that capitalism reaches a postindustrial stage of development in which structural contradictions lead to endemic breakdowns that eventually result in other forms such as socialism.

The Common Market has stimulated economic growth by promoting trade within the Community through the reduction of tariffs and by coordinating Community advantages and protection in terms of the outside world. Initially, the EEC stimulated a wave of American investment in the Community on the theory that buying into the domestic industrial sector would prevent the Europeans from locking the Americans out of Europe's postwar economic growth. On the micro level the effect of the Common Market's structure on industrial relations among its members is to promote competition and develop cross-national policies on the part of the employers and trade unions. The task of harmonizing national industrial policies has become more difficult and complex with the growth of multinational corporations and multinational union organizations, which bring together American, Japanese, and other national interests in addition to those of Common Market members. This trend often comes into conflict with the basic principle of the Treaty of Rome: to create a market based on free movement of the factors of production, including capital. Large industries can often benefit from economies of scale and lower unit costs, which increase both productivity and profitability. Such economic factors stimulate mergers, leading to charges of monopoly that the European Commission must oppose on principle but compromise on in practice. Large firms provide models for labor policy and have a major impact on management–labor relations in the Common Market.

The harmonization of Common Market industrial policies remains more of an ideal than a reality. While the EC claims to be committed to codetermination, equal pay for equal work, and a reduction in differences in working conditions, there actually has not been a significant narrowing of wage differentials between nations because of the Common Market. Each country works out its own codetermination and equal-opportunity policies.[26]

Paradoxically, given the commitment to the politics of redistribution in this egalitarian era, a more effective harmonization of industrial policy by the Common Market might make economic relations more equal but less productive as Common Market red tape is added to national bureaucracies, limiting the flexibility of investors, entrepreneurs, and corporate strategies. The commitment to full employment, for example, could aggravate the severe inflation problem in Western Europe and reduce productivity and economic growth. Growth, after all, depends on increasing the amount of input into the production process or increasing the effectiveness of the conversion of inputs into outputs. More frequently, European economic growth has been a result of the second factor—greater effectiveness in the use of existing resources. And this effectiveness is likely to suffer from increasing governmental regulation and a primary commitment to full employment above all else. The ideological atmosphere of the times suggests that a stronger Common Market might well tilt toward redistribution at the expense of productivity, meaning that Western European societies may become fairer at a slower rate of growth, with less flexibility to help nations outside the Common Market club.

REGIONAL AND GLOBAL CONSTRAINTS

The Common Market transacts some 40 percent of the world's trade, half of which is with nonmember nations, and possesses some 30 percent of the world's reserve currency. The population of the nine Common Market countries is greater than that of either the United States or the Soviet Union. And in terms of world exports and imports of gold, special drawing rights (SDRs), and convertible currency reserves, the Common Market outstrips both superpowers. In short, the Common Market's potential bargaining power in international affairs is formidable, particularly on economic issues. Only in the strategic realm of military strength does the EEC fall significantly short of superpower strength, its clout being conditioned by its vulnerability to the benign Soviet threat.

But potential power is not actual power. Actual power depends on a united front in foreign policy, a unity that is difficult to achieve because of the domestic disarray in European economies. (During the 1973 energy crisis, as we have seen, concern with oil security sent the French scurrying to make a separate deal with Middle Eastern producers, undermining the possibility of bloc unity.) Past colonial ties with Third World countries create differing national interests within the EEC. The financial dispute over Community agricultural policy (i.e., a dispute over 70 percent of the EEC budget) is deep-seated, particularly from the British viewpoint, since Britain has relatively few farms to benefit from EEC subsidies and is forced to import much of its food from outside the EEC: it pays in more than it receives from the Common Market. EEC projections of net financial gains and losses indicate that by 1980 Great Britain (the Community's third-poorest member) will replace West Germany (the richest member) as the EEC's largest contributor. Britain, West Germany, and Italy will be net losers, while the other six members will be net gainers. Such structural and financial differences have made it difficult to establish an effective European monetary system and have created different perspectives on policy toward north–south issues between industrialized and less developed nations in the Yaounde and Lomé Conventions, in which a number of concessions were made to stimulate economic growth in the Third World.

The Lomé Convention

The first Lomé Convention, signed on February 28, 1975, was the world's largest regional agreement, linking over 500 million people in the industrialized European Community and the developing countries in Africa, the Caribbean, and the Pacific (ACP). This conference was praised as a new model for relations between industrialized and developing countries and was based on the principles of equality and economic interdependence. It provided a Common Market guarantee for the raw-materials export earnings of fifty-three developing countries (the STABEX system) to insure ACP commodity exporters against bad years, and made EEC capital and technical assistance available to them through a Center for Industrial Development. The Lomé Convention covered everything from trade, industrial development, and financing to institutional cooperation, and symbolized a brave Western effort to control economic forces in the difficult recessionary period following the oil cartel crisis. In terms of foreign-policy bargaining power, Lomé provided the Common Market with a concrete achievement at the United Nations' Seventh Special Session on Development and International Economic Cooperation held in 1975. The United States, the Soviet Union, and Japan had nothing to compare with it. The renewal of the Lomé agreement when it expires on March 1, 1980, is likely to include provisions for human-rights principles, protection of European investments in the uncertain atmosphere of some of the developing countries, and minimum working standards along the guidelines provided by the International Labor Organization. A Fisheries Protocol is also under consideration to cope with the countries that have introduced 200-mile limits and conservation measures. The bargain to be struck here would allow developed countries the right to fish in certain territorial waters of less developed countries in exchange for financial compensation and help in developing local fishing industries. In general, the developing (ACP) countries are looking for more Common Market aid, which amounted to only $2 per person annually under the first Lomé agreement, as well as better terms of trade and a greater rate of transfer of technology, in return for providing Europe with raw materials and the greatest share in the expanding markets of developing countries.[27] The bargaining will continue to be tough, but without Common Market unity it would be tougher if not impossible.

The European Monetary System

Common Market unity can never be taken for granted, as the story of the creation of the European monetary system (EMS) in 1978 makes clear. Some observers ranked this development as the most important event in Western Europe in the past twenty years. At the very least, the EMS negotiations symbolize the inevitable process of bargaining between strong and weak political economies in Western Europe and the regional and global constraints affecting such interactions.

The European monetary system was created through a Franco–

German initiative when the leaders of West Germany and France realized that the divergence in monetary policies and interests between the American and Western European political economies was becoming so great that it could threaten the survival of the Common Market unless something was done. In the 1950s there was a predictable constancy in the external constraints laid down by the special West German (and European) relationship with the United States. This predictability was based on fixed exchange rates, a stable gold price, the persistent attempt by the most important Western economies to achieve equilibrium in external payments, and free trade within the world market economy (except for restricted trade within the Soviet bloc and with China). All of these assumptions went by the boards in the 1970s, overwhelming the world political economy with a variety of uncertainties. In August 1971 the United States unilaterally shifted the world economy from a system of fixed exchange rates based on the 1934 price of gold ($32 per ounce), with the dollar as the basic international reserve currency, to a system of floating exchange rates cut off from gold, with the dollar's value and role cast into a state of indefinite uncertainty. The basic problem was that there were too many dollars (or too much liquidity) in the world economic system: if everyone turned in dollars for American gold at once, as the system promised, the United States would be able to cover one-third of the outstanding dollars. To cover the deficit allowed them in the past by the dollar's role as an international reserve currency, the Americans had printed too many dollars. The world economy was flooded with liquidity, and worldwide inflation was the inevitable result.

The unilateral devaluations of the dollar in 1971 and 1973 compounded this uncertainty and the quadrupling of world oil prices in 1973 not only increased energy prices but had a deflationary impact, draining purchasing power from the rest of the world. Nevertheless, most nations reacted with anti-inflationary policies because the oil price rises were feeding world inflation. This drive to fight inflation was based on an understanding between the United States, Japan, and West Germany, which broke down in the midst of the recession of the 1970s. When the Germans realized that they could no longer count on the United States, they turned to Europe to try to create a zone of monetary stability in the form of the "snake in a tunnel" currency agreement, in which the northern members of the EEC agreed to keep their currencies within a narrow band of fluctuation. With the passage of time this arrangement came to be seen as a Deutschmark zone (DMZ) surrounded by satellites of weaker currencies. Since France was out of the snake and the agreement was not hooked formally into the EEC, it was not as effective as the Germans wished.

In 1977 the dollar fell in value and the German mark shot up, threatening eventually to raise the prices of German exports to the point at which they would no longer be competitive on the world market, and to make the mark an informal international reserve currency, which the Germans did not want. Flight from the dollar meant flight to other currencies, primarily the mark, the Swiss franc, and the Japanese yen. The West Germans feared that they were losing domestic control of their economy, particularly given the international pressure on them to cut their large trade surplus by intervening to stimulate domestic demand. The German initiative to realize a European monetary system was largely an effort on their part to recover monetary stability by creating a European zone that was buffered from dollar fluctuation, and to force other Western European economies to intervene domestically as well for the sake of stability, taking some of the weight from German shoulders. In this sense the German strategy is fundamentally a defensive one whose purpose is to preserve their view of equilibrium and domestic constraints, which has rewarded them with steady growth, limited inflation, and a relatively low level of unemployment during the postwar period.

The French joined in the German EMS initiative both out of belief that an external restraint might help in achieving monetary stability at home and out of fear of leaving leadership in monetary affairs entirely to Germany. The French have a tradition of monetary discipline, and they hope that the EMS might be one way of returning in some measure to the system of fixed exchange rates that they would like to recover. The French desire for status is also satisfied by having a Franco–German initiative responsible for the EMS, rather that just a German one. So in 1978 meetings at Copenhagen, Bremen, and Aachen resulted in a formal proposal for an EMS by the two strongest European currency countries, whose stake in the stability of the status quo was the greatest. The French and the Germans presented the rest of the Common Market members with a *fait accompli* and confirmed the thesis that nothing significant can happen to further the process of European integration without the support, if not the leadership, of the Franco–German axis.

The West Germans and the French proposed the "parity grid" system of exchange rates, according to which each currency is bound to every other currency, as in the old snake. The string between each pair of currencies is elastic in this system, but the exchange rate is allowed to move only 2.25 percent to either side of a central rate before central banks in both of the countries involved have to act to bring their currencies back into the permitted band width. The advantage of this system from the German point of view is that both the strongest and the weakest currencies involved are 50 percent responsible for intervening in their domestic political economies within a narrow framework of stability. The weak-currency countries, particularly Britain and Italy, objected to this system of forcing as much responsibility on the weak as on the strong (as they saw it). Instead, they supported an alternative "basket system" based on a weighted average of all EEC currencies called the European unit of account for central banks (ECU). This is, in effect, a reserve asset replacing part of the excessive dollar reserves; it has the potential to become a European currency.

The conflict between the parity grid and basket systems was resolved by a Belgian proposal that combined the two systems by using the basket system within the parity grid system as an indicator of divergence (called the rattlesnake) that would signal central banks to begin intervening at 75 percent of the 2.25 percent limit of flexibility allowed on either side of the central rate. West Germany, France, Denmark, the Netherlands, Belgium, and Luxemburg agreed to this system on December 5, 1978, when the European monetary system was officially adopted in Brussels. The agreement also approved the ECU for settling accounts between European partners, together with a financial-cooperation fund of $35 billion to stabilize participating currencies. Britain decided not to participate actively (except for partial use of the reserve system), and Italy and Ireland held out for more financial-aid concessions. Later, after some informal aid concessions Italy joined the EMS officially despite the abstention of the Communist party from the Christian Democratic government's decision.

At the beginning of 1979, as the EMS was scheduled to go into effect, the French pulled out of the arrangement on the ground that the European Common Agricultural Policy (CAP) unduly benefited West German farmers. In part, this attempt by the French to bring the controversial agricultural issue to the fore by using the EMS negotiations as an instrument was forced upon President Giscard d'Estaing by anti-EEC political pressure among potential right-wing supporters or competitors (notably Paris's Mayor Chirac, who was Giscard's prime minister before they split and formed antagonistic groups). However, in March 1979, when EEC leaders met for a summit meeting in Paris, where the outcome did not look promising, Giscard d'Estaing suddenly reversed his position without apparently gaining concessions. This reversal permitted the EMS to start immediately, making the French-sponsored summit a historic success and demonstrating once again the French diplomatic ability to use the European-integration process in subtle ways to further French status, if not France's objectives. All the Common Market nations except Britain were part of the EMS opening, agreeing to work to keep their currencies in the 2.25 percent range of flexibility from the central rate, except for Italy and Ireland, which were permitted a 6 percent range.

The launching of the EEC's joint float against the dollar was an auspicious sign of the Common Market's potential power in global political-economic matters.

The bargaining process in the EMS negotiations made explicit the conflict between the strong- and weak-currency countries, between the politics of productivity and the politics of redistribution. West Germany and France represented the strong currencies and the politics of productivity, desiring to promote stability and to control inflation. Their cooperation was made possible by the conservative economic stance of Social Democratic Chancellor Helmut Schmidt and his friendship with the moderate Republican President Giscard d'Estaing, whose right–center coalition had survived the challenge of the left-wing parties in the spring 1978 elections. The British and the Italians, the weak-currency leaders, attempted to use the technical EMS agreement for a politics of redistribution to help their nations make the domestic adjustments necessary to bring their currencies back into the legal limit when needed. The Italians, for example, asked for 8 percent flexibility instead of 2.25 percent and were granted 6 percent initially as an incentive to join the system. Both the British and the Italians pushed for resource transfers in terms of cash benefits rather than loans, given their heavy public debts. The British even bargained for lower interest rates on paying back the debts that are caused indirectly when a strong-currency country like West Germany affects weak-currency countries negatively by exchanging a strong currency for weaker ones to bring down the value of the strong one.

The future of the EMS depends on the ability of its members to harmonize their domestic political-economic policies more closely, an extremely difficult task. The Italians fear, for example, that the EMS may be used as a stick to thump discipline into the weak political economies, which could lead to nationalistic anti-EMS reactions. For the British, the timing of the EMS negotiations was awkward, since the British government was facing an election in 1979 and the majority of the British public was profoundly skeptical about British membership in the Common Market, much less the European monetary system. The EMS issue illustrates that the "incremental-trap" strategy of the European Commission to bring about European integration through the back door by using technical economic issues will not work in the long run without at least the passive support of national elites, if not their mass publics. Western Europe is polarized between the politics of productivity (or the right) and the politics of redistribution (or the left), and more often than not this politicalization has reduced the supranational concept of European integration to a realistic consensus on the lowest common denominator of national economic interests.

NOTES

1. David Calleo and Benjamin Rowland, *America and the World Political Economy* (Bloomington: Indiana University Press, 1973), p. 123.
2. "The Continental Challenge," *The Economist*, February 4, 1978, p. 78.
3. Robert Heller, *The European Revenge* (New York: Scribner's, 1975), p. 7.
4. Richard N. Coudenhove-Kalergi, *Europe Seeks Unity*, ed. Arnold Zurcher (New York: New York University, Institute of Public and Regional Studies, 1948).
5. Michael Balfour, "From Tribe to National State: The First Reich," in *West Germany* (New York: Praeger, 1968), pp. 15–16.
6. Frederick H. Hartmann, *Germany Between East and West—The Reunification Problem* (Englewood Cliffs, N.J.: Prentice-Hall, 1965), p. 16.
7. The concepts of zero-sum and variable-sum games were first developed and applied to economic cooperation by John Von Neumann and Oscar Morgenstern in *Theory of Games and Economic Behavior* (Princeton, N.J.: Princeton University Press, 1947).
8. *Der Spiegel*, no. 41 (October 9, 1963), 36–39, trans. James Richardson in *Germany and the Atlantic Alliance* (Cambridge, Mass.: Harvard University Press, 1966), p. 11.
9. As cited in F. Roy Willis, *France, Germany and the New Europe 1945–1967* (New York: Oxford University Press, 1968), p. 298.
10. See R. Isaak, "National Bargaining and Regional Integration—De Gaulle," in *Individuals and World Politics*, (North Scituate, Mass.: Duxbury Press, 1975), pp. 177–199.
11. European Communities, Statistical Office, *Basic Statistics for Fifteen European Countries: Comparison with the United States of America and with the USSR* (Brussels, 1961), pp. 95–98.
12. See *Euro-Barometre*, no. 5 (July 1976), polls surveying public-opinion trends in the Common Market countries.
13. See "Europe's High Risk Challenge," *New York Times*, July 30, 1978.
14. Hartmut Berg, *Zer Funktionsfähigkeit der Europäischen Wirtschaftsgemeinschaft* (Göttingen: Vandenhoeck & Rupprecht, 1972).
15. Michel Crozier, Samuel Huntington, and Joji Watanuki, "The Governability of Democracies," Report to the Trilateral Commission, May 1975. Published as *The Crisis of Democracies* (New York: New York University Press, 1975).
16. M. Jean-Claude Morel, "Problems and the Future of Economic Development in the European Communities," presentation at the Institute on Western Europe, Columbia University, September 9, 1976.
17. Clyde Farnsworth, "Joblessness Among Youths Is Raising Worry in Europe," *New York Times*, December 13, 1976.
18. "EC Sets New Goal: Full Employment Within 4 Years," *The Bulletin* (New York: German Information Center), June 29, 1976, p. 180.
19. Hans von der Groeben and Ernst-Joachim Mestmäcker, eds., *Verfassung oder Technokratie für Europa* (Frankfurt: Athenäum Fischer Taschenbuch Verlag, 1974), pp. 100–101.

20. Campbell Balfour, *Industrial Relations in the Common Market* (London: Routledge & Kegan Paul, 1972), pp. 122–123.
21. Paul Romus, "Regional Policy in the European Community," in John Vaizey, ed., *Economic Sovereignty and Regional Policy* (New York: Wiley, 1975), p. 128.
22. Commission of the European Communities, *Report on the Role of Public Finance in European Integration* (Brussels: April 1977), p. 12.
23. Paul Lewis, "As in America, Europeans Want Benefits Not the Taxes," *New York Times*, July 30, 1978.
24. "Europe's Mixed Economies," *The Economist*, March 4, 1978, pp. 92–93.
25. "Gradations of European Growth," *The Economist*, January 14, 1978, p. 85.
26. Balfour, pp. 11–13.
27. Peter Blackburn, "Getting Ready for Lomé II," *European Community*, no. 208 (July–August, 1978), 35–38.

Chapter 7
Comparative Political Economy

The ideal types of pure capitalism, based on the bare minimum of government designed to provide limited public goods and security of private property, and pure socialism, based on the government ownership and operation of all economic resources, are really empty boxes with no real-world examples to be found in them. Instead we have a great variety of intermediate states, which are in fact quite difficult to classify along this simple spectrum.
— Kenneth Boulding, *The Economy of Love and Fear*

The study of comparative political economy is actually the comparative study of mismanagement: How does one nation's failure to learn differ from that of another's? Put positively, the aim of comparative political economy is to develop effective strategies for coping with change that balance productivity and redistribution orientations for the harmonious benefit of all who live in the society. If there must be costly choices, how should the resulting costs and benefits be coordinated and distributed for the future good of all?

The richest Western European country is West Germany. Its political economy is dominated by the *managerial strategy* of coping with change. That is, the political-economic order is viewed as an equilibrium that must be maintained by anticipating future changes and problems in order to organize effective means for coopting them in advance. The main objectives of this strategy are stability and power. In West Germany's case power is defined as increasing the nation's capacity to control its own destiny following the postwar occupation, which still haunts the West German people. West German objectives are covered by certain typical façades: Europeanism, social ethics, economic virtue, and universal theories. Most West Germans accept the socioeconomic structure inherited from the war period, giving them an apolitical domestic consensus and stability that allows their considerable skills and energies to be focused on export markets and "the economic miracle." Working, saving, and investing flow naturally from the political culture. Productivity is almost inevitable as long as these assumptions hold. In West Germany's social-market economy the social consensus conditions the market, keeping the society stable and the economy manageable.

In contrast, the focus of France is on an administrative economy of cultural supremacy. The French stress the *entrepreneurial strategy* of coping with change, a strategy highlighted by joint state and industry ventures. The main objectives are the creation of wealth and status (and redistribution of these within the French family). Typical façades disguising these ends include the ideology of the primacy of French culture, ideological fashions, and the avant-garde. The French have maintained their belief in their cultural supremacy regardless of military loss and economic change, using French grandeur and nationalism as a noncompromise bargaining stance to skew the rules of the political economy of the Common Market in their direction. The French are astute at taking high risks in order to acquire wealth and maintain status, and they know how to keep the value of what they have.

The British have a socialized economy in crisis. They have specialized in the *bargaining-up strategy*, aiming to renegotiate the best deal they can on the basis of old conditions. Their objectives are to preserve their status and independence against the constant threat of downward mobility. Typical façades masking these objectives include propriety, the aristocratic ethos, and advocacy of a social superego, culminating in the attempt to set standards for proper upper-class social behavior. The British hang on to their old traditions and infrastructures despite the competitive socioeconomic and technological changes that have occurred since the war. They adapt by belt-tightening rather than meaningful structural reform. Perhaps the product they sell best is their culture. North Sea oil is likely to pay them for *not* adapting, consolidating their structural problems and supporting mismanagement.

Italy has a political economy of disenchantment. The Italians use the *bail-us-out strategy* of coping with change, aiming to have others pick up the bill as long as possible, knowing that Western European countries need Italy's large consumer market if not its continued membership in NATO. The typical Italian façades are perhaps the most colorful—*la dolce vita*, an air of nonchalance, the dazzle of spectacle. Beneath these masks their objective is to maintain their existing life style, a philosophy they call realism. And they have a keen eye for opportunities for upward mobility. Throughout the economic crisis of the 1970s, the Italians proved to be remarkably successful at maintaining their life style and consumption patterns even when one could almost hear Nero's violin in the background. After all, the etymology of the word *crisis* in Italy is "passage"—life as a continual transition.

The bureaucrats of the Common Market (the Commission of the European Community) also have a design for coping with change: the *incremental-trap strategy.* Their objective is supranational power for the sake of a united Europe, which is to be achieved by trapping nations into giving up more of their sovereignty behind their backs. The façades that they find most useful include the ideology of functionalism and the image of a supranational bureaucracy subservient to national desires. Unlike the nation–states on which they depend, they would adapt the European organization and its members to cope more effectively with contemporary change. But in the future, as in the past, these Eurocrats are likely to be outvoted. Even areas of great supranational potential like the European monetary system may well end up as compost heaps of parochial national strategies.

In sum, the strategies of the four largest European political economies are designed more to maintain the substructures (of psychocultural modes, values, and ideology) and the infrastructures (of socioeconomic productivity, labor relations, and transportation) of the past than to adapt to anticipated change in the future. The greater the perceived social change, the more the conservative impulse to preserve continuities pushes policy options upward to the superstructural level (of governmental interaction, economic bargaining, and party coalitions) and the more difficult collective learning or adaptation becomes. West Germany, Italy, and France all managed to break away from their normal conservative strategies for short periods after World War II, for a time were called "economic miracles," but then settled back into habitual patterns. And with ordinary strategies there cannot be any extraordinary outcomes.

Economic miracles depend on reducing costs at home (through efficiency) and increasing opportunities and benefits abroad (through effectiveness). A managerial strategy at home must be mixed or alternated with an entrepreneurial strategy abroad. West Germany and France have been the most successful at this politics of productivity, but in these nations, as in the rest of Western Europe, an era of redistribution has set in. The priority of redistribution is reaffirmed by the bureaucracies of the Common Market, which compound domestic red tape with regional regulations. Many effective European managers and entrepreneurs flee to the United States, "the last stronghold of capitalism," along with European capital seeking the highest rate of return after taxes. Future economic miracles are unlikely in Western Europe as long as productivity continues to be exported.

The basic assumption of the theory of comparative political economy suggested here is that the motivation to adapt to change or to resist it, which may be understood in terms of existing social structures and the trade-offs between redistribution and productivity, are not accidental, but are in large part the predictable outcomes of certain historical phases of political-economic development. By linking psychocultural modes with political and social structures to arrive at bargaining patterns and value priorities in policy making, systems theory can be exploited for its positive contributions of macroexplanation and "feedback." But one must go beyond this equilibrium-oriented perspective to include micro aspects of sociocultural change and strategy. The notion of the national political economy as a system with distinct boundaries and capabilities for coping with environmental change is a useful one, but it is not sufficient to pin down specific nuances of change, behavior, and strategy. For this, a more dynamic modernization model that taps into psychocultural modes, time frames, and bargaining codes is necessary.

Three phases of modernization that are recognized almost universally are the agricultural, the industrial, and the postindustrial. All of the countries examined in this book have entered the postindustrial phase, although Italy mixes earlier phases with advanced development. Agricultural economies not only focus on agriculture as their chief economic preoccupation but also tend to be past-oriented, traditional societies with diffuse role structures and affective ties to the family and a landed aristocracy. As these societies enter the industrial phase, the elites become future-oriented, concerned with transferring as much labor and capital from agriculture to the industrial sector as possible, and the population becomes sorted into specialized role structures. Legal–rational and contractual relationships replace traditional affective loyalties. Finally, the transformation from the industrial phase to the postindustrial phase involves a further shift out of agriculture and even out of manufacturing activities in the industrial sector, with an increasingly heavy focus on service and high-technology businesses and a present orientation on the part of the majority of consumers, complemented by minorities of past-oriented farmers and future-oriented industrialists.

In market-focused democratic societies such as those in the Common Market, the shift from industrial to postindustrial development also involves a replacement of market functions by government intervention as the democratic majority increases social demands for redistribution and public services. In short, the society first succeeds as a "free-business enterprise" and only thereafter succeeds as a democracy of equal participation. This democratization of the market-oriented economy through increasing government intervention makes equal opportunity and social justice possible, but at a cost of fiscal drag on the profit-oriented growth sector of the economy. Postindustrial economies pay for redistribution with productivity and economic growth.

In comparing industrial political economies such as those in the Common Market, the chief domestic problems have to do with different phases of development in various economic sectors of each society and with different redistribution–productivity trade-off strategies. Foreign economic-policy comparisons take these domestic factors as givens and become more complex because of the interdependence of all nations on the world market and because of the dependence of even the superpowers on other nations for their own security. The distinction between domestic and foreign policy collapses, however, when one compares the potential bargaining power of countries in the world political economy or when one seeks to discover which countries have been most adept at learning to cope with the traumatic socioeconomic changes that make the late twentieth century the age of uncertainty.

At a certain point in their industrial development, nations appear collectively to realize that there are trade-offs between social improvements at home and economic effectiveness abroad. Postindustrial development implies an increasing consciousness of *costs* within one's family, business, or national unit, whereas what goes on outside these units in the general market is oriented toward *benefits*—profits, new markets, trade, aid, and technological transfers. Leaders of postindustrial market-oriented economies therefore become shrewd negotiators who ask in each situation that comes up, How can I either cut or share the domestic costs within my nation while increasing the international benefits available in the world economy? Effective leaders bargain to maximize the collective life chances of their people, focusing on the critical issues of economics and security and using cultural and social concerns as masks for their material interests.

However, the world political economy rarely presents the leaders of the Western industrial nations with zero-sum game situations in which what one gains the other loses exactly. Most of political economy is a variable-sum game in which the payoffs, at least in the long term, are better for the whole community if everyone cooperates on certain issues. For example, if the Germans, who have a great trade surplus (exporting much more than they import), want cooperation from the French or Italians on lowering their subsidies for agricultural goods within the Common Market, they may have to promise to stimulate their domestic economy in an effort to bring their balance of trade more into balance. From the viewpoint of German foreign policy this is a difficult dilemma, since Germany's trade surplus in part substitutes for its lack of nuclear military capability as a symbol of security and bargaining power in international relations, just as it does for the Japanese. Moreover, it is not easy to get thrifty people who fear another 1920s inflation to suddenly start buying foreign goods that they may not need. Yet German policy makers will try to stimulate their economy anyway (e.g., by cutting taxes), for not doing so might cost them more in agricultural subsidies than staging an effort to increase domestic demand. Their basic concern has to be preventing the international animosity caused by Germany's large trade surplus from closing markets. The country needs to maintain exports for the future, particularly since exports account for one quarter of West Germany's gross national product (the highest export dependence of all major Western economies).

The German case is a significant example, since many people in Western Europe view the West German political economy as a model to emulate—a relatively free democracy with steady growth, low inflation, and limited unemployment. But the balance between the politics of redistribution and the politics of productivity is a delicate one in West Germany. In the booming 1960s the West Germans continued to build up a generous social program of social security, pension, health, and unemployment insurance. The recession of the 1970s called this program into question: Could the country afford these benefits for everyone they were committed to in the long run if economic growth and productivity began to decline? The dilemma of the cost of "fringe benefits" was further illustrated when Volkswagen set up a plant in the United States because labor costs (wages plus fringe benefits) were cheaper there than in West Germany, even though wages alone were lower in West Germany than in the United States. High labor costs at home mean more input for the same output, adding up to higher export prices and a threat to productivity.

The West German psychocultural mode of learning involves anticipating problems in advance in order to maintain the existing order or equilibrium. This social-market economy is helped by the extremely negative experiences the German people have had with inflation in the twentieth century, which stimulates them to save in the present and invest for the future. Anthropologist Gregory Bateson uses the concept of "deutero-learning" to describe the way people learn to learn (or learn learnings) in one culture or context compared to another. A critical task for political economists in Europe appears to be to investigate why the Germans have effectively learned from their economic experience and continue to do so at an efficient rate. The next question is whether such learning experiences can be duplicated by other nations in any other context short of world war. The only other alternative appears to be the idea of *New York Times* reporter Flora Lewis, who half-jokingly suggested that the only way to get other European nations to adopt the German economic model would be to fill them full of Germans.

The concept of "learning political-economic learnings" is a critical one in an era of rapid change when effective adaptation can mean need satisfaction, productivity, and better life chances for thousands of people. For the concept implies that the more often people repeat certain effective learning experiences, the faster they learn in similar situations the next time. Conversely, bad habits also consolidate and make unfortunate people in less advantaged learning contexts likely to fall into self-fulfilling patterns of failure and ignorance. Effective management, in short, is best taught in a well-managed context.

Different systems of learning or learning contexts are typical of different phases of modernization. For example, advanced industrial democratic states with market-oriented economies appear to go through a cycle of learning patterns. The state begins the postindustrial phase as a semiefficient system for the management of capital and investment, diffusing into an entrepreneurial corporate pluralism that thrives on cutting costs at home to maximize benefits abroad. But as this system of sophisticated industrialization develops and succeeds, resulting in a politics of productivity and economic growth, dispossessed or mismatched groups and workers down the class scale begin to organize to get a greater share of the higher standard of living, forming militant unions that push wages up. Wage hikes, in turn, raise production costs and export prices as the collective-bargaining process confronts the politics of productivity with the learning patterns of a politics of redistribution. Inflation and unemployment rise together. Exports fall as they become overpriced on the world market. Investment begins to leave the country (the "investment learning pattern") seeking cheaper labor markets and social environments with less governmental and union interference. A socioeconomic crisis then occurs in the free-enterprise form of political economy as it is made more complex by the increase in social demands placed upon it by democratic interest groups (the "democratic participation learning pattern"—consumer advocates, clean-air proponents, antinuclear demonstrators, and so on). This phase has been labeled the "overloaded democratic government" stage and now characterizes most Western European democracies, the United States, and Japan.

At this juncture the problems of society are pushed up to the superstructural governmental level for resolution, where only ad hoc, short-term strategies are available given the shifting governing coalitions in Western democratic states. More meaningful substructural and infrastructural reforms become difficult, if not impossible, as they are opposed by bureaucracies with vested interests in the status quo. People identify their life chances with bureaucratic jobs and arrangements and fear that eliminating unnecessary bureaucracies will increase the unemployment rate, just as cuts in state subsidies to ailing industries that are no longer productive or competitive are avoided as long as possible. The "welfare state learning syndrome" sets in with calls for a politics of redistribution, and the learning process called bankruptcy is forgotten along with the politics of productivity. Increasingly weak private firms are taken over by the government and turned into public corporations, which as often as not are a mix of social virtue and economic vice that don't do much for the gross national product. The service industries become popular as domestic manufacturing declines, often together with a drop in foreign confidence in the domestic economy and a devaluation of the currency.

These learning patterns each have their distinctive logics: the old traditional logic focusing on the costs at home and past experience (the agricultural phase) is replaced initially by the new future-oriented logic of industrialization, investment management techniques, legal–rational processing, and technological research and development. In France and Italy these old and new logics exist side by side in constant combat, stalemating the society and the government in the process. The new logic of modernization looks beyond costs to benefits abroad, seeking export-oriented growth, industrial expansion, a multinational imperial strategy. But in the process the new logic creates an antithesis—call it third-force logic. This antithesis combines a small-is-beautiful concern with the quality of life at home with an empathy for Third World countries in need of economic help abroad—even if it means cutting into one's own country's balance-of-trade surplus or domestic stability.

Third-force logic is, of course, represented by many schools. These range from a fundamentally conservative group of people who unite with others out of a physical concern for their environment and health over all else to terrorists who seek to destroy existing social structures in the hopes of initiating a fascist reaction followed by a social revolution. From the technocratic viewpoint of the "new logic" of modernization, the behavior of ecologists, terrorists, student rebels, militant labor unions, and strikers is all "irrational"—the behavior of people who are not malleable and refuse to adapt to the rules of the game or "learn to learn" as a matter of tactics, if not principle, even if the price is high. But these minorities are the exceptions that both prove and change the rule. They see through the maintenance strategy of the systems-overload model used by economic and political elites. From their point of view the model does not look forward to a healthy balance between productivity and redistribution priorities, between industrial and social needs, but becomes the symbol and rationalization for an almost desperate "holding action" to shore up the waning power of elites threatened by uncertainty and social change. The reified overloaded-systems model comes into violent confrontation with the nihilism of the terrorists, one advocating productivity and stability now above all else for the sake of economic growth even at the cost of less redistribution, and the other demanding redistribution now for the sake of social justice regardless of the costs in productivity or economic growth. Since terrorists are aware that they are vastly outnumbered and cannot win by following the regular rules of the game, they seek to subvert those

rules, hoping that their antithesis will help bring in a new revolutionary order of redistribution. The bourgeois middle class is frightened by
this political conflict and battens down its hatches, hanging on to what
it has, while the terrorist minority believes that existing wealth and
stability must be sacrificed as necessary costs of the new order they
hope to help bring into being.

Another variation of third-force logic is a less violent form of the
politics of redistribution represented by the Italian communist Gramsci's notion of "ideological hegemony," referring to the determinative
and repressive aspects of the new logic of modernization. But in analyzing European policy making today one discovers more than one
ideological hegemony, each logic becoming imperial in its own way
and blind to all other logics. In the 1950s C. P. Snow talked about the
conflict between "the Two Cultures"—the scientific and the literary—
without meaningful communication between them. The 1970s have
been marked by a conflict between productivity and redistribution
world views, each with distinctive logics, each with an ideological
hegemony it would impose on people. Economic growth and social
justice have been polarized into a heated ideological conflict, even
though one is at some point dependent on the other. The specializa-
tions in postindustrial society increasingly take on an ideological
flavor—the conservative, productivity-minded "business school"
group versus the social-conscience, redistribution-minded coalition. It
is as if economic needs could be split off from social needs, the making
of money from its distribution, profit from cost. Productivity and redistribution need to exist in dynamic equilibrium, but instead they are
polarized into enemy camps. Rather than well-managed postindustrial
societies that balance industrial and social policy, the political climate
encourages pendular swings between one priority (growth) and
another (employment and equal opportunity), frustrating the political
center, which usually governs.

The logics one finds in postindustrial societies—the old alongside the
new and the third force—are also the logics that split the world political economy. The Third World nations, representing a mix of the old
and third-force logics, contend that the First World countries, dominated by the new logic, have had unfair advantages and opportunities
in the nineteenth and early twentieth centuries as the first industrial
nations that were equipped to exploit the world's resources and markets. The International Monetary Fund is one First World response to
this dilemma, but its credit goes more to ailing First World nations than
to needy Third World countries. The Lomé Convention of the Common Market is another, but it, too, is not oriented toward the fundamental redistribution desired by the developing nations. Rather, it
seeks to stabilize Third World resource supplies and markets for First

World countries in return for development technology and aid to help stimulate Third World productivity. Still, the Lomé Convention is a hopeful step in providing a context within which developing countries can learn "new logic" learnings from developed political economies and developed nations can adapt to the Third World redistribution perspectives of resource and market suppliers whose cooperation will be vital to future European prosperity.

The First World countries also bring contradictions in logic to the bargaining tables at economic summit meetings. Such a summit was held in Bonn, West Germany, in 1978 and was attended by the heads of West Germany, France, Italy, Great Britain, Japan, the United States, and the European Community. These leaders all desired to avoid entering a new recession before they had left the last one behind, and they promised to combat inflation while stimulating moderate economic growth. But West Germany and Japan had massive trade surpluses that destabilized the world political economy from one direction, whereas the United States had a large trade deficit that undermined stability from the other. Although President Carter had been one of the foremost rhetorical advocates of free trade, the remedy for the American balance-of-trade deficit was actually a mercantilist strategy: Increase exports, reduce imports, and cut unemployment at home, regardless of the consequences for other nations. In the long run, of course, the United States and other advanced industrial countries should benefit from a free world market, since they have the production, management, and sales capacity to make the greatest use of world markets. But in the short run the Americans are apt to let the dollar float as low as they can in order to make their exports cheaper and reverse the trade deficit.

There have been pressures on the Germans and Japanese to import more (if not export less) to reduce their balance-of-trade surpluses. But again a logical contradiction emerges. Asking them to export less (as the Americans have suggested) is an indirect form of protectionism, a limitation on free trade. Yet continuing to let such large surpluses grow in an unstable economic environment will not stimulate confidence or encourage investors—prerequisites for a world economic recovery. Nor is the creation of the European monetary system, largely a reaction to the instability of the dollar, a sufficient means for this end.

The power and limits of the European Community as a bargaining unit in the world political economy were highlighted at the economic summit of major Western industrial nations in Tokyo in 1979. In a preparatory meeting the Common Market resolved to clamp a freeze on its oil imports until 1985, holding down imports to their 1978 levels. The EC's action was largely due to the rapid 1979 price hikes by the oil-producing OPEC nations, many of whom represent Arabs furious over the Israeli–Egyptian peace treaty in which the West, particularly the United States, was heavily involved. But American officials initially but unsuccessfully rejected the Common Market oil-freeze plan since it excessively favored Europe over the United States, Canada, and Japan for two reasons. First, the oil from the North Sea, which the Europeans share, is growing and expected to peak in 1985, giving the EC "a privileged sanctuary." Second, the freeze plan allows consumption to rise in Europe and, therefore, does not constitute an effective response to the Organization of Petroleum Exporting Countries, which has pressed the West for meaningful cuts in the use of oil. The 15 percent oil price hike at the 1979 OPEC meeting in Geneva served to help stimulate an economic recession in the Western industrial countries, which is not expected to last as long or to be as severe as the recession provoked by the 1973–1974 quadrupling of oil prices, since Western economies are at different points in the economic cycle, not all synchronized toward a downturn as they were in the mid-1970s. But given the structural economic difficulties of the four largest EC nations and their unwillingness to adapt easily to changed circumstances, the recession is apt to last longer and run deeper than anticipated.

At bottom, the theory of political economy suggested here is a bargaining and learning theory. Motivations, structures, bargaining codes, past policies, and global opportunities and constraints are the key variables that cluster to determine the potential power and strategy of each national political economy at any particular historical moment. As political economies modernize from the agricultural to the industrial phase, the dominant time frame motive shifts from a past orientation to a future orientation; cost efficiency strategies are slowly displaced by investment and innovation strategies as leaders learn that increasing national bargaining power means focusing on the industrial sector and export growth. And as political economies develop further from the industrial to the postindustrial phase, the dominant time frame motive for most people shifts from the future to the present, set off by minority factions of past-oriented farmers and future-oriented industrialists. The four postindustrial societies analyzed here—West Germany, France, Great Britain, and Italy—are therefore all to some extent awkward coalitions among the present, the past, and the future, with the large democratic majority made up of present-oriented consumers who want the greatest benefits for the least cost. Such conflicting motivations are reflected in voting patterns: in the late twentieth century advanced Western societies are typically governed by delicate party coalitions led by narrow majorities.

However, there is no such thing as a clean break from the agricultural phase to the industrial phase, or from the industrial to the postindustrial. Each nation becomes something of a museum of old structures and obsolete behavior patterns, giving it a unique pattern of development. One reason old substructures of values and economic infrastructures are so difficult to change is that they have become respected traditions over time, habitual patterns in which citizens have invested their psychological commitment as well as material resources and careers. Modernization always involves trying to teach old dogs new tricks, and old dogs are shrewd enough to find a way around such disruptive innovations in their lives if at all possible. For old-timers, what economists call "sunk costs" apply not only to tangible assets that they have invested in old businesses and ways of doing things but also to invaluable time, energy, and experience that they have put into certain patterns: resisting change from their perspective not only makes sense but often seems to be a survival imperative if they do not want to see everything they have stood for washed away. The national policy-making cases analyzed here suggested that these patterns of resisting change are what predominantly distinguish one nation's political economy from another's and that it is by no means certain that such resistance does not pay off for many groups of people, particularly in the short run.

The past behavior patterns, structures, and experiences of each member of the Common Market color its learning context and set an optimum bargaining strategy for those conditions. The Common Market itself provides an additional learning context that is more than the sum of the national contexts of its members. The existence of the Common Market and its supranational Commission and small budget demonstrate daily to both members and outsiders that political economy is indeed a variable-sum game as long as a cooperative framework provides Community ground rules and assurance that national sacrifices will result in benefits for everyone, including the nation that makes the sacrifice. It is this certainty of payoff in the long run that is so important for national cooperation. Little is done for nothing or for good will alone, as the British, Irish, and Italians made clear in initially refusing to join the EMS. Within the variable-sum game of the Common Market, the ground rules have already been loaded by the first nations to set up the system. Without what must seem to others (like the British) to be excessive subsidies for French agriculture, France would probably not find sufficient national interest in the Common Market to remain a member. West Germany's dominant industrial role was also preordained when the Common Market was first established. German motivation to contribute energy, personnel, and funds to the joint enterprise is directly related to the advantages for West Germany's national interest and export markets of hiding national economic power behind a regional ideology of "Europeanism," of so identifying West Germany with the Community's interest that despite envy for German success, no other member of the Community can claim that West Germany has not given its fair share. West Germany has been the largest net financial contributor to the EEC, although it is projected that Great Britain is taking over this role.

Italy entered the Common Market with the same structural split that it has today between the developing, agricultural South and the richer, industrial North. More than most countries, Italy benefits from the European Social Fund, which aims to ameliorate such regional differences, and Italy's credit rating when it comes time to borrow from other European countries is also higher because of its Common Market membership. Great Britain represents a late entry into the Common Market framework and has the reservations of someone who enters a poker game late with the feeling that most of the chips have already been distributed. As the third-poorest member of the EEC, Britain does not relish the prospect of becoming its largest net contributor. Constantly worried about getting a better deal, particularly because of the radical shift involved in its relationship with Commonwealth and EFTA allies, Great Britain's leaders have occasionally threatened to pull out of the Common Market in order to reassure the skeptical British public that they are negotiating for the best possible arrangement on almost a daily basis.

The smaller national members of the Common Market are perhaps most supportive of this supranational framework because it provides them with a possibility of sharing in a kind of superpower economic status and international bargaining position that they could never muster alone. They have much less to lose and actually do gain more financially from Common Market membership. Still, on particular issues affecting their own domestic economies they can be as stubborn and as shrewd as their more powerful colleagues.

The Common Market has great potential bargaining power in the world arena and is the only regional organization with the universally recognized authority to sign international treaties as a unit. The EEC has demonstrated its diplomatic clout as a bloc in the Lomé Convention, in economic summit meetings with the Japanese, Canadians, and Americans, in its rapprochement with the People's Republic of China for joint deterrence of the Soviet threat, and in its United Nations staff coordination. If the European monetary system works, it will have important international effects. But the nations that make up the Common Market will achieve superpower economic status only if they learn bloc bargaining patterns that enable them to function as an increasingly effective unit—a possibility that neither the Soviet Union nor the United States takes lightly. Indeed, one of the main ulterior motives American diplomats might have for supporting the expansion of the Common Market to take in Greece, Turkey, Spain, and Portugal is to diffuse the Common Market's bargaining power. Paradoxically, this diffusion motive is also behind some of the strategies of Common Market members themselves. The French, for instance, would come closer to the Gaullist vision of a "Europe of separate states" by expanding the Common Market to such an extent that in pragmatic terms this could be the only possible result. Nevertheless, expanding the Common Market as projected would undoubtedly have the effect of coopting former dictatorships (Greece, Spain, and Portugal) into the Western democratic club on a more lasting basis. Such expansion is likely to occur in the 1980s, since most Common Market members believe the short-term political gains would outweigh the significant initial economic costs, and eventually there might well be economic gains for the whole Community as well. But the expansion will inevitably have the effect of funneling more Western European resources and energies into "the EC Club," leaving less for those outside it, like the Third World.

Lately attention has focused on the possibility that advanced industrial democracies with mixed market-oriented economies, such as those of Western Europe, reach a stage of democratization that overloads their political-economic systems, making it increasingly difficult for them to cope or to be governed effectively. Structural contradictions in capitalism are said to be responsible for this state of affairs, according to socialist interpretations of the overloaded-government thesis. But the difficulty is that noncapitalistic, nondemocratic political economies are overloaded as well by the traumatic changes of the late twentieth century. The structural contradictions in European societies must be compared with the antithetical logics at work in non-Western European societies.

One development hypothesis that does emerge from the European cases examined here is that countries that have focused on the politics of productivity (with economic growth as the top priority) at the expense of the politics of redistribution—such as in the ten-year "economic miracle" phases of French and Italian development after the war—set themselves up for a militant left-wing reaction calling for a politics of redistribution. This tendency was reinforced by the unitary government structures of France and Italy, where redistribution between regions for the sake of social justice is more automatic and less visible than in nations with federal structures. In the federal structure of West Germany, for example, redistributive economic policies (such as welfare and education) must be negotiated with regional and local governments as explicit issues before funds are allocated. The call for more redistribution where it is less visible is not an unexpected result of these structural differences within nations and is likely to be more popular with the democratic majority than the call for more productivity, which often demands austerity measures to bring down the rate of inflation. Similarly, the West German criticism of redistributive politics on the local and regional level is more clearly heard. In part this is because of the federal system and the consequent bargaining required down the line, making West Germany's conservative tendency toward productivity and tax cuts and away from redistributive politics more understandable from a structural perspective.

A dynamic equilibrium between the politics of productivity and the politics of redistribution may be the optimum theoretical model for advanced, democratic mixed economies of the West European variety. But in actual politics equilibrium is the exception and not the rule. In everyday political life politicians and economic managers must go one way—say toward redistribution—rather than another. Only in West Germany does there seem to be a broad social consensus on the virtues of preserving equilibrium for its own sake regardless of changes (or, indeed, because of them). Not accidentally, the West German political economy is held up as a model of dynamic equilibrium. Still, each country's optimum developmental strategy depends on its own given political culture and traditions. In this sense the French and Italian strategies should not be underrated. Both of these Latin countries threw all their resources and energies in one direction at a certain critical moment after the war—toward productivity and economic growth. Not to have done so would have meant to continue to focus on costs at home and on redistributing what existed at a time that was ripe for greatly expanding the existing economic pie with future-oriented risks and investments. The postwar recoveries of France and Italy depended on this high-risk strategy of going all out for economic growth and productivity.

The social structure, political culture, and ideologies prevalent in Great Britain did not permit a concentrated productivity risk of the Latin variety. The result was a stop-and-go strategy of painful adjustment rather than clear alternations between productivity and redistribution. If this comparative pattern continues, the French and Italians may be able to afford the period of redistribution they have entered, whereas the British may not. For there is at least the hope, based on past French and Italian behavioral patterns, that these nations can once again swing all their energies behind a politics of productivity and economic growth after redistributing enough to convince their populations that their future life chances and standard of living will suffer without further economic growth. The muddling-through policy of the British, on the other hand, may lead them to a continuous strategy of mediocre compromise—democratically praiseworthy but economically disastrous. North Sea oil is not likely to pull them out of this traditional political-economic pattern but instead may reinforce it, with good fortune paying off bad management when the reverse may be required.

Comparative political economy may be understood as the study of strategic learning theories whereby nations try to achieve a dynamic equilibrium between productivity and redistribution by alternating between a focus on investment, production, entrepreneurship, and export expansion and a counterfocus on sharing costs and benefits at home in order to improve the life chances and living conditions of their citizens. Regional organizations and the world political economy are basically means for such national ends. The European experience suggests that power depends on productivity, which is what makes redistribution possible. The good life may be closer to social justice than most people believe.

SELECTED BIBLIOGRAPHY

Acquaviva, Sabino, and Santuccio, Mario. *Social Structure in Italy*. Translated by Colin Hamer. Boulder, Colo.: Westview Press, 1976.

Almond, Gabriel, and Verba, Sidney. *The Civic Culture*. Princeton, N.J.: Princeton University Press, 1963.

Balfour, Campbell. *Industrial Relations in the Common Market*. London: Routledge & Kegan Paul, 1972.

Balfour, Michael. *West Germany*. New York: Praeger, 1968.

Barzini, Luigi. *The Italians: A Full Length Portrait Featuring Their Manners and Morals*. New York: Atheneum, 1964.

Beer, Samuel. *British Politics in the Collectivist Age*. New York: Knopf, 1967.

Bell, Daniel. *The Cultural Contradictions of Capitalism*. New York: Basic Books, 1976.

Beyme, Kaase, Krippendorff, Rittburger, and Shell, eds. *German Political Systems—Theory and Practice in the Two Germanies*. Beverly Hills, Calif.: Sage, 1976.

Butler, David, and Stokes, Donald. *Political Change in Britain*. New York: St. Martin's, 1971.

Calleo, David. *The German Problem Reconsidered*. Cambridge: Cambridge University Press, 1978.

Calleo, David, and Rowland, Benjamin. *America and the World Political Economy*. Bloomington: Indiana University Press, 1973.

Caporaso, James. *The Structure and Function of European Integration*. Pacific Palisades, Calif.: Goodyear, 1974.

CERC. *Dispersion et Disparités de Salaries Entrance en Cours des Vingt Dernières Années*. Paris, 1976.

Cockburn, Claude. *The Autobiography of Claude Cockburn*. Harmondsworth, Middlesex: Penguin, 1967.

Cohen, Stephen S. *Modern Capitalist Planning—The French Model*. London: Weidenfeld & Nicholson, 1969.

Commission of the European Communities. *Report on the Role of Public Finance in European Integration*. Brussels, April 1977.

Cook, Chris, and Ramsden, J., eds. *Trends in British Politics Since 1945*. New York: St. Martin's, 1978.

Crozier, Michel. *The Bureaucratic Phenomenon*. Chicago: University of Chicago Press, 1964.

Crozier, Michel, Huntington, Samuel, and Watanuki, Joji. *The Crisis of Democracy*. New York: New York University Press, 1975.

Dahrendorf, Rolf. *Society and Democracy in Germany*. Garden City, N.Y.: Doubleday, 1967.

Deutsch, Karl. *France, Germany and the Western Alliance.* New York: Scribner's, 1967.

Di Palma, Guiseppe. *Surviving Without Governing: The Italian Parties in Parliament.* Berkeley: University of California Press, 1977.

Earle, John. *Italy in the 1970s.* London: Newton Abbot, David & Charles, 1975.

Epstein, Klaus. *The Genesis of German Conservatism.* Princeton, N.J.: Princeton University Press, 1966.

Edinger, Lewis J. *Politics in West Germany.* Boston: Little, Brown, 1977.

"Eurobarometre." Polls surveying public opinion trends in the EEC countries, published by the Commission of the European Communities in Brussels.

European Commission. *The European Community and the Third World.* Brussels: European Community, 1977.

European Community, Statistical Office. *Basic Statistics for Fifteen European Countries: Comparison with the United States of America and with the USSR.* Brussels, 1961.

Forschungsgruppe Wahlen E.V. *Bundestagswahl 1976: Eine Analyse der Wahl Zum 8. Oktober 1976.* Mannheim: Institut für Wahlanalysen, 1976.

Franko, Lawrence. *The European Multinationals.* London: Harper & Row, 1976.

Freymond, Jacques. *Western Europe Since the War: A Short Political History.* London: Pall Mall, 1964.

Fuà, G. *Occupazione e Capacità Produttiva: La Realtà Italiana.* Bologna: Mulino, 1976.

Geiger, Theodore. *Welfare and Efficiency: Their Interactions in Western Europe and Implications for International Economic Relations.* Washington, D.C.: National Planning Association, 1978.

Goguel, F., and Grosser, A. *La Politique en France.* Paris: Libraire Armand Colin, 1964.

Habermas, Jürgen. *Toward a Rational Society.* Boston: Beacon Press, 1970.

Hagen, Everett. *On the Theory of Social Change.* London: Tavistock Publications, 1964.

Hall, Edward. *Beyond Culture.* Garden City, N.Y.: Doubleday Anchor, 1976.

Hallett, Graham. *The Social Economy of West Germany.* New York: Macmillan, 1973.

Hankel, Wilhelm. *Währungspolitik.* Stuttgart: W. Kohlhammer, 1971.

Hanrieder, W. F., and Auton, G. P. *The Foreign Policies of West Germany, France, and Britain.* Englewood Cliffs, N.J.: Prentice-Hall, 1980.

Harrison, R. *Europe in Question—Theories of Regional International Integration.* London: Allen & Unwin, 1974.

Hartmann, Frederick H. *Germany Between East and West—The Reunification Problem.* Englewood Cliffs, N.J.: Prentice-Hall, 1965.

Hartmut, Berg. *Der Funktionsfähigkeit der Europäischen Wirtschafts Gemeinschaft.* Göttingen: Vandenhoeck and Rupprecht, 1972.

Hayward, Jack. *Planning, Politics and Public Policy. The British, French and Italian Experience.* London and New York: Cambridge University Press, 1975.

Heidenheimer, Arnold, Heclo, Hugh, and Adams, Carolyn. *Comparative Public Policy.* New York: St. Martin's, 1975.

Heller, Robert. *The European Revenge.* New York: Scribner's, 1975.

Holt, Stephen. *Six European States—The Countries of the EC and Their Political Systems.* New York: Taplinger, 1970.

Hoffmann, Stanley. *Decline or Renewal: France Since the 1930s.* New York: Viking, 1974.

Huffschmid, Jörg. *Die Politik des Kapitals.* Frankfurt: Suhrkamp, 1969.

Institut Universitaire des Hautes Etudes Internationales. *Europe 1980: The Future of Intra-European Relations.* Bruges, 1972.

Isaak, R. *Individuals and World Politics.* 2nd ed. North Scituate, Mass.: Duxbury Press, Wadsworth, 1980.

Katzenstein, Peter, ed. *Between Power and Plenty.* Madison: University of Wisconsin Press, 1978.

Kohl, W. L., ed. *Economic Foreign Policies of Industrial States.* Lexington, Mass: Lexington Books, 1977.

Kolinsky, Martin. *Continuity and Change in European Society: Germany, France and Italy Since 1870.* New York: St. Martin's, 1976.

LaPalombara, Joseph, and Blank, Stephen. *Multinational Corporations in Comparative Perspective.* New York: Conference Board, 1977.

Ledeen, Michael. *Italy in Crisis.* Beverly Hills, Calif.: Sage Publications, 1977.

Lee, Roger, and Ogden, Philip. *Economy and Society in the EEC.* Lexington, Mass.: Lexington Books, 1977.

Lindberg, Leon, and Scheingold, Stuart. *Europe's Would-Be Polity.* Englewood Cliffs, N.J.: Prentice-Hall, 1970.

Lipset, Seymour Martin. *Political Man: The Social Basis of Politics.* Garden City, N.Y.: Doubleday Anchor, 1963.

Longepierre, Michel. *Les Conseillers Généraux Dans le Système Administratif Français.* Paris, 1971.

MacFarlane, J. *Issues in British Politics Since 1945.* New York: Longman, 1975.

Mackay, D. A., and Mackay, G. F. *The Political Economy of North Sea Oil.* Boulder, Colo.: Westview Press, 1975.

Macridis, Roy. *French Politics in Transition—The Years After De Gaulle.* Cambridge, Mass.: Winthrop, 1975.

Marris, Peter. *Loss and Change.* New York: Pantheon Books, 1974.

Mauriac, François. *De Gaulle.* Garden City, N.Y.: Doubleday, 1966.

McClelland, David C. *The Roots of Consciousness.* New York: Van Nostrand, 1964.

Metraux, R., et al. *Some Hypotheses About French Culture.* New York: Research in Contemporary Cultures, Columbia University, 1950.

Le Monde. "Les Elections Législatures de Mars 1978: La Défaite de la Gauche." Special supplement.

Mosse, George. *The Nationalization of the Masses.* New York: Howard Fertig, 1975.

Muth, Hans Peter. *French Agriculture and the Political Integration of Western Europe.* Leiden: Sithoff, 1970.

Organization of Economic Cooperation and Development. *The Industrial Policy of France.* Paris, 1974.

Parkin, Frank. *Class Inequality and Political Order: Social Stratification in Capitalist and Communist Societies.* New York: Praeger, 1975.

Paterson, William. *Social Democracy in Post-war Europe.* New York: St. Martin's, 1974.

Potthoff, Erich, Bleume, Otto, and Duvernell, Helmut. *Zwischenbilanz der Mitbestimmung.* Tübingen: J. C. B. Mohr, 1962.

Probert, Belinda. *Beyond Orange and Green: The Political Economy of the Northern Ireland Crisis.* 1978.

Pryce, Roy. *Politics of the European Community.* Totowa, N.J.: Rourman and Littlefield, 1974.

Robertson, Arthur Henry. *European Institutions—Cooperation, Integration, Unification,* 2nd ed. London: Stevens, 1975.

Romus, Paul. *Economic Sovereignty and Regional Policy.* New York: Wiley, 1975.

Rosenthal, Glenda. *The Men Behind the Decisions: Cases in European Policy-Making.* Boston: D. C. Heath, 1975.

Richardson, James. *Germany and the Atlantic Alliance.* Cambridge, Mass.: Harvard University Press, 1966.

de Savigny, Jean. *L'Etat Contre les Communes?* Paris, 1971.

Scalfari, E. *Razza Padrona.* Milan: Feltrinelli, 1974.

Schonfield, Andrew. *Modern Capitalism.* New York: Oxford University Press, 1965.

Schuchman, Abraham. *Codetermination, Labor's Middle Way in Germany.* Washington, D.C.: Public Affairs Press, 1957.

Schweigler, Gerhard Ludwig. *National Consciousness in Divided Germany.* Beverly Hills, Calif.: Sage Publications, 1975.

Stamps, Norman. *Why Democracies Fail: A Critical Evaluation of the Causes for Modern Dictatorship.* Notre Dame, Ind.: University of Notre Dame Press, 1957.

Stern, Fritz. *The Politics of Cultural Despair.* Garden City, N.Y.: Doubleday Anchor, 1965.

Thoenig, Jean-Claude. *L'Ère des Technocrates.* Paris, 1973.

Vernon, Raymond. *Big Business and the State: Changing Relations in Western Europe.* Cambridge, Mass.: Harvard University Press, 1974.

von der Groeben, Hans, and Mestmäcker, Ernst-Joachim, eds. *Verfassung oder Technokratie für Europa.* Frankfurt: Athenäum Fischer Taschenbuch Verlag, 1974.

Wallace, W., Wallace, H., and Webb, C. *Policy-Making in the European Communities.* London: Wiley, 1977.

Willis, F. Roy. *France, Germany and the New Europe, 1945–67.* London: Oxford University Press, 1968.

Zysman, John. *Political Strategies of Industrial Order: Industry, Market and State in France.* Berkeley: University of California Press, 1977.

Periodicals

Affari Esteri
Les Annales du Marché Commun
Atlantic Community Quarterly

Bulletin Européen
Comparative Political Studies
Comparative Politics
The Economist
Euromoney
Europa-Archiv
European Community
European Economic Community—Bulletin
European Journal of Political Research
The German Tribune
Journal of Common Market Studies
Journal of European Integration
Journal of Political Economy
OECD: Economic Outlook, Main Economic Indicators
The OECD Observer
Politique Etrangère
Revue du Marché Commun
Lo Spettatore Internazionale

Appendix
Political-Economic Events

Federal Republic of Germany—Political-Economic Events

Political parties: SPD (Sozialde-
mokratische Partei Deutschlands), in coalition with FDP,
favors governmental policy of
competitive economy, but planning to protect individual from
uncontrolled economic interests; CDU/CSU (Christlisch-
Demokratische Union) focuses
on private property and individual freedom, then equality
(CSU in Bavaria); FDP (Freie
Demokratische Partei) stands
for democratic and social liberalism—individual focus of
state and economy; DKP
(Deutsche Kommunistische Partei) represents Marxism-Lenin-
ism; NPD (Nazionaldemokra-
tische Partei Deutschlands) is a
nationalistic right-wing or neo-
Nazi party.

Area: 95,543 sq. mi. or 248,624
sq. km., or the size of Wyom-
ing. Population (1979):
61,310,000. Unemployment: in
1978, 3.5%; highest rate, 1955–
1973: 4.9% in 1955; lowest in
1973, 0.9%.
Average annual growth rate
(GD),** 1964–1979: 3.5%.
Imports: 9.3% of world (2nd
after U.S.) in 1976; 13% of GDP
in 1955; 23.5% in 1977.
Exports: 11% of world (2nd
after U.S.) in 1976; 13.7% of
GDP in 1955; 26.4% in 1977.

1948

Wirtschaftswunder—economic
miracle establishing social market economy (virtually uncontrolled scope to free enterprise);
GNP rises by over 80%; moderate wage demands facilitate
economic growth; Erhard minister of economics; until mid-
1960s no major fiscal-policy
measures taken to stimulate
economy.

1949

Grundgesetz or Basic Law formu-
lated by *Lander* parliamentarians
in Council; Federal Republic of
Germany established, but no
formal sovereignty until 1955,
when it also joined NATO; Adenauer as first chancellor.
European Coal and Steel Community formed.

1951

Signing of Rome treaties establishing EEC and EURATOM;
Bundestag elections: CDU winner in coalition with German

1957

Social-security system rein-
forcement: pensions tied to cost
of living and growth in national
income; Cartel Act—first at-

party (DP)—a small party
unable to win seats after 1957.

SPD adopts Bad-Godesberg
Plan—abandonment of
Marxism.
Willy Brandt chosen as SPD
candidate for chancellorship.
Erection of Berlin Wall; *Bundestag* elections: CDU wins majority in coalition with FDP.
Adenauer resigns, Erhard
elected to chancellorship.
Bundestag elections: CDU winner in coalition with FDP; Erhard (CDU) as chancellor.
FDP withdraws from coalition;
CDU chooses Kiesinger for
chancellorship in alliance with
SPD, Brandt as vice-chancellor,
forming the Grand Coalition
party to pass the Emergency
Decrees; student unrest in
Frankfurt and Berlin.

Bundestag elections: SPD in coalition with FPD form majority;
Brandt as chancellor.
Ostpolitik—first formal talks
with Eastern Europe, treaties
signed with Soviet Union and
Poland confirming existing
frontiers.

1959

1960

1961

1963

1965

1966

1967

1968

1969

1970

tempt to control contemporary
trend toward concentration in
German economy.

Since currency reform of 1948,
first slackening of growth rate
(GNP falls by .02%) and fall in
industrial production; new government passes Stabilization
and Growth Law, which gives
government far-reaching control of overall spending,
medium-term growth
planning—marks growing interventionism, change from social-market economy.
Currency crisis: Germany resists pressure to revalue
D-mark.
Continuation of crisis: Brandt
decides to revalue D-mark.

D-mark revalued by 9.29%.

1971

D-mark is floated against international currencies.

1972

Basic Relations Treaty signed with DDR;* coalition in *Bundestag* loses majority, election called; SPD elected, for the first time largest party in *Bundestag*. Both FRG* and DDR join UN.

Establishment of European "snake in the tunnel" monetary arrangement: maximum margin of fluctuation between two EEC currencies 2.25%.

1973

Anti-inflation program launched to combat effects of worldwide recession.

1974

Willy Brandt resigns after discovery that his personal assistant had been working for DDR minister of state security; succeeded by Schmidt, former minister of finance.
Bundestag elections: SPD loses position as largest party in *Bundestag*, SPD/FDP coalition retains slender majority. Schmidt reelected chancellor.

Unemployment climbs to 800,000, or 3.5% of labor force. Immigration of most foreign laborers stopped.

1976

Balance-of-payments surplus declined from $10 billion in 1974 to $3 billion.

1977

Increasing terrorism culminates in kidnaping of industrialist Schleyer in September; October hijacking of Lufthansa jet, stormed successfully at Mogadishu by special German police unit.

Decline of the dollar; German and Japanese supportive interventions in December.

1978

Signature of 25-year cooperation between FRG/USSR during Brezhnev's visit to Bonn: Western economic summit in Bonn in July. Choice of Franz Joseph Strauss by CDU to contest 1980 election vs. Schmidt signals conservative resurgence. U.S. and China pressure Schmidt to increase defense spending and ease *Ostpolitik.*

Establishment of swap arrangement between U.S. and Deutsche Bundesbank.

1979

European monetary system set up to protect European currencies from dollar fluctuations. Slowdown of German economy owing to energy crisis. Heavy flow of German investment capital to U.S. and South America.

*DDR = East Germany; FRG = West Germany.
**GDP = gross domestic product—private consumption on the economic territory.

France—Political-Economic Events

Political parties: Union des
Democrats pour la République
(UDR): Gaullist party from
1968, allied with RPR; Union
pour la Democratie Française
(UDF): Giscard coalition of Republicans, social-democratic
center, and others; Rassemblement pour la République (RPR):
formed after Chirac resigned as
PM in 1976, part of Giscard's
governmental majority; Parti
Radical et Radical-Socialiste: reformist party that stands with
presidential majority; Centre
des Democrates Sociaux (CDS):
created in 1976 by merger of
Centre Democratie et Progrès,
part of governmental majority;
Parti Republicain (PR): formed
in 1977 of independent republicans and three pro-Giscard
groups; Mouvement des So-
ciaux Libéraux (MSL): created
in 1977, split from RPR to appeal to moderate socialists and
non-Chirac Gaullists; Parti Socialiste (PS): stands for socialist
planned economy, nationalization of critical industries and
full employment; Parti Commu-
niste Française (PCF): small
left-wing revolutionary party.

Area: 211,208 sq. mi. or 547,626
sq. km., or 4/5 the size of
Texas. Population (1976):
52,893,000.
Unemployment: in 1978, 5.3%;
highest rate 1955–1973: 2. 4%
in 1972. Average annual growth
rate (GDP*) 1969–1979: 4.2%.
Imports: 6.9% of world in 1976;
11% of GDP in 1963; 21.6% of
GDP in 1977.
Exports: 6% of world in 1976;
10.2% of GDP in 1963; 16.1% of
GDP in 1963; 21.4% of GDP in
1977.

1944

Provisional unicameral government under de Gaulle; national
referendum rejects return to
prewar regime.

1945

Election for formation of Constituent Assembly, de Gaulle
resigns; 4th Republic born after
referendum approving legisla-
tively strong Constitution (26
Cabinets formed during life of

Republic); outbreak of war in
Indochina lasting eight years.

1946

Nationalization of electricity,
gas, Renault; Bank of France,
Air France under state
supervision.

1947

Until 1949—unrest, communist
strikes.

Until 1952, the first Monnet
Plan of economic recovery, modernization under slogan "Modernization or Downfall."

1949

NATO formed; Council of Europe formed at Strasbourg.

1950

Postwar economic boom
marred by inflationary trend,
thereby weakening franc and
undermining international competitiveness; protected economy—economy sheltered from
outside competition by high
tariffs, sheltered internally by
heavy government subsidiza-
tion; French economy: largest
agricultural nation in Europe
after Soviet Union, but dispro-
portionately narrow industrial
base.

1951

Birth of European Coal and
Steel Community.

1952

Rejection by France of European Defense Community.

1954

Problem of Indochina ended by
Geneva Convention: Indochina
divided into North and South
regions; beginning of insurrec-
tion in Algeria.

1956

"Suez Crisis"—abortive intervention.

1957

EURATOM and EEC treaties
signed.

1958

End of 4th Republic: insurrec-
tion in Algiers, threat of civil
war, de Gaulle invited by President Coty to form government,
invested as prime minister to
rule by decree for six months,
leaders of 4th Republic abdicate
to avoid civil war; new constitution approved by referen-

Birth of the "new franc"; de
Gaulle's liberalization reforms.

dum, strengthened executive; general election: victory for Gaullists (UNR), de Gaulle elected president.

France explodes first atomic bomb in North Sahara.

1960

Extremely high rate of economic growth from 1961 to 1971, GNP grows at annual average rate of 5.8%; continuation of generally large governmental role in economy—planning controlled by Commissariat General du Plan, which instituted a series of economic plans as "indicators"; setting growth targets; aiming to improve international competitiveness of French industry by restructuring.

1962

Evian agreement for end of Algerian War approved by national referendum.

1963

France breaks off negotiations for British entry into Community.

1965

Elections: de Gaulle does not win on first ballot; second-round results: de Gaulle 55% of popular vote, Mitterand 44%; from mid-1965 until 1966, French withdrawal from some Community activities.

1966

France announces withdrawal from NATO.

1968

The May crisis: serious revolt of students and workers threatens Republic for approximately one month, but collapse of student movement, disunity among left, general strike eventually settled by large wage increases; National Assembly elections give UDR clear majority.

Aftereffects of crisis: unbalanced budget, weakened franc, de Gaulle forced to adopt severe austerity measures.

1969

De Gaulle resigns after defeat in referendum on regional reform; June: Georges Pompidou (UDR) elected president with 44% of popular vote.

Pompidou devalues franc by 12.5%, Giscard d'Estaing appointed minister of finance.

1971

Under Pompidou, the Sixth Plan (to 1975) encourages industrial expansion and technological development to combat inflation.

1972

"L'Affaire Aranda" involving administration in planning and development payoff scandal; political scandal involving Premier Chaban-Delmas in tax avoidance; signature of "Programme Commune" of left-wing parties.

General election; Gaullists threatened by "Union of the Left"; a reduced majority.

1974

France hosts Western economic summit at Rambouillet.

1975

French economy suffers in world economic crisis, −2% growth rate in 1975.

1976

Jacques Chirac resigns as prime minister, replaced by Raymond Barre; student unrest.

High inflation continues into 1976 at over 11%; removal of franc from "the snake"; Barre introduces "austerity plan" and some redistributive reforms.

1978

March elections: Giscard defeats disunited left.

Barre cuts subsidies for industry and asks for social reforms.

1979

France serves as host of European summit in Paris that results in actual beginning of the European monetary system. First direct parliamentary elections result in victory for supporters of Giscard and defeat for the Gaullist Chirac. Government's dubious interference with election results leads Mitterand to withdraw from European Parliament. Anti-Barre sentiments build up among left.

Giscard advocates freezing European oil imports at 1978 levels after oil price hikes by OPEC cartel; freeze approved by other European leaders at 1979 summit. France joins EMS. Third year of Barre's austerity plan ends with rising unemployment, double-digit inflation, and a widening trade deficit resulting largely from increased energy costs.

*GDP = gross domestic product.

Great Britain—Political-Economic Events

Political parties: Conservative and Unionist party: aims to preserve religion, freedom, and the Constitution, pro defense and free enterprise, antisocialist, supports adequate social services; Labour party: a democratic-socialist party standing for social justice, planned economy and classless society, strong union ties; Liberal party: stress on liberty, prosperity, and security, focus on the individual; Communist Party of Great Britain: aims to substitute public ownership for the capitalist system; National Front: a nationalist and racialist party with new popularity; Plaid Cymru: Welsh nationalist party, protects Welsh interests; Scottish National party (SNP): promotes independence for Scotland and Scottish control of natural resources.

Area: 94,250 sq. mi. or 244,108 sq. km., or the size of Oregon. Population (1978): 55,880,000. Unemployment: 1978, 6.8%; highest rate 1955–1973: 3.9% in 1972, 2.8% in 1973. Average annual growth rate (GDP*) 1969–1979: 2.1%. Imports: 5.9% of world in 1976; 16.0% of GDP in 1963; 28% of GDP in 1977. Exports: 5.0% of world in 1976; 14.1% of GDP in 1963; 29% of GDP in 1977.

1945

Elections: Labour majority, Clement Atlee prime minister.

1946

Nationalization program: Bank of England, coal industry, electricity, and inland transport.

1948

Establishment of British welfare state. National insurance scheme started, social-security scheme set up, aid from Marshall Plan begins.

1949

NATO agreement signed in Brussels; Ireland proclaims itself a Republic, leaves Commonwealth.

1950

Until 1960, slow growth rate: average GNP per capita rises only 2.1%.

Elections: Conservatives in office, Churchill prime minister, winning also in 1955 and 1959, each time with a larger majority.

1951

Under Churchill, denationalization of steel and road transport; in the 1950s, liquidation of the British empire.

King George VI dies.

1952

Queen Elizabeth II crowned.

1953

Britain's adhesion to South East Asia Treaty Organization.

1954

Churchill resigns, replaced by Anthony Eden.

1955

The "Suez Crisis": general disapproval of the Anglo–French intervention leads to change in orientation of British foreign policy.

1956

1957

Inflation threat leads government to turn to fiscal controls; by 1960, improvement in economy to 3% growth rate.

Britain applies for membership in EEC, by January 1963 negotiations break down owing to de Gaulle's protest.

1961

Death of Hugh Gaitskill, leader of Labour party, replaced by H. Wilson; "The Profumo Affair": Conservative government suffers embarrassment, but Prime Minister MacMillan regains popularity through his contribution to Nuclear Test Ban Treaty; MacMillan resigns, Lord Home chosen by Queen to replace him.

1963

Economy has slowed to a standstill—unsuccessful, unpopular programs to stimulate it, but production lags, wages and prices rise.

Election: Labour wins majority of only 4 in House of Commons, Harold Wilson PM.

1964

Labour government puts through emergency measures budget.

Election called by Labour government to gain greater majority, which it received—97 seats.

1966

1967

Pound devalued—leads to price, wage increases; unemployment rises to 3.6% compared to average 1.7% for 1960–1966; trade union concentration; 70% of union membership converges in 18 unions—over 100,000 members each.

1968

Industrial expansion: commitment of Labour government to technological and efficiency improvement.

1969

Economic stability threatened by wildcat strikes and student demonstrations as manifestations of general social discontent.

1970

Elections: Conservatives gain surprise victory, majority of 30 in Commons—Heath, new leader of Conservatives, as PM; unrest continues in Northern Ireland, violence increases.

Oil discovered under bed of North Sea; by early 1970s Britain's per capita GNP 10% below European average, attempts at higher level of growth by stimulating demand lead to repeated crises in balance of payments and consequent squeezes on credit, wages rising at annual rate of 20.8%, prices at 10.4%.

1971

Powers of Stormont Parliament in N. Ireland suspended for one year because of continuing crisis; Conservatives pass Industrial Relations Act to modernize structure.
January 1: Britain formally enters EEC.

1973

Oil crisis: Britain in recession, by 1975 a 25% annual rate of inflation.

1974

Election: Labour wins 5-seat majority, H. Wilson as PM, end of state of emergency called by Conservatives, 5-day work week restored; October: another election to improve Labour's position, still no clear majority.

National referendum: Britain votes 2:1 to stay in Common Market.
Wilson resigns, succeeded by James Callaghan (Labour party); in return for certain concessions government makes agreement with Liberal party, renewed for 1977–1978 parliamentary session.

1975

1976

Government introduces anti-inflationary measures, agreement on wage hike limitation.

1977

Partial economic recovery, economy managed on lines recommended by IMF; pound floated upward; 800,000 barrels per day of high-quality North Sea oil produced.

1979

National elections forced by Conservative-inspired vote of no confidence in Labour government. Conservatives win election. Margaret Thatcher becomes prime minister. Leadership struggle in Labour Party between Callaghan and left-wing MP Tony Benn follows.

Britain is only European Community country that does not join the European monetary system.
New Conservative budget aims to cut state subsidy for industry, increase investment incentives, trim taxes, increase defense spending. Government begins denationalization of British Aerospace, BNOC, and other large concerns.

*GDP = gross domestic product.

Italy—Political-Economic Events

Political parties: Democrazia Cristiana (DC): populist party, focus on centrist position; Partito Comunista Italiana (PCI): largest communist party in Western Europe, stands for democratic socioeconomic reform and an independent foreign policy; Partito Socialista Italiano (PSI): stress on left, service to working class, claim that socialism, democracy, and individual freedom are inseparable; Partito Socialista Democratico Italiano (PSDI): splinter party of PSI composed of former social democrats, to the right of PSI; Partito Liberale Italiano (PLI): stress on freedom in public and private affairs; Partito Repubblicano Italiano (PRI): strongly economic oriented, technocratic, pro-Europe; Partito Radicale (PR): leftist party acting as pressure group—study groups, congresses, publicity on issues: reformist, libertarian; Sudtiroler Volspartei (SVP): largest of the ethnic-based regional parties; Democrazia Proletaria (DP): ran as united far-left party in 1976 elections, encompassing Pdup manifesto, Autonomia Operaiao, Lotta Continua, and Movimento dei Lavoratori per il Socialismo; Movimento Sociale Italiano–Destra Nazionale (MSI–DN): rightist "order" party, anticommunist, neofascist elements.

Plebescite: monarchy abolished, Italy becomes republic; de Gas-

Area: 116,318 sq. mi. or 301,225 sq. km., or slightly larger than Nevada.
Population (1978): 56,690,000.
Average annual growth rate (GDP*) 1969–1979: 3.4%.
Unemployment: 1978, 7.2%; highest rate, 1955–1973: 5.5% in 1959, 3.7% in 1973.
Imports: 4.6% of world in 1976; 16.7% of GDP in 1963; 26% of GDP in 1977.
Exports: 4.9% of world in 1976; 11.2% of GDP in 1963, 28% of GDP in 1977.

1945

1946

Industrial output one quarter of prewar level.

peri (DC) heads government of
DC, PSIUP, PCI, PRI.
End of participation of PCI in
governmental majority—until
1960, DC lead government with
center-party coalitions.

1947

Marshall Plan aid begins; classical liberal approach to economic policy until 1965,
primary reliance on free market, stable currency, trade
liberalization.

Constitution establishing bicameral republican government
comes into effect.

1948

1950

Establishment of "Cassa per il
Mezzogiorno" to narrow eco-
nomic gap between North and
South.

1951

1952

Prewar levels of production.
Until 1962, "economic
miracle"—doubling of national
income; rapid growth of industrial production due to low
labor costs—export oriented,
average GDP growth rate
5–6%.

Death of de Gasperi, succeeded
by Fanfani; government promotes "Legge Truffa" giving
extra seats to any electoral bloc
or party having over 50% of
votes, DC fail to achieve majority, law repealed.
Settlement of Trieste question—
administration divided between
Italy and Yugoslavia.

1953

1954

Exodus from land in the South,
1954–1969: half of agricultural
workers abandon countryside.
Ministry of State Participations
created, controlling state-
owned corporations (IRI, ENI,
etc.).

1956

EEC, EURATOM treaties
signed at Rome.
Beginning of rapprochement toward left: victory of Nenni's
autonomist group within PSI in
Congress; 1959, DC Congress:
Aldo Moro elected secretary—
favored opening to left.
Election of Tambroni (DC)
center–right coalition, ended
by mass antifascist, antigovern-

1957

1958

Entry into EEC permits Italian
labor migration to EEC
countries.

1960

ment demonstrations; first center–left Fanfani (DC): DC, PSDI, PRI; PSI abstaining but in support of government.

1961

"Green Plan": government investment and aid to agriculture, especially depressed areas.

1962

Nationalization of electric industry.

1963

Discontent due to low wage rates, lack of social reforms; in elections, right and left gain at expense of DC; until 1970 no significant reforms, strikes and labor unrest grow, student agitation.

Inflation and balance-of-payments deficit, Moro government introduces measures to restrain consumption; recession, new Moro administration: investment to overcome recession.

1965
1969

The "hot autumn" strike wave.

First economic plan developed. Severe inflation and economic stagnation.

1970

Colombo's (DC) center–left coalition: divorce, finance laws, and "Statuto dei Lavoratori": relieved worker injustice, gave trade unions more leverage; but deterioration of economy, government resigns.

1972

State-owned industries now account for half of total national industrial investment.

1973

Election: short-lived Andreotti (DC) center–right coalition; then center–left DC, PRI, PSDI under Rumor (DC); PCI and trade unions have tolerant attitude; government enacts crisis economic policies.

Italy badly hit by oil crisis due to heavy dependence on foreign energy—by 1974, trade deficit almost treble that of previous year.

PRI withdraws from coalition over economic policy; referendum on divorce law—large majority in favor; formation of weak Moro coalition.

1974

1975

First-year economy fails to expand: austere measures lead to severe recession in industry—reflationary measures introduced.

1976

Moro's government resigns after withdrawal of PSI; elections, PCI over 34%, DC 38%—Andreotti forms government assured of abstention of PCI deputies.

Lira falls about 25% on the dollar; Andreotti government passes austerity measures to cope with continuing economic crisis.

1977

Four months of negotiations, then conclusion of "programatic accord": allows opposition significant role in policy making but no direct role in government.

Large IMF loan received in return for pledge of public-expenditure reduction, limit on inflation rate.

1978

Resignation of Andreotti cabinet due to withdrawal of opposition support, government reformed after negotiations; kidnaping of Aldo Moro by Brigate Rosse, later found dead; approval of abortion law; Brigate Rosse members tried and sentenced; regional elections, PSI increased support.

Balance of payments in surplus, growth 4%; government parties approve three-year spending plan, "Piano Pandolfi": combat inflation, stimulate growth.

1979

Election: Communists lose over one million votes, dropping to 30.4%; first national PCI electoral setback since WW II. DC drops to 38.3%. PSI gains five new seats. Victory for small center parties: Social Democrats up to 3.8%, Republicans stay at 3%, Liberals up to 1.9%. Radical party triples vote to win 14 new seats for 18-seat total.

Partial economic recovery based on small businesses. Italy joins the European monetary system with an exceptional 6% range of fluctuation.

After 89 days without a government, Francesco Cossiga (DC) forms coalition with small parties; imposes energy rationing.

*GDP = gross domestic product.

The European Community—Political-Economic Events

		Area: 587,794 sq. mi. or 1,519,050 sq. km. Population: 258,777,000. Unemployment (1979): 5.5% Average annual growth rate (GDP*) 1966–1976: 3.7%; 1963–1973: EUR 6,** 5.0%; EUR 9,** 4.5%. Imports: % of world in 1976 = 36.1%; 1973: EUR 6 = 32.1%; EUR 9 = 41.7%. Exports: % of world in 1976 = 35.1%; 1973: EUR 6 = 34.6%; EUR 9 = 42.5%.
ECSC Treaty comes into force. EEC and EURATOM Treaties come into force.	1952 1958	
	1959	First tariff cuts on movement of goods within Community. Abolition of quotas on industrial goods.
Applications for membership received from U.K., Denmark, and Ireland; "Bonn Declaration" of Six aiming at political goals.	1961	
	1962	European Agricultural Guarantee and Guidance Fund (FEOGA) comes into effect.
Breakdown of negotiations for accession of U.K. Yaounde Convention of association with developing countries comes into effect. Crisis: partial withdrawal of French government from Community institutions over political and institutional future of Community—EEC fails to meet deadline on financing of Common Agricultural Policy (CAP). France agrees to resume place in Community. New applications for membership received from U.K., Denmark, and Ireland; de Gaulle vetoes British application once more, leading to deadlock in	1963 1964 1965 1966 1967	Mansholt Plan for common grain prices agreed upon. Completion in Council of a series of agreements introducing the main elements of CAP.

negotiations; institutions of
ECSC, EURATOM, and EEC
merged in implementation of
Merger Treaty of 1965; Rome
summit meeting.

1968

Establishment of customs
union and introduction of
Common External Tariff (CET);
free movement of labor begins.

1969

Hague summit: establishment
of Davignon Committee for
study of closer political cooperation.

Report of Davignon Committee
on Political Cooperation Procedure (PCP) submitted; new
round of negotiations for acces-
sion of four countries begin.

1970

Council agrees on final regulation on financing of CAP.

1971

General System of Preferences
introduced affecting imports
from 91 developing countries.

1972

Referendum in Norway rejects
EEC membership, referendum
in Denmark approves membership; summit conference in
Paris establishes wide range of
future objectives for the Community; social fund revised:
new scheme allowing more
general assistance.

Council of Ministers approves
the establishment of the currency "snake": narrowing of
fluctuation margins.

1973

Denmark, Ireland, and U.K. ac-
cede to the EC; adoption of
common commercial policy toward Eastern Europe.

System of free-trade agreements with EFTA introduced;
European Monetary Cooperation Fund set up overseeing
narrow-margin (2.25%) system.

1975

Referendum in U.K. approves
Common Market membership;
until 1977, negotiation of a series of joint technical projects—
Euro–Arab dialog; Greece
submits application for
membership.

Payments of Regional Development Fund begin compensating
for unequal rate of development in different regions in the
Community; single system of
value-added tax (VAT) applied.

1976

Tindemans report on European
Union published; Lomé Con-
vention (following Yaounde
Convention) comes into force;
Council of Ministers agrees to

direct elections every five years of European Parliament (EP), set first election date: May–June 1978.

1977

Introduction of customs union, EEC-EFTA; Spain and Portugal submit applications for membership.

1978

European Council, Copenhagen: failure of member states to meet target date—EP elections rescheduled to June 1979.

European Council, Bremen: French–German proposals for European monetary system (EMS).

1979

Direct European Parliament elections for first time. Center–right parties predominate. Germany and Britain raise issue of common European defense; rebuffed by France.

EMS begins to operate for all Common Market nations except Britain.

Britain slows own growth to export 100,000 barrels of North Sea oil per day to EEC, which agrees to limit daily imports from outside Community to 9.4 million barrels per day through 1985. EEC begins antitrust crackdown on state-controlled companies in Common Market.

*GDP = gross domestic product.
**EUR 6= original 6 Common Market members; EUR 9 = current 9 members.

Index

About the Author

Robert Isaak is Associate Professor of European Studies and Political Economy at The Johns Hopkins University, School of Advanced International Studies at the Center in Bologna, Italy. He has taught at a number of American universities and is the author of three other books on politics: *American Democracy and World Power* (St. Martin's Press); *Politics for Human Beings* (with Ralph Hummel); and *Individuals and World Politics*.

Dr. Isaak has lived in Europe on and off since he was sixteen, when he won a national essay competition that sent him to Switzerland. Two years later he studied for a year in Heidelberg on a journalism fellowship. He received his B.A. from Stanford University in 1966 and his Ph.D. from New York University in politics in 1971. In 1972 he was a Faculty Sponsor for the London School of Economics Comparative Government Program, which took him to London, East and West Berlin, Dresden, Moscow, and Leningrad. He divides his summers between the Neckar Valley and the Mediterranean Sea.

This book was written under the auspices of The Institute on Western Europe and The Research Institute on International Change, both at Columbia University, which supported the research behind it from 1975 through 1978. Since then the author has taught graduate seminars in Comparative European Political Economy Systems and West European Integration at the Johns Hopkins Center in Bologna.